# The Experimental Study
# of Personality

# The Experimental Study
# of Personality

Douglas P. Crowne

*University of Waterloo*
*Ontario, Canada*

 LAWRENCE ERLBAUM ASSOCIATES, PUBLISHERS
1979    Hillsdale, New Jersey

DISTRIBUTED BY THE HALSTED PRESS DIVISION OF
JOHN WILEY & SONS
New York    Toronto    London    Sydney

Lawrence Erlbaum Associates, Inc., Publishers
365 Broadway
Hillsdale, New Jersey 07642


Distributed solely by Halsted Press Division
John Wiley & Sons, Inc., New York


**Library of Congress Cataloging in Publication Data**
Crowne, Douglas P
  The experimental study of personality.

  Bibliography: p.
  Includes indexes.
  1. Personality—Research.  I. Title.
BF698.C744      155.2'07'24      78-32009
ISBN 0-470-26664-3

Printed in the United States of America

*To my parents*

IRVING H. CROWNE

MARGARET P. CROWNE

# Contents

# Preface

Experimental research in personality is now so vast and many-faceted that nearly every serious student is limited to an area of specialty, and there are few personality psychologists whose ken is so catholic as to span the entire discipline. The range of theoretical concepts and problems to investigate is very great, encroaching as it does on other areas of psychological inquiry—motivation, development, and learning, to name but three. There is a diversity of research methods so broad that I cannot think of a principal methodological procedure that is not represented in the personality literature. Finally, personality psychologists have searched widely for subject populations suitable—or even sometimes ideally fitted—for the investigation of particular experimental questions. What this can mean to the student who is beginning the study of personality is exposure to a bewildering and disorganized sea of facts that seems to shift according to the view of the moment. The lack of a comprehensible perspective can be very disheartening, leading to abandonment or to a premature focussing of interest on a small set of problems and their associated concepts and experimental techniques.

There are, I believe, some principles that can help to guide the study of research in personality. Those principles concern the approach to experimental problems. A well-grounded understanding of research methods, their logic, and something of the strategy of their application can bring an important sense of order to the study of personality research. But research methodology by itself is severely abstract, and it does not give the insight linking method with theoretical conceptualization that we, student and teacher, mutually seek. Research methods as they have been actually employed, however, tell a different story and I think, indeed, a far richer story than simply the recital of their findings would tell.

Thus, this book is chiefly built around the principal methods used in the experimental study of personality. I have chosen several research areas that seem to me to represent both creative and in some cases problematical application of research designs. In each chapter, I have tried to present major experiments in some detail—tried, really, to let them mainly give the account of the research problem or concept. I have tended to select good examples rather than bad ones in the belief that the adage about fighting sin by immersing oneself in it is advice that can get one hopelessly lost in errorful ways. Sin is informative up to a point, and so there are some sinful examples of research in most of my chapters. Precept, though, is better, and I have both chosen research I think exemplary and made much of its noteworthy features. My choice of research areas was influenced by another consideration. I wished to represent something of the conceptual range of the experimental study of personality, and so I have included chapters on questions of classic importance—conflict and repression—as well as chapters reviewing more recent research on the socially relevant concepts of need for approval and internal versus external control of reinforcement. This does not in any way make a representative sample except in the specific senses discussed in the final chapter. Two chapters differ from this plan. In Chapter 1, I have dealt with the distinctive problems that confront the study of human personality and with the nature of personality. Chapter 2 is a detailed analysis of research method and strategy. It does, however, consider a research area: Some of the major studies of the drive theory of anxiety are used as a vehicle for the discussion of questions of method.

The period during which this book was written was a reflective one for me, in which my thinking was strongly influenced and changed. I came to a greater understanding of experimental design and research strategies and came to appreciate more fully the need for the interplay of research methods in personality. My thinking about the logic and strategy of research has been influenced significantly by Karl Pribram, whose great breadth of interest and ability to weave clinical insight with experimental sophistication I very much admire. I am pleased to record my appreciation.

A number of friends and colleagues have read various chapters, and I have been much aided by their comments. They include Julian Rotter, Amerigo Farina, Herbert Lefcourt, David Rosenhan, and Ian Steele Russell.

My wife, Sandra, has read and heard every word and drawn laborious figures. My friends and colleagues who gave me assistance are, each of them, authors; they will understand the priority of my acknowledgment. My writing has been made easier in many ways, large and small, by the thoughtful generosities of my department through its thoughtful and generous chairman, Robin Banks. The last phase of writing and editing has been helped by a sabbatical leave fellowship in the MRC Unit on Neural Mechanisms of Behaviour and in the Department of Psychology, University College, London. I wish to express my gratitude to Ian Steele Russell and to Professor George C. Drew.

*London, England*                                    **Douglas P. Crowne**

# The Experimental Study
# of Personality

# 1

# The Scientific Study
# of Personality

## ABSTRACT

*The scientific study of personality shares fundamental attributes and methods of inquiry with all science. It also has some distinctive features that set it apart. The uniqueness of personality research derives from man's study of himself: the psychologist belongs to the class of objects he or she investigates. We begin by considering a number of obstacles to scientific inquiry that follow from this fact.*

*The remainder of the chapter is concerned with the nature of personality, personality theory, and methods of personality study. Personality is defined as* an organized system of potentialities for behavior, *and the implications of that definition are developed. The importance of studying human behavior as the product of* situation–person interactions *is stressed. The important concepts of* personality structure *and* personality dynamics *are defined. Theories are discussed as conceptual systems which make empirical claims about observable events. The claims of theory should be sufficiently specific to enable their truth or falsity to be established. Personality theories are conceptual systems for the whole range of significant human behavior. Their inclusiveness, however, poses problems for specific behavioral prediction, and personality psychologists develop* miniature theories *to account for limited classes of behavior.*

*The chapter concludes with a brief overview of methods in the experimental study of personality. Experimental and correlational methods are introduced (they are taken up in detail in Chapter 2) and contrasted with the clinical method as procedures for the scientific study of human personality.*

## INTRODUCTION

Nearly everyone is convinced that he or she holds the key to understanding the behavior of fellow mortals. We each have our own looking-glass, as it were, which gives back a reflection of our own certitude of understanding ourselves, a reflection which we bend to the task of comprehending others. "Not everyone," wrote Freud (1940), "is bold enough to make judgments about physical matters; but everyone—the philosopher and the man in the street alike—has his opinion on psychological questions and behaves as if he were at least an *amateur* psychologist [pp. 282–283]." Nearly everyone is convinced, that is, that he or she commands a particularly insightful version of a common-sense view of human behavior until the common-sense theory runs smack into enigma and mystery.

Paradoxically, we are not all abashed over our areas of ignorance of the nature of the physical universe, while all of us—philosopher, man in the street, and psychologist—concede only grudgingly our uncertainty about human behavior. We are hardly newcomers at the game—man has been the object of his own scrutiny from the dawn of recorded history and certainly long before that. What is it that makes the task so difficult? Why is it that the great periods of discovery of laws regulating the physical universe and the physiology of living organisms as well have yet to meet their parallel in the discovery of a similarly expansive network of laws by which we might come closer to understanding the nature of human behavior?

It was Ebbinghaus' famous remark that "Psychology has a long past, but only a short history." Although we can trace the inquiry into human affairs back to antiquity, the scientific study of behavior is a phenomenon of the nineteenth and twentieth centuries. The science of behavior, human and infrahuman, is a Johnny-come-lately, and the study of personality by the plainly objective methods of science is a chapter in "the proper study of mankind" of the last 60 or 70 years. The task of any science is to describe and explain the phenomena that fall within its boundaries—to classify and categorize, to observe the empirical regularities that occur among phenomena, and to account for these regularities by the fewest explanatory concepts possible. Psychology has simply tackled its phenomena a good deal later than the physical sciences, and the psychology of personality has come to the task of studying the behavior we all think we understand anyway even later.

## OBSTACLES TO THE STUDY OF HUMAN BEHAVIOR

The scientific study of human behavior is not only a latecomer, but is confronted as well by some distinctive obstacles that do not plague other sciences or plague them much less. These obstacles are all occasioned by the single fact that psychologists, unlike other scientists, are in the uniquely difficult positon of studying objects that are in myriad ways similar to themselves. Mandler and Kessen (1975) put the matter this way:

> Science may be viewed as an organized system of statements about objects and events. Just as other scientists look at and listen to slides, stars and whooping cranes, the psychologist looks at and listens to the behavior of organisms. As a scientist he makes statements about the events which he has observed. In this respect he does not differ from the bacteriologist, astronomer, or ornithologist. The psychologist, however, soon faces a confusion not normally shared by his scientific colleagues, a confusion derived from the fact that he also happens to belong to the universe of objects which he is observing [p. 34].

## The Scientific Language of Psychology

Quoting Bergmann (1950), Mandler and Kessen (1975) wish it clearly understood that "*the behavior scientist and his subjects do not, in principle, speak the same language* [p. 36]." That is to say, the language by which psychologists describe the objects of their observations—people—is not the language people use to describe or talk about themselves. The scientific language of psychology is a language *about* certain events—behavior—and the concepts invented by the scientist to account for those events. It is a language distinguished by its objectivity; it appeals for that which can be observed, for precise definitions, and more generally for the use of words that can be clearly linked to observables. In this, psychology differs not one bit from any other science which must develop a precise set of terms about its objects under observation. What people do or what they say about themselves—their behavior, including *verbal* behavior—may be interesting and important as observations *about* people, but these things are the factual, empirical grist out of which the psychologist's conceptions about behavior are made, not the conceptions themselves.

Although we take an enormous step forward by recognizing this necessary partition between observer and object of observation, the matter is not so neatly resolved. Psychologists are brought up in the culture of their fellows, sharing an organized system of perceptions, thought, and language. They become scientists only by learning to differentiate themselves in their role as psychologists, adopting the objective methods and the objective language of description of science. But this is never an easy task, and it is an especially difficult one in psychology. The everyday, vernacular language on which one grew up and one's everyday, common-sense perceptions and notions about the way people behave and why, can exercise a potent influence on an individual's approach to the subject matter of psychology. Common-sense, everyday conceptions of human behavior are likely to have some major frailties. The language of description is vague and not precise, and its behavioral referents (or ties to observed behavior) are often unclear. Common-sense explanations of behavior are prone to oversimplifications in which richness and complexity—and often any utility for the purpose of prediction—are sacrificed in favor of a too ready understandability (see, for example, Mischel, 1973, pp. 263–264). How many times have you heard, "Oh, she's just doing that to attract attention," or "People don't like him because he's too pushy." Faced with the extraordinary response repertoires of human beings, the structural complexity of human organisms, the intricate and often subtle interactions of man and environment, and the changeability of those interactions, it is little wonder that psychologists occasionally lapse into such temptations as these.

## From Person Perception to Psychological Theory

We often make judgments about other people on the basis of assumed similarity or contrast. The process of understanding another is based on our *assumptions* about the similarity of their experiences to ours; or, because we have some basis for believing that other persons are different than we are, we understand their experiences by the contrast with our own. We fail to ask about the specific nature of their experiences and about its relation to observed behavior. We ascribe motives to another's behavior on the basis of our understanding of our own motives. Thus, "He's like me (or not like me), and if I were in his shoes I would do the same thing (or, I wouldn't dream of doing that)" becomes the essential premise for much of our understanding of others. I do not mean to imply that assumed similarity may not provide some fruitful hunches about behavior and its motive forces; I am saying that is is not a sufficient basis for psychological theory, and it is one form of oversimplification that lies in wait for the psychologist. Similarity–contrast leads to the construction of stereotypes. The stereotype is a blunted instrument for understanding, based as it is on unexamined assumptions. It is a poor substitute for careful observation and discrimination.

*The Problem of Emotional Commitments.*    Human beings, in distinction to other objects of observation, are capable of arousing strong feelings which may make objectivity difficult and influence the direction of thinking about human behavior. We do not ordinarily become as emotionally embroiled with non-person objects as we do with persons, and thus the tasks of objectivity and the careful accounting of facts in theoretical formulations of non-person phenomena are greatly eased. Our own experiences may incline us to strongly emotional views not only of particular persons but of major groups of people or perhaps people in general. The caption of a famous cartoon by William Steig, "People are no damn' good," is a facetious overstatement but it captures the point. The effect of an intensely emotional commitment to a particular view of people is forcefully if sadly evidenced in biased attempts to prove the innate intellectual inferiority of the black from data that cannot be interpreted to support that conclusion (for a careful, scholarly review of this problem see Loehlin, Lindzey, and Spuhler, 1975).

Another outcome of strongly-held beliefs about the nature of man is shown in Brown's (1965) powerful characterization of the ideological personality studies of Jaensch (1938) in Nazi Germany and their American antidote, the studies of *The Authoritarian Personality* (Adorno, Frenkel-Brunswik, Levinson, & Sanford, 1950). A set of characteristics which Jaensch interpreted as weak, indecisive, and effeminate, traits of such inferior peoples as the Jews, the American researchers established as the characteristics of liberal, democratic, and more reflective individuals. Jaensch found a contrasting personality, the J–type: masculine, a rugged individual of firm, hard perceptions and beliefs, whose psychological characteristics were beautifully adapted to the cause and ideology of Nazi Germany. To the authors of *The Authoritarian Personality,* Jaensch's tough J–type was the person likely to hold ethnocentric and authoritarian attitudes, the anti-democratic or Fascist personality. As Brown notes:

> Unquestionably there was some gratification for American social psychology during this period [immediately following World War II] in the theory of the authoritarian personality which exposed the fear, the stupidity, and the sadism in nationalistic and reactionary politics. Was there perhaps also some distortion of truth in the service of values? If so, it was not so blatant as Jaensch's, not so obviously unsupported by evidence, not in the service of the state, perhaps not there at all [p. 479].

This was, as Brown vividly shows, research recruited in a cause, less blatantly and for honorable reasons by the American psychologists, flagrantly and for venal ones by the Nazi Jaensch. In the latter case, clearly, it was research whose facts were made to fit the mold of a prior and emotionally charged commitment to a set of views about man's behavior.

There is one more way in which our observations and interpretations of behavior may be imperiled by the force of affect. It is sometimes difficult to recognize in behavior or in theories of behavior matters about which the tuition of culture and our own specific experiences have created strong fears and aversions. Despite the intense distaste, mistrust, and actual disbelief that greeted Freud's investigations and theories—he once (1916) remarked that psychoanalysis "forfeited the sympathy of every friend of sober scientific thought, and laid itself open to the suspicion of being a fantastic esoteric doctrine eager to make mysteries and fish in troubled waters [p. 22]"—he stoutly insisted that psychoanalysis was charged with no less a duty than to follow wherever the facts as they were known at the time might lead. That, of course, is the task of the science of personality, the task of any science. To pursue such a quest runs the risk of insulting our sensibilities about man and leading us to interpretations of behavior that may uncomfortably remind us of those things about ourselves we would far rather not have to confront.

## Observer and Observed

This chapter began with the suggestion that it is quite wrong-headed to indulge the comfortably lulling fiction that what motivates behavior bends easily to understanding. All of the evidence that the study of personality has amassed prescribes a different conclusion. Human behavior is highly complex, to be understood by no simple set of principles. The difficulty of the task is compounded by the fact that man, even with his marvelously astute capacities, faces some mountainous obstacles in making himself the object of his own observation. We have seen some of the major obstacles in the paragraphs above; there is one more now to add to the list.

In studying members of his own species, the psychologist is part of the context in which the object of observation is behaving. The psychologist's presence and observation inevitably influence the behavior of the observed. Each psychologist is a unique individual and will represent to some degree a unique configuration of stimuli for the person whose behavior is being studied. This will be true despite careful efforts to standardize the psychologist's own behavior from person to person. One psychologist wears a mustache, moves about his tasks briskly, and tends to be somewhat brusque in his transactions with others; another is slightly balding, rather nervous and fluttery, and habitually diffident in his interpersonal interactions. The effect of the psychologist's unique stimulus value will be to introduce some unspecifiable variation in the behavior of subjects. Thus, in part, the behavior observed by any psychologist is peculiar to that person–psychologist interaction; the more complex that interaction, the more probable these distinctive features are. I do not mean to say that all behavior is distinctive to a particular situation, never to be repeated, but I do mean that to a degree, probably a small one, observer–subject interactions are not exactly repeated.

*Awareness of Being Observed.*  There is another aspect to this general problem. Humans, especially the intelligent and sentient ones we typically study, are sensitive to observation and self-conscious about their behavior. Aware of being studied, their behavior may be changed in significant respects. If I tell you, or if you happen to surmise, that I am interested in how you behave when you are angry or anxious or frustrated in the pursuit of some goal, your behavior is likely to reflect that awareness and to differ perhaps from your angry, anxious, or obstacle-overcoming behavior in more natural circumstances when you are not conscious of being scrutinized. Your behavior when you are being watched will contain some elements of how you think I would like to see you behave, how you ought to behave, or what you would like me to think of you. This is more of an issue in research on some kinds of problems than on others. In research on learning, for example, we are reasonably safe in assuming that the subject's self-consciousness about being observed will play less of a role in his behavior. Research in personality, however, is apt to be concerned with behavior about which people do have strong feelings, and it is much more vulnerable to a person's investment in behaving for the psychologist in ways that suit the person's own purposes. Typically, this problem is handled in experiments by disguising their real purpose, making the experimental manipulation or critical procedures seem to be incidental occurrences. If your exposure to psychological research has led you to wonder why psychologists sometimes seem to be calculating and devious, this is why: the psychologist wishes to observe behavior as it would naturally and spontaneously occur, and to do so must thereby convince the subject that something else is being investigated. It happens that subjects sometimes manage to acquire an idea of the hypothesis under investigation, and they may vary their behavior within the limits of their abilities and understanding to fit what they believe to be appropriate, or perhaps what they think the hypothesis demands. A considerable amount of research in personality and in social psychology has been criticized on precisely these grounds—that many or most of the experimental subjects became aware of the purpose of the experiment and the hypothesis under investigation, and in their understandable desire to be good subjects, contributing useful data, gave unwitting confirmation to the hypothesis (Orne, 1962). It is clear that if this is the case in an experiment, we do not know what the true fate of the hypothesis would have been. Unless we are specifically interested in the investigation of behavior when the subject *is* aware of being observed, this is a potential source of error in research.

These two points—that the observer has a unique stimulus value for the observed, and that the behavior of the observed may reflect *his* understanding of the purposes for which he is being observed and whatever motives may be engaged for him—are genuine, but not insurmountable, problems. While a particular psychologist presents a different face to the subject than any other psychologist, he or she is also manifestly like other psychologists, and other people in general, in myriad ways. This is so much so that, in general, experimental results are not likely to vary much from one investigator to another on these grounds if the procedures of an experiment are carefully replicated. The second point is answered by not providing experimental subjects with knowledge of the behavior under investigation or the hypothesis of the experiment. We can carefully examine the procedures of an experiment being planned for any clues that might be given to subjects about its true concern. This effect, then, can be minimized, although through increasing public knowledge of psychological research larger numbers of potential subjects become sensitized to the kinds of disguises psychologists use to solve this problem. There are alternative approaches to the study of personality that may greatly diminish awareness of being observed or avoid the issue altogether. We can sometimes take the experimental study of personality out of the laboratory into important life situations where self-consciousness may be eclipsed by salient and onrushing events. We shall explore examples of studies in naturalistic and clinical settings in conflict (Chapter 3), stress (Chapter 4), and internal versus external control (Chapter 7). Another possible solution to the problem is to use nonhuman subjects for basic experiments that may provide significant analogues to the questions of human behavior we wish to solve. The conflict studies of Chapter 3 exemplify this approach.

*A Question of Ethics.*    Some ethical problems of considerable moment lurk behind the psychologist's deception of his subjects. If the deception is successful, subjects may unwittingly engage in behavior they would not wish to expose to view. Suppose the psychologist successfully arouses genuine and intense anger or fear, or induces the subject to respond in ways that the subject would regard as reprehensible. What happens to the subject at the conclusion of the experiment? Of these two issues—the deceptions of the psychologist and the instigation of potentially disturbing behavior—the latter is the more easily resolved. In a statement of ethical principles adopted by the American Psychological Association (1973b), psychologists have obligated themselves to ensure that no subject ever leaves an experiment in a more disturbed state than when he began it, nor is any subject exposed to potentially dangerous procedures without full knowledge and consent beforehand. Here is the ethical principle concerning the protection of experimental subjects from possible harm (American Psychological Association, 1973a):

> The ethical investigator protects participants from physical and mental discomfort, harm and danger. If the risk of such consequences exists, the investigator is required to inform the participant of that fact, to secure consent before proceeding, and to take all possible measures to minimize distress. A research procedure may not be used if it is likely to cause serious and lasting harm to participants [p. 79].

What kind of answer can be given to the first question? The principle is that:

> Openness and honesty are essential characteristics of the relationship between investigator and research participant. When the methodological requirements of a study necessitate concealment or deception, the investigator is required to ensure the participant's understanding of the reasons for this action and to restore the quality of the relationship with the investigator [p. 79].

Perhaps you have already considered the other side of the issue: Were psychologists deprived of experimental manipulation, some terribly restrictive fetters would be placed on research, especially personality research, and our knowledge would surely advance more slowly and more uncertainly. How are these issues to be resolved? Is there any way to reconcile the rights of the research subject to privacy and to protection from externally-imposed stress and the need of the psychologist to know? At this point, it may be that we can only argue that it is not an easy matter to arbitrate. Society justly incurs an obligation for the scientific endeavors of some of its members, and perhaps this is one of them: not an unbridled obligation to be subjected to any investigative whim of the scientist, but a serious obligation that members of the society accept, recognizing the ethical boundaries the scientist binds himself to observe.

## Reprise

It is no simple matter, I have been arguing, to begin the study of personality. The central point of the foregoing pages has been that when man studies his own species he must struggle both with problems encountered in the study of the physical universe and with some that only man himself poses as an object of inquiry. An objective language of description of events is a difficult and exacting achievement; to develop such a language and to apply it objectively when persons are the events to be observed is an achievement even harder won. People are skittish about what they will permit to be observed, are capable of extraordinary variability in their behavioral repertoires, and have a splendid capacity for self-consciousness which unfortunately can frustrate the observation of natural behavior in the psychologist's artificial situations. People's feelings become aroused to influence their perceptions, sometimes even when they are strongly committed to objectivity. These are, however, stones in the path, not impassable barriers: cautions to be observed and not signs to turn back.

## WHAT IS PERSONALITY?

The business of this book is research in personality—the sorts of concepts investigated by the psychologists of personality, the methods of their investigations, and the substance of their findings. For these purposes, we might accept what personality psychologists investigate as a definition of personality itself. There is a vast body of research to point to, and it would be a simple and plausible claim that personality is what the personality theorist makes it and what the personality researcher directs his investigations toward. There are some questions, however, that such a strategem would not enable us to answer. What is personality and what is not personality? What kind of experiment is a personality study, and what belongs to some other field of psychological inquiry? Why, indeed do we set personality apart as a separate area of study?

## A Definition of Personality

Although we might in part understand what personality is by the kinds of concepts represented in the research described in this book, the term personality means more than those individual concepts. The following definition stakes out the boundaries of personality in saying something about how we approach its study. *Personality is the organized system of potentialities for behavior.* To say that personality refers to an organized system is to recognize that we observe organization and unity in behavior. This is an old theme in personality—that human behavior is not segmental, fragmented, and discrete. People show consistency in their behavior, over time and across different situations. The same person is recognizable in the most different of social contexts, and we can also observe the continuity of behavior over the extraordinary range from early childhood to old age. We may note in addition that personality is concerned with the whole person: not just with intelligence or certain attitudes or a few motives, but with all these things and more and with the effects of their interactions on behavior. It is important, however, to distinguish the clinical analysis of a single personality, in which we look for the keys to understanding a whole, functioning person, from the way the research scientist approaches the investigation of personality.

Scientific research in personality is necessarily piecemeal. We isolate a given behavioral event for study both because we wish to know the separate and independent effects of each personality variable and because experiments in which many variables are manipulated are difficult to design, control, analyze, and interpret. The single variable study which enables us to understand behavior of interest and significance is important and worthwhile at this stage in the development of personality psychology. The stage at which we shall be able to investigate the single and joint effects of a number of variables in multivariate experiments is further ahead. Thus, the personality psychologist's one-variable-at-a-time investigations do not imply a fragmented, mechanistic conception of personality, but follow instead from the necessities of a research strategy that will permit the design of feasible and intelligible studies.

The other key phrase of the definition stresses potentialities for behavior rather than behavior itself. The study of personality is distinctively stamped by the concepts we develop to give behavior meaning. It is the inferences from behavior about what impels and directs it—its potentialities—that give the broad and general understanding of behavior that is the hallmark of personality. Personality psychology is less content than many other areas of psychological inquiry to study behavior in a largely empirical, minimally theoretical way.

Personality psychologists often investigate learning or perception or physiological processes. What distinguishes such experiments from those of the learning or perception or physiological psychologist? In contrast with these investigators, the psychologist of personality tends to base research on concepts that differentiate individuals, concepts that reflect stable and generalized modes of behavior, concepts that enable the prediction of a wide range of behavior. The interest of the psychologist of learning or perception is in the processes and conditions associated with change and maintenance of behavior within these areas, that of the physiological psychologist in the structures of the nervous system responsible for behavior. The difference, then, lies in the emphasis on the sources of difference between persons versus the basic processes and conditions of a phenomenon. Ultimately, of course, the study of personality must get down to the fundamental processes and conditions of personality development and behavior change, and then the distinction becomes blurred.

What kinds of concepts qualify as the behavioral potentialities of personality? Personality concepts deal with behavior that:

1. Is of social importance—not necessarily of social value, but behavior that is significant in interpersonal interactions. Frequently in personality we deal with responses, such as the behavioral outcomes of anxiety, that are associated with forms of personality disturbance, although it should be clear that the study of personality is not restricted to the study of abnormal behavior.
2. Differentiates persons, contributing to the distinctive profiles of individuality.
3. Is consistent and stable over time; we tend not to be interested in behavior that changes readily.
4. Is trans-situational, occurring in many rather than few situations.

## Situation-Person Interactions

Although personality is concerned with the sources of individual differences and their outcomes, its lens is focused on a wider image than the internal processes of persons themselves. What we observe—our behavioral raw material—is the product of situation–person interactions. We see a great array of individual differences among people, but we also see people responding to situations of great variety. Is it possible to conceptualize a person quite apart from the situations in which we observe that person behaving? I shall say baldly that it is not. The concepts we use to represent persons are abstractions from behavior. They derive from observations of behavior that are embedded in situations. That is true when we see someone differentiate one situation from another, and it is also true when we see that person respond in a consistent way in very different, discriminable situations. We must recognize, as Mischel (1973) points out, "the crucial role of situations (conditions)... as informational inputs whose behavioral impact depends on how they are processed by the person [p. 279]." Situations are of powerful import to behavior. But we also need to remember that "*the effects of experience,*" as Wiggins, Renner, Clore, and Rose (1971) say, "*are always modified by the organism to which they occur* [p. 40]."

So, we may take it that we cannot approach the understanding of personality without giving meaningful recognition to the fact that behavior occurs in a context that gives it substance and meaning. Perhaps, though, you have some objections that are not satisfied: you say, "Surely, there are some things that truly make a person, some things characteristic or essential about him, without which he wouldn't be that person at all." Lewin (1935) would have had an answer to such a challenge, accusing you of static Aristotelian thinking—the kind of thinking that explains the behavior of an object as an inherent property of the object itself and misses the dynamic relations of events and their environments or fields. Lewin pointed to the Galilean revolution in science in trying to persuade psychologists to turn out of an old Aristotelian rut. One example he used was from Galilean physics itself:

This decisive revolution comes to clear expression in Galileo's classic investigations of the law of falling bodies. The mere fact that he did not investigate *the heavy body itself,* but the process of "free falling or movement on an inclined plane," signifies a transition to concepts which can be defined only by reference to a certain sort of situation (namely, the presence of a plane with a certain inclination or of an unimpeded vertical extent of space through which to fall). The idea of investigating free falling, which is too rapid for satisfactory observation, by resorting to the slower movement upon an inclined plane presupposes that the dynamics of the event is no longer related to the isolated object as such, but is seen to be dependent upon the whole situation in which the event occurs.

Galileo's procedure, in fact, includes a penetrating investigation of precisely the situation factors. . . . The list of situations involved (free falling, movement on an inclined plane, and horizontal movement) is exhausted and, through the varying of the inclination, classified. The dependence of the essential features of the event . . . upon the essential properties of the situation . . . becomes the conceptual and methodological center of importance [p. 29; italics mine].

Psychological concepts, no less than physical ones, are defined "by reference to a certain sort of situation." It is not people we study but behavior-in-situations, not angry persons but aggressive behavior in more-or-less aggression-arousing situations. If you understand the notion of interaction, there should be no mistake about what sparks behavior—the person or the situation. Behavior is a function of neither separately. Personality concepts are defined by behavior observed in situations. Situations themselves are defined by the behavior we observe. Even the instinctive behavior of organisms—the defense of a private territory by the male stickleback or robin, or the burying of nuts by a squirrel—is, as the ethologists say, an innate action pattern triggered or released by a specific stimulus event (Eibl-Eibesfeldt, 1970). Such innate, mechanical responses, which do not require a learning history, do demand an environment, a stimulus situation, for their performance just as the complex and purposive action patterns of human personality do.

It is not inconsistent with what I have been insisting about the situation–person interaction to say, as I did above, that personality concepts refer to stable behavior generalized across many situations. Of course there is stability and cross-situational consistency in behavior; yet remember that it is the fact that we observe a person behaving consistently in a number of different situations that enables us to mark the person as consistent or to detect situational descriminations.

## Personality Structure and Personality Dynamics

We need to take up one final definitional question, the distinction between personality structure and personality dynamics. It is a useful distinction for understanding how we use theoretical concepts in the study of behavior and the kinds of functions we assign to them. In defining personality, I said that we recognize an organization and unity in behavior in our conceptualizations about it. Personality theories give personality a systematic and organized structure which reflects our assumptions about how personality is put together. We use concepts like "ego" or "habit" or "psychological needs," which are linked in their functions to other concepts—"superego," "drive," and "expectancy." Personality structure refers to the particular concepts of a particular theory of personality and the way these concepts function within the larger system, the way they are articulated with each other. These concepts and their linkages to other concepts in the system enable us to make sense out of our observations of behavior and to make meaningful predictions. The concepts and their linkages function very much like the articulated segments of a crustacean's shell. If each segment does its job well and if it is joined with other segments so that the organism can get about its business, all is well. But imagine a lobster, some of whose body segments are malformed and poorly articulated with other segments, so that every time it reaches out a claw to protect itself its tail goes up. This lobster, you would have to say, is doomed to a short, unhappy life—and so it is with the theoretical structure of personality theories. Structural elements are either functional and functionally related to other elements or the system is slated for extinction.

Personality structure is in principle no different than the organized system by which physics views its phenomena. The units of physical description may be particles of matter—molecules and atoms and subatomic particles—each having particular properties and each having a specified place and certain functions within the larger system. So it is with the conceptual materials and the means of their acting together which make up the theoretical description of personality. Personality structure may be applied to the description of an individual personality, and in so doing we take the terms of a given personality theory and put them to the task of understanding a person's behavior. The structure of that individual's personality is conferred by the structure of the concepts we use to describe him or her.

There is a way in which the term personality structure is sometimes used that I do not mean. For some psychologists, personality structure refers to the most general and unchanging characteristics of a person, especially those characteristics that place the person in a class or identify a personality type. So, if you happen to run across such a statement as, "The underlying structure of his personality is schizophrenic," or something like it, you should recognize another usage, one not intended here.

Personality dynamics is more difficult to define than personality structure, for it is widely used to refer to a number of things. It is sometimes used, especially by psychoanalytic writers, to describe only Freudian dynamics—the defense processes or mechanisms by which intolerable ideas and wishes are barred from consciousness. Occasionally, the terms seems merely to be an honorific, expressing little more than the conviction that if it's dynamic it's got to be good. Neither of these things are what I shall mean by personality dynamics. One is too restricted a meaning, and the other really has no meaning at all.

Personality dynamics refers to the *processes* by which behavior comes about—*how* it is acquired, maintained, and changed. The directing and energizing of behavior—the forces that push it an channel it one way rather than another—are the substance of personality dynamics. Dynamics is the property of a concept, and it says something about the way in which that concept functions. Personality dynamics is concerned with process: with how the ongoing stream of behavior develops, changes, or maintains its course. There are theoretical conceptions of personality that do not make use of dyanmic or process concepts. Type theories, for example, tend to emphasize a static structure of personality and are more concerned with the description of stable characteristics than with the analysis of change. Perhaps you will have already anticipated me by branding such theories as Aristotelian—I should not object.

## WHAT IS PERSONALITY THEORY?

It should now be clear that an attempt to define what personality "really is" as if it were an immutable property of the person, indissoluble with his very being, is a very unrewarding experience—as personality psychologists have painfully discovered. The task will be much less frustrating if we recognize that a scientific definition of personality—or of any other phenomenon examined by science—represents a particular way of viewing events. The regularity, order, and system of personality are properties conferred by a theory and the assumptions it makes. Personality is a construction of the observer, as hypothetical and as contrived as fiction. How, then, does it differ from genuine fiction, which doesn't masquerade as science? What does the science of personality have to offer that is not already splendidly evident in a fine novel that intuitively portrays the faces of a person?

## The Nature of Theory

Perhaps I have said this too abruptly and boldly: If our constructions of personality are fiction then there is nothing to believe, there are no facts to stand on, and only imaginative mirages remain. What's more, alongside a good novel, scientific descriptions of personality seem really rather dull. To go further, if the psychology of personality is science, then it must follow that all of science is some fanciful creation, and that cannot be. Fiction, by definition, is not true. Of course, there is a popular notion which pits theory against practice, implying that when it comes right down to knowing what is once-and-for-all true one had better depend on good old practical knowledge and leave theorizing to the fuzzy mind in the ivory tower. How can the dilemma be solved? Is the man in the street correct in this tough-minded disdain of theory, or is there a way in which fictive theory communes with hard fact? In a brief description of science, Einstein (1940) once suggested an answer in a way I very much admire.

> Science is the attempt to make the chaotic diversity of our sense-experience correspond to a logically uniform system of thought. In this system single experiences must be correlated with the theoretic structure in such a way that the resulting co-ordination is unique and convincing.
>
> The sense-experiences are the given subject matter but the theory that shall interpret them is man-made. It is the result of an extremely laborious process of adaptation: hypothetical, never completely final, always subject to question and doubt.
>
> The scientific way of forming concepts differs from that which we use in our daily life, not basically, but merely in the more precise definition of concepts and conclusions: more painstaking and systematic choice of experimental material; and greater logical economy. By this last we mean the effort to reduce all concepts and correlations to as few as possible logically independent basic concepts and axioms [p. 487].

Einstein says that the tension between fact and theory is really no tension at all—indeed, that facts outside a theory are disorganizing and confusing to the senses. How do we get from fact to fiction or the other way around, and is there any way of telling, apart from literary merit, whether the theoretical constructions of science are good or bad fiction? It is true that both scientific theory and honest-to-goodness fiction are constructions of reality; but having fashioned an image of reality, one stops content while the other anticipates the next step. Both theory and fiction evolve from experience and give that experience order and meaning. Theory and fiction say something about how things "out there" (reality) work. There, however, the parallel ends. Theory, but not fiction, has a check: From it, if it is good theory, can be derived *predictions* about a phenomenon, statements about events not yet observed or not yet accounted for.

A theory is a set of statements consisting of assumptions about the lawful operation of the phenomena it is concerned with. These statement posit certain states or forces or processes (such as our psychological concepts of habit and drive, ego defense, or innate releasing mechanism) which are abstractions from events, inferred from those events, and designed to explain them. As a set of assumptions, theory cannot be proved or disproved, but we can determine whether the empirical propositions deduced from a theory— hypotheses about events actually to be observed—are true or not true. Thus, the check of theory is *falsifiability:* The claims of the theory are *potentially* disconfirmable. That must seem like a strange way of putting it, to emphasize that a theory can be wrong and to suggest that we set up conditions in which its falsity will be evident. That is exactly what we do, for the reasons that Popper (1962) gives in the following propositions:

> It is easy to obtain confirmations, or verifications, for nearly every theory—if we look for confirmations. . . .
> A theory which is not refutable by any conceivable event is nonscientific. Irrefutability is not a virtue of a theory (as people often think) but a vice.
> Every genuine *test* of a theory is an attempt to falsify it, or to refute it. Testability is falsifiability; but there are degrees of testability: some theories are more testable, more exposed to refutation, than others; they take, as it were, greater risks.
> Confirming evidence should not count *except when it is the result of a genuine test of the theory;* and this means that it can be presented as a serious but unsuccessful attempt to falsify the theory. . . .
> Some genuinely testable theories, when found to be false, are still upheld by their admirers—for example by introducing *ad hoc* some auxiliary assumptions, or by re-interpreting the theory *ad hoc* in such a way that it escapes refutation. Such a procedure is always possible, but it rescues the theory from refutation only at the price of destroying, or at least lowering, its scientific status. . . .
> One can sum up all this by saying that *the criterion of the scientific status of a theory is its falsifiability, or refutability, or testability* [pp. 36-37].

Now this is a stringent requirement, and Popper himself acknowledges that there is value in a theory that is not strictly falsifiable. Such a theory may have heuristic value, stimulating ideas that eventually take form in a new or modified theory about the same phenomena that is potentially falsifiable.

There are other criteria of scientific theory, one of them being that we expect the language of theory to be objective. The terms of a scientific theory are precise, their meaning and usage clear and unambiguous. But the hardest test of scientific theory is how successful it is in producing propositions (hypotheses) about observable events and how well, for a given theory, we can specify the conditions under which these propositions would be true or false.

I am aware that theory is not universally held in high esteem among members of the scientific community. One eminent psychologist, Skinner, has argued (see, for example, Skinner, 1950) that the constructions or models of behavior that psychological theories represent are unnecessary and probably misleading. As one part of a more complex argument, he suggests that we confine ourselves to the investigation of lawful regularities in behavior and let theory come after the relationships are known. Such a view of theory, however, does not adequately describe the history of science, in which theories as *predictive* systems have played a compelling role. It is further true that the scientific study of personality is a strongly theoretical enterprise; the research you will encounter in this book is research testing theoretical propositions. Without getting further involved in the disagreement over the utility of theory and theoretical concepts, it can be said with certainty that theory directs much of scientific activity, and to eschew theory in personality would be to render it a barren wasteland.

## Theories of Personality

Personality theories are several competing brands of a nearly universal scientific commodity. They share, more or less, the attributes of theory described above. Among the variety of contemporary personality theories, each has its frailties. All of them are heuristic, some compellingly so, organizing the data of personality in intriguing and suggestive ways. On the other hand, no single personality theory can presently give an account of all the known data of personality in a convincing way, meeting the requirement of objectivity and producing testable (and confirmed) hypotheses about behavior. That we have a number of theories of personality, each with its own special view and limited predictive capability, should not be a disturbing or even surprising state of affairs. Theoretical diversity is a powerful stimulus to research, and when personality theories are sufficiently developed to permit tests of competing claims we can gracefully retire those whose claims are falsified.

What sets personality theories apart from other psychological theories? As a class, personality theories are general behavior theories. The point to be emphasized is the generality, the inclusiveness, of personality theories: Ideally, their concern is with all human behavior. This is, of course, an incredibly vast undertaking, one not achieved by any personality theory.

Most personality theories are capable of handling some phenomena, are incapable of predicting others, and appear simply to ignore some events within the broad area. Kelly (1955) coined a term to describe this characteristic selectivity of theories in the range of phenomena they deal with. He called this the "focus of convenience" of a theory, and by that he meant the range of events actually encompassed by the theory, the range of events the theory does well in explaining.

One of the risks confronting personality theories is that in trying to be so all-inclusive, the power to predict specific behavior in some areas is weakened. To account for the enormous range of personality, the concepts of a theory must have broad generality. At the present level of our knowledge, however, such generality is achieved only at the price of a reduction in specificity—a reduction in the ability of theories to produce specific and testable hypotheses over most of the potential range. Generality imposes a great strain on personality theories, a strain increased by the fact that we now seem to require greater precision and accuracy of theory than we used to. Thus, a personality theory that does a good job of predicting conflict behavior may have little that is precise and specific to say about attitudes toward the self; another theory manages self-regarding attitudes (the self-concept) well, but its terms cannot be translated into concrete, operational definitions of variables in the area of conflict. A third theory may have some suggestive and even exciting ways of representing behavior generally, but it simply doesn't generate predictions that can be confirmed or disconfirmed. The last theory, as Kelly (1955) picturesquely put it, should be a "candidate for the trash can"—and rather soon.

Theories with a strong dynamic or process emphasis might seem to be not quite so hard-pressed by the generality problem, since their concepts deal with general principles of behavior change and maintenance regardless of the particular nature of the behavior. Personality, however, involves highly complex behavior and behavioral relationships, and the application of general principles to the prediction of such complex patterns is a difficult task. A learning theory may describe self-esteem as a habit system, for example, but that is an unexciting solution, and unless some distinctive predictions emerge it is not likely to be a very useful one. If this learning theory can describe self-esteem as generalized expectancies about personal competence in attaining need satisfaction that develop as a result of specific experiences of success and failure, reward and punishment, it may make predictions that can be falsified. The theory now begins to take a fair risk.

As a consequence of the predictive problems of personality theories, psychologists turn to the development of smaller-scale theories to account for behavior not easily explained by major theories. Although a large amount of personality research involves the testing of hypotheses derived from the general behavior theories of personality, not all personality research is so closely linked to broad theory. A very large proportion of personality research tests the hypotheses of a single concept or a small number of related concepts. These are theories on a miniature scale, their inclusiveness limited to particular kinds of behavior. Often these miniature theories are tied to a larger personality theory, but that is not always the case. This book contains several examples of miniature theory. One of them is anxiety–drive theory, which we consider in the next chapter; another is the concept of need for approval, reviewed in Chapter 6.

The development of miniature theories to explain behavior not precisely accounted for by full-scale theories leads to a certain amount of diversity and fragmentation. Some investigators pursue research on need achievement, others study anxiety, and for still others the concern may be problems of stress. Large bodies of separate and distinct research findings grow, and the problem of assimilating them and linking them together has now become considerable. While the fragmentation of personality research does make it difficult to see where we are going and to develop a coherent picture of personality from research findings, there is actually less diversity and fragmentation than you might be led to expect. This is mainly because miniature theories tend to be influenced by the fundamental assumptions about human behavior of the major theories—assumptions, for example, about the nature of motivation, the role of learning, and the processes involved in such covert or unconscious phenomena as defense and fantasy. In this sense, the inclusive theories of personality exercise a pervasive role.

## Theory and Method

There are two great research traditions in the experimental study of personality. One is the investigation of individual differences. Its principal research method is *correlational*. Relationships among behavioral measures are studied to test theoretical hypotheses. The other tradition is experimental. Here, the conditions believed to be responsible for a behavioral phenomenon are experimentally varied. Chapter 2 compares the logic and the strategies of these research methods, their respective strengths, and their weaknesses in a review of a classic series of studies on anxiety and drive.

I do not mean to imply that there are two thoroughly separate and independent avenues of personality research. While these two paths have diverged in psychology, the study of individual differences and the experimental manipulation of conditions by which to observe the predicted occurrence of a phenomenon are genuinely complementary, as Cronbach (1957) long ago reminded psychologists:

> Individual differences have been an annoyance rather than a challenge to the experimenter. His goal is to control behavior, and variation within treatments is proof that he has not succeeded. Individual variation is cast into that outer darkness known as "error variance."...

The correlational psychologist is in love with just those variables the experimenter left home to forget. He regards individual and group variations as important effects of biological and social causes. . . .

The spell these particular . . . methods cast upon us appears to have passed. We are free at last to look up from our own bedazzling treasure, to cast properly covetous glances upon the scientific wealth of our neighbor descipline. Trading has already been resumed, with benefit to both parties [pp. 674–675].

In personality, the correlational and experimental approaches are even more closely interwoven, and necessarily so. The personality investigator can no more afford to ignore individual differences than disdain the situations and experiences that shape behavior. In fact, there is an increasing emphasis in personality research on combining the correlational study of individual differences with experimental manipulation, and we see individual differences investigated as a function of experimentally varied conditions or situations. The experimental design is thus set up to explore a true situation–person interaction.

*The Clinical Method.*   Personality theories provide conceptual schemes for the systematic study of behavior, but that is not their only function. There is another one, rooted more deeply in their history. Personality theories began to take form in the last quarter of the 19th century as clinical theories focused on disturbed behavior and its treatment. Such men as Charcot, Janet, Breuer, and Freud struggled with the problem of behavioral disturbances that were not satisfactorily explained by the physical structure and disease concepts of medicine. Fumbling and uncertain in the beginning, these efforts gradually led to the development of a kind of medical psychology, a strange new breed hardly recognizable as medicine or psychology and accepted by neither. Personality theory began to be formalized with the development of psychoanalysis, a system of thought offering both an explanation of neurosis and a method for its treatment. Psychoanalysis grew as a system, coming in the 1920s to be a rich, complex, and all-embracing general behavior theory. Other theories of personality began to emerge, starting with two psycho-analytic dissidents, Adler and Jung, shortly before the first World War. A number of other influences shaped the development of theory in personality: The study of individual differences, especially in intelligence and ability; Gestalt psychology, with its emphasis on holism; the psychological study of child development; and the experimental psychology of learning. Many of these influences came later, after personality had arrived at the study of general, as well as abnormal, behavior. Personality theories no longer occupy the maverick role they once did, and they have taken an accepted and indeed prominent place in the mainstream of psychological thought.

Theories of personality began by fishing in the dark and troubled waters of disturbed behavior, however, and they owe their existence to the discoveries of the clinic and the therapeutic couch. The observations and concepts that came out of the clinic were intended to serve an immediate and compelling purpose—the understanding and treatment of disturbed behavior. These remain a major function of personality theory.

The research method responsible for the early developments in personality theory was the case study or clinical method, the study in depth of a single person. For the study of individual personality, it has an appealing advantage over the experimental techniques of the laboratory: It is an approach to the person as a whole, functioning being, and it attempts to understand behavior in an integrated, personalized way. Why is the case study method not the primary method of choice in the investigation of personality? The answer lies in the adequacy of the case study as a method of scientific research. The case study is legitimately a *research* method if the investigator acts like a scientist in studying a case. It is surely a research method when it is set to the task of developing new theoretical analyses of little-understood phenomena. It is also research when the investigation of single cases is used to test the hypotheses of a theory already existing. How good a method of research is it?

Does the clinician do the same things a scientific investigator does? And are they done as well as the exacting requirements of scientific method demand? The scientific study of behavior begins with observation and an attempt to systematize what is observed. So does the clinician. We may note that the clincian is faced with a constraint on his or her behavioral observations: The person typically comes to the clinician, whose observations are limited to what the person says and how it is said—the person's expressive style. If, in the course of the study of a person, the clinician wants to know how that person responds in the actual give-and-take of his or her family, when the person becomes angry and to what degree of intensity, or what kinds of situations bring on strong apprehension and anxiety, the clinician must ask. There must also be some criteria for deciding whether the answers are veridical, and if not, why the answers came out as they did.

Both participants influence what is observed. The clinician's subject—the patient—has the evaluation of self at stake in the process, and this self-portrayal will reflect the patient's own purposes. One can shade a portrait to bring out nuances: Irritability becomes righteous indignation, or obsessive doubt turns into circumspection in the face of genuine uncertainty with but a few strokes of the brush. All of us develop some artistry of this kind, and it is often applied without full awareness. Clinicians themselves affect what is observed in several ways. For our purpose here, the most important way is by selecting from all too many things to attend to the events that are significant. The clinician's theory selects in advance certain kinds of behavior as grist for the interpretive mill, and these are the things on which attention is focused. Yes, as a clinician one may miss observations of great potential significance because one's theory is too restrictive and choosy. On the other hand, an astute clinician may pick up striking and untoward responses, even though not conceptually prepared for them. But the clinician does select, as individual purposes and theory direct.

Observation is only the start of the process; a simple catalogue of behavior won't do, for that is too disorganized to digest. If the clinician is to begin to understand, the next step must be conceptual—the formulation of a hypothesis. Exactly how the hypothesis is formed is something of a problem. Obviously, both the observations made by the clinician and the theoretical concepts determine the hypothesis, but to be able to say how the two are combined so that others can reproduce the result is not yet an achievement of the clinical method. I do not mean this to disparage the considerable amount of research on clinical inference and theoretical analyses of the processes involved (for example, Bieri, Atkins, Briar, Leaman, Miller, & Tripodi, 1966; Sarbin, Taft, & Bailey, 1960), but it has to be recognized that the hypothesis-forming behavior of the clinician is an exceedingly difficult problem.

However uncertain we are about how this occurs, the clinician does form hypotheses. If you have a hypothesis, the only reasonable thing to do with it is to test it, and clinicians are reasonable people. Clincial hypotheses are tested by pitting them against observation, by seeking evidence that would confirm or deny them. Sometimes, tests are based simply on further observation, with the clinician noting the generality of the behavior in question or the presence or absence of other behavior implied by the hypothesis. Sometimes, they are conducted by a kind of manipulative experimentation in which the clinician makes a prediction of this general form: "If I do this, thus-and-so will happen," "thus-and-so" being a consequence specified by theory. The clinician may probe to see if there is a reaction commensurate with the expectation implied by the hypothesis. Once, as a neophyte therapist, I said to an unhappy young woman who had given most of an hour to a wistful portrait of her perfect mother—"a beautiful Southern lady who always wore white gloves" and who never seemed to be around when a little girl most needed her attention, "It must be hard to realize how much you hate your mother." It was a daring strategy for someone with as little experience as I had, and the reaction was startling and dramatic. There was a stunned silence for perhaps thirty seconds (it seemed to me like thirty minutes) and then, all at once, the tears came and she burst from the door crying, "I guess you had to do that." I could imagine her running in front of a car or performing some other desperate act in her anguish, a tragic ending of her career, and I imagined the swift conclusion of mine. She returned the following week smiling and cheerful, apparently relieved—or so I took it to mean—of a terrible, repressed burden. Was this confirmation of my repression-of-anger hypothesis, a vivid instance of the returns of the repressed? And in the sudden release of feelings hitherto unseen, was it confirming evidence for the concept of repression?

What the clinician does seems a close parallel of the scientist's procedures. The clinician observes, formulates hypotheses which imply predictions (I was pretty sure I was going to get some kind of reaction, and it wasn't going to be easy acceptance), and puts these to test. How much confidence can we place in the process—in the understanding of a person that arises from it, or in tests of theoretical propositions based on the investigation of single cases? If we compare the clinical method to experimental methods, two criteria suggest themselves—replicability and control. Experimental methods demand that relationships demonstrated between variables or causal sequences of events be *potentially* replicable or repeatable by others. This is a requirement that the conditions under which observations are made be clearly specified. Research findings themselves must be in *fact* replicable if they are to remain part of the body of scientific knowledge. Scientific research is properly obsessive in the precise, objective description of the conditions of observation and the measurement procedures by which phenomena are defined. It is operational in its definition of concepts by explicit procedures of measurement. In Stevens' (1939) tough-minded words, "Only those propositions based upon operations which are public and repeatable are admitted to the body of science. . . . A term denotes something only when there are concrete criteria for its applicability; and a proposition has empirical meaning only when the criteria of its truth or falsity consist of concrete operations which can be performed upon demand [pp. 27–28]." Replicability can be achieved only when the conditions for a phenomena are describable and described.

The discovery of lawful relationships depends on fulfillment of a second mandate: Control of potentially influential variables. A variable is controlled in an experiment when it is not allowed to vary so that its potential effects can play no role. The process of repression, as Freud (1915) described it, involves keeping from consciousness those thoughts and feelings whose acknowledgement would powerfully arouse anxiety. The process, however, is private and unobservable, and the demonstration of repression requires an observable criterion. Suppose we define the outcome of repression as the unavailability of a response clearly expected in some situation, say an anger-instigating one. We could then design an experiment to test the repression phenomenon—an experiment in which we attempt to arouse the sort of intense feelings that repression might well interfere with. We badger experimental subjects with critical and unfair personal attack. We might refine the experiment by predicting repression only among subjects with certain personality characteristics. Now, the absence of the anticipated response for a specified group of subjects will reveal the occurrence of repression. Is repression, however, the only possible interpretation that could be placed upon the failure of anger to appear? Unfortunately, one other highly likely possibility is that anger is not repressed—banished from consciousness and hence unavailable—but simply withheld. In fact, the situation of the subject in an experiment is one that might well lead him to hold back a response not ordinarily made to scientists and university professors. Thus, an alternative and equally likely possibility, perhaps an even more plausible one, is the withholding of a response deemed by the subject inappropriate in the circumstances. A control for response-withholding could rescue the phenomenon of repression in this experiment; without it, we have no way of determining why anger did not appear, and the experiment is hopelessly ambiguous.

Does the clinical method meet the criterion of replicability, and are sufficient controls employed in the clinical study of persons? Can the clinician specify the conditions under which observations are made and hypotheses tested, and can controls be built into the case study method so that its conclusions are unambiguous? On warm spring days I sometimes see from my window a class of art students sketching a campus landmark. I have never dared to go outside and peer over each shoulder, but if I did I imagine I would discover the small pond they draw depicted in amazing variety. Each artist would capture some facet unseen or deemed unimportant by others; in each sketch there would be a new and undiscovered pond. The clinician, of course, is not an artist, and the criteria by which clinical work is judged are not the subjectives ones of art criticism; but perhaps the analogy is not entirely unfair if it suggests the difficulty of the clinical method. The clinician is, at one and the same time, observer, interpreter of what is observed, and by the tests carried out, arbiter of the correctness of these interpretations. It is an extraordinarily complex task: There are myriad potential influences on the behavior of the person being studied, and there is grave difficulty even in specifying what observations impinge on the clinician's consciousness. Without question, the clinician attempts to bring scientific procedures to bear by employing concepts and techniques that are recognized by many other clinicians and whose definitions and uses are part of a common body of knowledge. The clinician is also likely to make the observations that many others would agree are important and to apply hypothesis-testing procedures with care. The question is: Is the picture constructed reproducible, and do tests of clinical propositions permit of no other interpretation? I shall not labor the issue. You must decide for yourself the adequacy of the clinical method; but whatever your conclusion, perhaps you will judge the slow, small, painfully-won achievements of experimental research in personality with due recognition for the importance of their accomplishment under the rigorous conditions demanded by science.

# 2 Some Questions of Method

## ABSTRACT

*This chapter is about methods in the experimental study of personality. We shall review two major approaches: The experimental method, which is called stimulus-response (S-R), and the correlational or response-response (R-R) method. The logic and strategy of the experimental method are contrasted with the logic and strategy of correlational studies. We shall see how inferences are made to theoretical concepts from S-R and R-R procedures, and examine the chief difficulties that can make research results uncertain.*

*These questions are developed by reviewing some of the research on the drive theory of anxiety. This research program made creative use of both S-R and R-R methods to study an important human experience and clinical phenomenon. It also encountered difficulties with theoretical inference. We shall examine the research, its methods, and the inference problems to see how theoretical inference can be made more secure. At the end of the chapter, the methodological lessons learned from the anxiety-drive studies are applied to two other approaches to the study of anxiety.*

## INTRODUCTION

Getting to know and understand someone involves such concretely familiar processes that we ordinarily don't bother to talk about them. We simply experience a growing certainty about another's probable feelings and behavior in those situations in which he is familiar to us. A scientific psychology of personality has moved a long way from this sort of concrete and intuitively obvious understanding of others. It is deeply concerned about methods of inquiry and the logic of those methods, and it is not concrete and intuitive but highly conceptual. Some very-high-level abstractions have gone into the design of an experiment so that concrete behavioral events can be transformed from observations to an abstract construct. We start with a conceptualization, move to observation of behavior regulated by strict operational conventions, record those observations in quantitative form so they can be subjected to statistical treatment, and finally arrive at conclusions inferred from these preceding steps about the status of the construct. These are complex processes requiring a careful set of rules about procedure and about permissible inference.

In this chapter we shall examine these processes and the basic rules that govern them. We shall consider the way experiments and correlational studies are designed, the kinds of inferences that may be drawn from them, and the nature and function of the constructs to which these inferences are made. There are two principal themes. The first concerns the nature of constructs and the logic and strategy of research. We shall need to understand what are called S–R (experimental) and R–R (correlational) types of research and some major problems of inference. The second theme is the R–R or correlational research design and the logic and procedures by which causal inferences are made from the correlation of response measures. To develop these themes, we shall follow a series of studies on the concept of anxiety to examine their rationale and design and to see how they hurdled—or stumbled over—the chief obstacles to theoretical inference.

## CONSTRUCTS AND THE LOGIC AND STRATEGY OF RESEARCH

The terms *construct* and *concept* are used interchangeably. There is some advantage to the word construct because in its verb form it means to build, and this is a helpful emphasis. Theoretical concepts are indeed "built"; they are conceptual edifices erected for theoretical purposes. The purpose that constructs serve is explanation, and they do so by bringing together, accounting for, and being able to predict a number of related phenomena. From a construct are derived predictions of the relations to be observed among events, and thus the construct anticipates them or at least some of them. Sometimes a construct genuinely predicts a relation hitherto unsuspected; more frequently, it predicts relations we have known about or had reason to suspect from casual observation outside the laboratory. A construct does not create relations among events. It is a conceptual device for organizing and understanding some quite diverse and ostensibly quite different phenomena. We judge a scientific construct by how successfully it accomplishes its task, by how successfully it *predicts* the events brought under its roof. A construct is thus one of three links in a causal chain. There is the antecedent or causal event, the caused event on the other side, and in the middle is the construct—the bridging or mediating link. Instead of using the language of cause and effect, which is simple but for these purposes problematical, let me instead say that we have on one side antecedent conditions, on the other the subsequent responses to be predicted, and the construct intervening.

## Anxiety and Drive

The experimental study of anxiety will help us with our analysis of constructs. The research on anxiety that we shall review illuminates the nature of constructs and their relations to antecedents and to behavior with especial clarity. Perhaps no other research program in personality has been as clearly and explicitly concerned with the processes of theoretical inference as this one. That explicit concern, some impressively successful experiments, and a few serious failings that marred the research make the drive studies of anxiety an ideal choice to explore some questions of method. The drive studies of anxiety grew from a theory of learning and the motivational concept, drive, that is one of its central features. Their purpose was to show that an important clinical phenomena and a pervasive human experience could be represented by a theoretical concept with broad and general implications.

*Anxiety.* To be anxious is a terrible experience, as many of us know, an imperative and sickening feeling from which escape is urgent and blindly uncertain. It has physical effects—heightened arousal that is felt in the pounding of one's heart, dryness of the mouth, muscular tremor, sweating of the palms, and that may be felt in gastric upset and diarrhea. If you have been anxious at times when you needed to use your mind, the experience will have impressed itself on you in another way: Cognition is impaired. Thoughts become jumbled, incoherent, and unrelated or sterotyped and repetitive. Thinking and learning may become impossibly difficult. Anxiety arouses. Anxiety disrupts. It is a potent and painful motivator. There is a vicious circularity about it. You are likely to react to the unpleasant bodily symptoms, the awful sense of urgency, and the disruption of thought and concentration with even greater anxiety. A small degree of anxiety is bearable and may facilitate thinking, learning, and performance. In general, however, when we speak of anxiety, it is the debilitating effects above that we have in mind. In the following excerpt, a student talks about his anxiety over an impending exam (Fischer, 1970).

> When I think about the exam I really feel sick . . . so much depends on it. I know
> I'm not prepared, at least not as much as I should be, but I keep hoping that I can
> sort of snow my way through it. He [the professor] said we would get to choose

two of three essay questions. I've heard about his questions ... they sort of cover the whole course, but they're still pretty general. Maybe I'll be able to mention a few of the right names and places. He can't expect us to put down everything in two hours. . . . I keep trying to remember some of the things he said in class, but my mind keeps wandering. God, my folks—What will they think if I don't pass and can't graduate? Will they have a fit! Boy! I can see their faces. Worse yet, I can hear their voices: "And with all the money we spent on your education." Mom's going to be hurt. She'll let me know I let her down. She'll be a martyr: "Well, Roger, didn't you realize how this reflects on us? Didn't you know how much we worked and saved so you could get an education? . . . You were probably too busy with other things. I don't know what I'm going to tell your aunt and uncle. They were planning to come to the graduation you know." Hell! What about me? What'll I do if I don't graduate? How about the plans I made? I had a good job lined up with that company. They really sounded like they wanted me, like I was going to be somebody. . . . And what about the car? I had it all planned out. I was going to pay seventy a month and still have enough left for fun. I've got to pass. Oh hell! What about Anne [girlfriend]? She's counting on my graduating. We had plans. What will she think? She knows I'm no brain, but . . . hell, I won't be anybody. I've got to find some way to remember those names. If I can just get him to think that I really know the material, but don't have time to put it all down. If I can just . . . if . . . too goddam many ifs. Poor dad. He'll really be hurt. All the plans we made—all the . . . I was going to be somebody. What did he say? "People will respect you. People respect a college graduate. You'll be something more than a storekeeper." What am I going to do? God, I can't think. You know, I might just luck out. I've done it before. He could ask just the right questions. What could he ask? Boy! I feel like I want to vomit. Do you think others are as scared as I am? They probably know it all or don't give a damn. I'll bet you most of them have parents who can set them up whether they have college degrees or not. God, it means so much to me. I've got to pass. I've just got to. Dammit, what are those names? What could he ask? I can't think . . . I can't. . . . Maybe if I had a beer I'd be able to relax a little. Is there anybody around who wants to get a beer? God, I don't want to go alone. Who wants to go to the show? What the hell am I thinking about? I've got to study. . . . I can't. What's going to happen to me? . . . The whole damn world is coming apart [pp. 121–122].

How does anxiety do its painful work? The drive theorists proposed that the effects of anxiety come about because drive is augmented. The anxiety–drive theory, thus, is an account of some specific things that happen when motivation is sharply increased.

*The Construct of Drive.*   The motivational concept of drive was conceived by Hull (1943) as a general state of activation to which specific needs such as hunger, thirst, sex, and pain avoidance contribute. Drive is a concept, an inferred and hence unobservable state of the organism. It is anchored to behavior by increases or decreases in the strength of response: With higher drive, response probability is greater, response amplitude is larger, and response latency is shorter. In the theory, drive acts through a multiplicative relation with another concept, habit (H). The product is expressed in a third concept, excitatory potential (E). The higher E is, the more likely a response is to be made. Thus,

$$E = f(D \times H).$$

Drive is also anchored in stimulus or antecedent conditions. The number of hours of food deprivation is one example of an experimental operation for varying the level of drive. So, in an experiment, drive might be manipulated by asking different groups of subjects to abstain from food for varying periods of time—no hours, four hours, and twelve hours. The increase in drive brought about by food deprivation will activate many habits; thoughts of food and eating should be among the strongest. Having subjects tell creative stories about semi-ambiguous pictures should bring out the food-related thoughts, and the longer the period of deprivation the more frequent these thoughts should be. One can see how drive bridges the gap between antecedent conditions and subsequent responses in Fig. 2.1 for this experiment.

| Antecedent Conditions | Intervening Construct | Subsequent Responses |
|---|---|---|
| Number of hours of food deprivation | _Drive_ × Habit Strength →E | Number of food-related stories told to semi-ambiguous pictures |
| (Manipulate) | | (Observe) |

FIG. 2.1.   The anchoring of drive in a hypothetical experiment.

Why do we need such an inference chain? Why could we not simply describe functional relations between variables at a purely observed or behavioral level, doing away with all theoretical inference as Skinner (e.g., 1950, 1953) has long and forcefully argued? After all, in the example above, "drive" means number of hours of food deprivation since it is explicitly tied to this variable, and it is similarly anchored to frequency of food themes on the response side. It seems legitimate to ask whether the theoretical concepts adds anything. Although this is a more complex problem than the answer implies, one major reason why it is difficult to dispense with constructs is that they mean more than the specific manipulations and observations of a particular experiment. The construct of drive involves a number of theoretical relations to responses and to various antecedent conditions; there are many potential sources of variation in drive in addition to food deprivation. On the response side, frequency is but one indicator of strength of drive. It is only an instance of many possible output measures—for example, response amplitude, number of trials to extinction, and response latency. As a construct, drive is not exclusively tied to one set of antecedents and consequents. Any given set represents larger classes of events which reflect the level of drive and which provide the behavioral means for inferring drive level and measuring its effects.

A series of experiments begun several years ago at the State University of Iowa explored the role of drive in simple learning situations involving aversive stimuli. They were experiments in classical defense conditioning. Their rationale proceeded as follows. In its simplest form, the construct of drive predicts that a threatening and painful occurrence like the administration of electric shock will produce a momentary increase in drive level. Since drive multiplies habit strength, we may observe the effect of shock-induced drive on the acquisition of responses. For example, the frequency of conditioned responses over the course of conditioning trials would provide an output or response index of drive. The higher the level of shock, the higher the drive; and the higher the drive, the greater the effect on the probability of making a response. The theory is almost but not quite as simple as this. It assumes that aversive stimuli produce emotionality, and it is emotionality that is responsible for the increase in the level of drive. The immediate effect of a painful stimulus is the arousal of a persisting emotional response, designated in the theory as $r_e$: The emotional response, in turn, produces a heightened state of drive. Schematically, aversive stimuli$\rightarrow r_e \rightarrow$D. This theoretical sequence is shown in Fig. 2.2.

Let's start in the middle of the diagram and work out to both sides. Three of the intervening constructs are now accounted for—the emotional response, $r_e$; habit strength, H; and drive, D. D multiplies H, and $r_e$ directly affects D but can influence H only through the multiplying effect of D. There is one more intervening construct to account for—excitatory potential, E. As Fig. 2.2 shows, the probability of making a response, R, on the response side of the diagram, is a function of excitatory potential. E is included because the theory

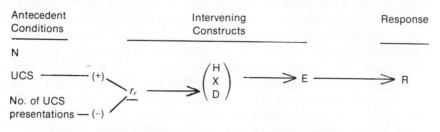

FIG. 2.2.   The antecedent, response, and intervening variables in classical defense conditioning. Note that the relation between UCS and $r_e$ is *positive*, while the number of UCS presentations is negatively related to $r_e$. (Adapted from Spence, 1958.)

recognizes that not every response tendency is strong enough to appear overtly. It is frequently the case in the early trials of learning that responses sometimes appear and sometimes do not. If they appear, habit strength and drive must be above zero—but how then to explain the failure of the response to appear on the next trial? E makes a place for learning to exist as a *potential* to respond.

For our purposes, however, we can simply recognize that R is a positive, direct function of E. The antecedent conditions in classical conditioning leading to changes in H, $r_e$, and D are listed on the left side of the diagram. N stands for the number of conditioning trials—that is, the number of trials on which the conditioned stimulus is presented and immediately followed by the unconditioned stimulus. In the Iowa studies, a tone or an increase in the brightness of a small illuminated disc in front of the subject was the conditioned stimulus, and a puff of air to the cornea of the eye was the unconditioned stimulus. R was a conditioned eyeblink. Drive, through the mechanism of $r_e$, is a function of two variables. One is the level or magnitude of the unconditioned stimulus, UCS—the greater its intensity, the more intense the emotional response and the higher the drive. The number of presentations of the unconditioned stimulus also affects the level of drive. At the time the theory was formulated and these experiments begun, it was well known that responses to painful stimuli tend to habituate over time. Thus, the level of response to repeated presentations of shock would tend to adapt and diminish with repetition. The Iowa theorists assumed that the number of UCS presentations affects D *inversely*—the greater the number of them, the weaker D becomes. It follows that giving the UCS alone for a number of trials preceding conditioning would produce an adaptation effect, and depending on the number of these adaptation trials the level of drive during the conditioning task to follow would be lowered.

*Emotionality.*    There is one matter to clear up before we proceed further. It is not intuitively obvious—at least it wasn't initially to me—why the concept of $r_e$ is necessary. Isn't this an unnecessary theoretical step, given that D is the effective multiplier of H? The problem is that a close look at the sequence of events in classical defense conditioning makes it clear that D by itself simply won't handle the events to be explained. To understand this we have to ask what D specifically means—how it is linked to a stimulus operation like a UCS and what kind of intervening process must be set off by the unpleasant occurrence of, say, an electric shock. To produce an effect on H, a given level of drive must be active at the *moment* the increment in H is to be multiplied. We run into difficulty right at the point at which the UCS increases D. In classical conditioning the conditioned stimulus, CS, precedes the UCS. As the conditioned response, CR, is gradually acquired, it is anticipatory to the occurrence of the UCS. So, on any trial it cannot be the

UCS which directly activates D, since conditioning is the acquisition of a habit which *anticipates* the UCS. Logically, we cannot have the motivational effect of D acting backward in time.

Suppose we assumed that a persistent emotional response is set off by the aversive UCS (and perhaps also by the general apprehensiveness that subjects might well experience in a strange and deliberately rather threatening experimental situation), lasting *at least* until the next trial. One can now see the necessity for $r_e$: It is an emotional reaction aroused by painful experience on previous trials. On any trial, after $r_e$ is established, it energizes D, which in turn activates H. Spence, Haggard and Ross (1958) further suggested that "this persisting emotional response may also get established as a CR to other cues in the general situation, possibly even to [the subject's] own verbal responses. These expectations, or fears, are assumed to keep a persisting level of emotional activity present that is, to an important degree, a function of the intensity of the UCS employed in the experiment [p. 405]."

*Some Theoretical Deductions.*   The basic statement of drive theory is now complete, and we can examine the sorts of deductions that may be made from it. The theory grew out of a wealth of previous research, and its constructs reflect already known laws. Spence (1966) called this an "*empirical construct type of theory*," noting that it "takes its start from the findings of laboratory studies of classical and instrumental conditioning [p. 445]." Thus, the meanings of H, $r_e$, and D, and the multiplicative relation of H and D, were intended from the beginning to recognize a number of already established empirical relations. N, UCS, and the number of UCS presentations were not dictated by the theoretical constructs as antecedent conditions; instead, the theory formalized and provided an integrated theoretical scheme for some empirical laws already known.

A basic hypothesis from drive theory is that the acquisition of conditioned defense responses is a function of UCS intensity, mediated by the effect of $r_e$ on D. The results of one experimental test are shown in Fig. 2.3. This was an eyeblink conditioning experiment in which drive was manipulated at two levels. There was a strong air puff group (1.5 pounds per square inch) and a weak air puff group (.25 pounds per square inch). If the air puff is noxious, as indeed it is, the strong-puff group should produce a higher level of conditioning. In addition, half of the subjects in the strong-puff and weak-puff groups were threatened by telling them that they might receive electric shocks during the course of the experiment. The anticipation of shock should produce a heightened $r_e$ adding a further increment to drive level. Thus, the strong-puff, shock-threatened group should the highest level of conditioning, and the poorest conditioning should be found in the weak-puff, non-threatened group. This is just what happens as you can see in Fig. 2.3: the threatened strong-puff group shows the highest percentage of CRs, and a very

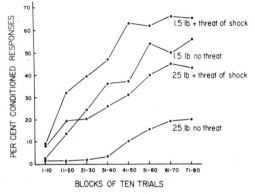

FIG. 2.3. The effects of UCS intensity and threat or no threat of shock on the acquistion of CRs in eyeblink conditioning. (Adapted from Spence, 1958.)

low level of conditioning is shown by the nonthreatened weak-puff group. A strong air puff without shock threat produced a somewhat higher level of conditioning than threat to the weak-puff group.

These results provide straightforward support for the theory: D varies with UCS intensity and the emotionality aroused by shock threat, multiplying H to determine the eyeblink CR. In fact, as Spence (1956; also Spence, Haggard, and Ross, 1958) found, an intense UCS increases both D and H. A clever experiment by Spence, Haggard, and Ross showed that H is directly affected by aversive stimuli and emotionality. This was another eyeblink conditioning experiment, with the reinforcing stimulus being an air puff. A high intensity group, Group H, got a strong air puff on each conditioning trial, and a weak air puff was presented alone (without the CS) on an equal number of randomly interspersed trials. The second group, Group L, got a weak air puff on conditioning trials and a strong puff on the randomly interspersed UCS-alone trials. Since both groups received equally strong air puffs in total, we would have to assume drive level to be the same for both. The difference lies in the specific pairing of strong or weak puffs with the CS on conditioning trials. Spence, Haggard, and Ross suggested that if there are reinforcing effects of the UCS on conditioning trials, Group H should develop greater habit strength than Group L and thus give a higher frequency of CRs. A third group in this experiment received a weak puff on both the conditioning and interspersed trials. This is Group LL, for which we should expect a very low level of conditioning. Fig. 2.4 gives the results. Group H shows a significantly higher percentage of CRs than either Group L or Group LL, and Group L is significantly better than Group LL. Spence, Haggard, and Ross pointed out that the cessation of a strong UCS produces a larger reinforcement effect than the cessation of a weak one. When the CS and UCS are paired, this differential reinforcement effect is responsible for the habit strength differences resulting in the superior conditioning of Group H. Group L, which got the strong air puff on the nonconditioning trials, is superior in its

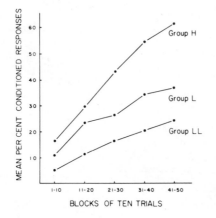

FIG. 2.4. The acquisition of CRs by three experimental groups: H (strong puff with weak puff interspersed), L (weak puff with strong puff interspersed), and LL (weak puff with weak puff interspersed). (Adapted from Spence, Haggard, and Ross, 1958.)

conditioning performance to Group LL, and this difference must reflect the effect of drive.

*S-R and R-R.* From the research we have examined so far, one can see that drive theory brings together several phenomena and gives them a very economical accounting. The drive construct, for example, effectively links the intensity of the UCS to the frequency of CRs, and it handles the adaptation effect of repeated aversive stimulation. The theory seems to deal very well with the simple learning situation of classical defense conditioning. In these experiments, drive has been defined by stimulus manipulations, and its response consequences have been observed. This is the classic form of the experiment, S-R experimentation, as Bergmann and Spence (1944) called it:

> Like any other scientist the psychologist is interested in discovering the empirical laws (functional connections) that obtain between the variables of his field. Unlike the physical sciences, however, behavior science at its present stage finds that its variables are divided into groups: on the one hand, the so-called response variables (R), and on the other, the group of experimentally manipulated variables (S). The functional relationships the behavior scientist is looking for are typically of the form
>
> $R = f(S)$ [p. 19].

Given that we have achieved some understanding of the nature of the stimulus and response variables, S-R research design converges very powerfully on constructs, with empirical anchors on both sides of the problem. Bergmann and Spence also pointed to another kind of empirical law, established by the correlation of responses:

$R_1 = f(R_2)$

This is called R–R research. Since an important part of research in personality is R–R in form, let's examine its strategy and logic and contrast it with the S–R experiment. We return to drive theory for this.

*The Link of Anxiety to Drive.*    Drive reflects all the needs acting on an organism at a given time. Hunger, thirst, sexual arousal, and a state of fear would summate to produce a total effective level of drive. Thus, a slightly hungry and moderately fearful college student who found himself a subject in the strong air puff condition in one of the Iowa experiments would have higher D than another subject, also in the strong-puff group, who had not missed breakfast and was less frightened by the experiment. It follows that persons who habitually tend to respond to a wide variety of situations with fear or anxiety ought to have higher D than those more calm and less anxiously aroused. Drive theory proposes, then, that anxiety is a contributor to drive and that the disposition to react in any situation with anxiety produces a higher level of D. It is important to recognize that drive theory is not equating anxiety and D—the state of anxiety may have many other effects beside the effect on D—but the theory does say that anxiety contributes to D by increasing emotionality. Now, if we could select two groups of subjects, one anxious and the other nonanxious, the anxious group should show superior performance in eyeblink conditioning. Taylor (1953), a student of Spence, undertook the problem of devising a method to select anxious and nonanxious subjects and to test this hypothesis.

*The Measurement of Anxiety.*    The measurement of personality variables is not easily accomplished. The inference to constructs from the responses of subjects is the key issue in R–R research, and the anxiety–drive studies have a special lesson to teach. How was anxiety measured? There were several possible options, among them clinical interviews, ratings of observed behavior, behavioral test procedures, physiological measures, as well as personality tests. Despite the potential alternatives, the personality test has far and away become the dominant method chosen in contemporary personality research. Personality tests have some important advantages. They are usually not time-consuming for the subject or the investigator. They are readily administered, and except for projective tests, easily and reliably scored. They are often not hard to devise. Personality tests have some important problems. I shall not mention them here, for they will occupy us later in the chapter.

Taylor's choice was a personality test—an anxiety questionnaire. She obtained a set of test items representing the symptoms of anxiety and emotionality from the Minnesota Multiphasic Personality Inventory (MMPI), a major personality test composed of a series of scales which are presumed to identify the principal symptoms and forms of behavior disorder.

TABLE 2.1
Some Illustrative Items from the Manifest Anxiety Scale[a]

I feel anxious about something or someone almost all of the time.
I am about as nervous as other people.
At times I have been worried beyond reason about something that really did not matter.
At times I feel that I am going to crack up.
My sleep is restless and disturbed.
At times I lose sleep over worry.
I am not at all confident of myself.
When embarrassed I often break out in a sweat which is very annoying.
I am often sick to my stomach.
I have diarrhea ("the runs") once a month or more

[a]From Taylor, 1953.

These items were given to a group of clinical psychologists along with a clinical description of the symptoms of chronic and severe anxiety. Item by item, the psychologists were asked to decide whether each one reflected some facet or symptom of anxiety as seen in the clinical description. Those items on which the judges agreed became the first version of the Manifest Anxiety Scale. Several revisions designed to increase the understandability of the items and the reliability of the test followed. The anxiety items were embedded among a much larger number of "buffer" or disguised items intended to mask the purpose of the test. This is customary, and it is related to the practice of disguising experiments to conceal their true purpose that we discussed in the last chapter. Several items of the MAS are shown in Table 2.1.

The items fall in several clusters. Some are direct statements of anxiety or nervousness, predictable in a measure of anxiety. Restlessness and difficulty in sleeping is another category—one that clearly follows from chronic emotionality and apprehension. Then, there are somatic symptoms—sick stomach, unusual sweating, and "the runs." These things are presumed to be among the effects of persistent emotional arousal, and Taylor's clinical psychologist judges agreed that they were.

The MAS looks like an anxiety scale, and the judges who selected the items were each convinced that they were choosing items expressing some of the major symptoms of anxiety. The test had its hard-nosed critics, however, who soon posed a difficult question for the Iowa researchers: how could there be assurance that the test *really* measures anxiety? Here is the defense offered (Spence, Farber, & McFann, 1956):

> One sort of criticism of our experiments has revealed a serious misunder-
> standing of their purpose and underlying logic. It is that since there is not
> independent evidence that the test really measures emotionality, and there is

evidence that the test scores correlate with other personality indices, it cannot legitimately be *assumed* that differences on the test reflect differences in drive level (D). To repeat again the reasoning of these experiments, the *hypothesis* is set up that the test scores reflect differences in emotionality and hence differences in D. This hypothesis is then tested by deriving, with the aid of other parts of the theory of learning, implications concerning differences to be expected in conditioning and various other types of learning situations. Confirmation of these deductions lends support to the theory, including the hypothesis about the relation of the anxiety scale scores to D. Obviously they don't prove the theory, just as any theory is never proved in science [p. 297n].

Thus, drive theory makes predictions about the relation between scores on the MAS and performance in learning tasks like classical defense conditioning. If these predictions are confirmed, the relation between anxiety and learning receives support, and the inference that anxiety is a contributor to drive is also supported. The argument is that an independent criterion of anxiety is unnecessary; neither is there cause to question the meaning of the scale because it correlates highly with measures of other personality variables. Note carefully that Spence, Farber, and McFann do not use the words "prove" or "confirm" but the very cautious construction, "lends support...." R–R research needs such cautiousness, and the reason why concerns the degree of confidence we can have that measures of individual difference variables unquestionably measure what they are suppose to measure.

Although Spence, Farber, and McFann's justification for the interpretation of the MAS would require no further evidence than that from the predicted relation of the scale to learning, Taylor took one more step. She argued that if the scale is a measure of anxiety we could expect psychiatric patients to score higher than nonpatient subjects. Her reasonable assumption was that neurotic and psychotic patients would exhibit more anxiety symptoms than undisturbed individuals. The prediction was confirmed. Subsequently, several studies found significant correlations between MAS scores and psychiatric ratings of anxiety based on clinical interviews with subjects (Taylor, 1956). So there appears to be some ground for accepting the MAS as an index of anxiety, and now the question is how the MAS–learning predictions fared.

*Anxiety, Drive, and Conditioning.*    Over a period of more than fifteen years, nearly thirty studies testing the hypothesis of a direct relation between conditioning performance and anxiety were conducted at Iowa and in other laboratories. Each of these investigations paralleled the basic procedures of the conditioning experiments we have already reviewed, except that level of anxiety as defined by MAS score was the major independent variable. In each of these studies, typically, there were two groups of subjects—a high-anxious group and a low-anxious group—selected from the extremes of the MAS

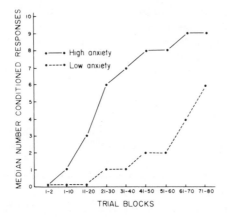

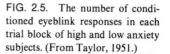

FIG. 2.5.   The number of conditioned eyeblink responses in each trial block of high and low anxiety subjects. (From Taylor, 1951.)

score distribution, usually the top 20% and the bottom 20%. The frequency of conditioned responses was greater for the anxious subjects than for the low-anxious subjects in the great majority of these studies (23 out of 27), and in more than half of them (15 studies) the difference between the anxious and low-anxious groups was significant. Fig. 2.5 gives the results of one of the original experiments (Taylor, 1951). Why weren't they all significant? I should simply like to pose the question at this point and come back to it when we evaluate the anxiety–drive theory research.

The MAS is not the only possible operation for assessing individual differences in anxiety and emotionality. The Iowa researchers sought other ways of determining anxious or emotional arousal, and I think it reflects well on their research program that they were not content to remain with a single instrument or procedure for varying drive. Remember that the theory interposes the concept of an emotional response, $r_e$, between drive-arousing antecedents and drive itself. As an emotional response, $r_e$ would involve changes in autonomic nervous system activity—increases in heart rate and blood pressure and changes in the electrical conductance of the skin. We could expect subjects who are more reactive autonomically—who would tend, for example, to show marked autonomic responses to mild stress—to condition more rapidly as result of a higher level of drive. Thus, another procedure for investigating inferred differences in drive was proposed by the Iowa researchers, paralleling but not identical to the MAS.

As an operational definition of emotionality, autonomic reactivity seems to be nearly ideal, since in the theory itself autonomic responses are assumed to be an integral part of $r_e$. It is unfortunate that such a simple and direct analysis is not warranted. There is a great deal of evidence to indicate that the same autonomic changes used to define an emotional response also occur to nonemotional stimuli (Graham & Clifton, 1966; Lacey, 1959). Also, as we shall see, the relation between MAS-defined anxiety and autonomic reactivity is equivocal. Nevertheless, a study investigating the relation of autonomic reactivity and conditioning needed to be done. It took several failures before the Iowa researchers found a method of scoring autonomic responsiveness that was sufficiently reliable and sensitive. The autonomic measure they finally adopted was one developed by Lacey (1956), called the *Autonomic Lability* index, which recognizes that patterns of autonomic arousal to aversive stimuli are frequently unique to individuals. Skin-conductance (the so-called galvanic skin response, GSR) and heart-rate recordings were taken from a large number of subjects during presentation of a mildly noxious stimulus. The GSR and change in heart rate following the noxious stimulus constituted the index of emotionality. High and low autonomic lability groups were made up from the top and bottom 30% of subjects on whom the autonomic measures were obtained, and subjects in these two groups were conditioned. The results nicely confirmed the prediction. Subjects who showed a high degree of autonomic responsiveness to the aversive stimulus performed significantly better in eyeblink conditioning. Runquist and Ross (1959) and Runquist and Spence (1959) replicated this finding, and in the latter experiment a measure of muscular tension also predicted conditioning.

*Anxiety–Drive Effects in Complex Learning.* What we have seen of the effects of anxiety and drive in learning situations has so far been restricted to the simple acquisition of a classically conditioned response. The theory has some interesting predictions to make in more complex learning tasks, where high drive does not have the same outcome as in classical conditioning. In classical conditioning, only one response is to be learned, the anticipatory eyeblink to the air puff. D multiplies a single H. What happens when there are a number of competing responses, only one of which is correct? D does not discriminate between habits; it multiplies all Hs impartially. When there is a heirarchy of habits and when the response to be made on a given trial is selected from many potential responses, D is a constant multiplier of all of them. The response with the highest H has the highest probability of occurrence. In the early stages of learning, before the correct response has become dominant, incorrect responses compete. If we have several potential responses that could be made, if each of them has a habit strength above zero, and if these habit strengths are all approximately equal in value, there is a high probability of an incorrect response. As learning proceeds, competing incorrect responses are gradually extinguished while the correct response increases in strength. Thus, a state of high drive has the paradoxical effect of impairing performance in the early stages of learning by increasing the probability of error, but facilitating learning once the correct response has come to dominate all its competitors. If you are a tennis player as I am, perhaps you remember how difficult it was when you were first learning to accomplish such a simple thing as returning a ball hit to you in midcourt. All manner of competing tendencies were evoked; the dominant responses should have included moving toward the ball, getting your feet into a stance sideways to it, bringing your arm back in a gentle arc, all leading to the satisfying outcome of a crisp and decisive forehand. What you did do was back up, overrun the ball, or forget to bring your arm back until it was too late, and if you were as anxious to play well as I was when I first suffered these exasperations it must have seemed that learning would never occur.

As you can see, the more competing habits there are and the stronger they are, the worse should performance be when drive is high. Over the years I have often wondered whether I should ever eliminate bad habits in tennis, and perhaps I should worry about a state of high drive. Anxiety–drive theory makes a plausible analysis of the effects of drive in learning to play tennis. It also capably deals with the cognitive interference experienced during high anxiety. The student, whose account of his anxiety–stricken state before an impending exam we saw earlier, complained of inability to think. His story is jumbled and disjointed, and it also seems to get stuck in the same track. The anxiety–drive interpretation is that high drive raises a number of thoughts and impulses above the threshold of awareness. Many of them are inconsistent and incongruous in the situation in which they are experienced; they appear because of the intensity of the drive state. Repetitive thoughts— the preoccupation with failure and his family's reaction—occur because of their prepotent habit strengths. He cannot stop thinking them or returning to them. Thus, his mind is filled with competing, irreconcilable, and disruptive thoughts that alternate with repetitive themes. It is not surprising that he has the experience of imminent disaster.

What kind of laboratory learning situation, where the experimental conditions can be well controlled, would permit us to observe the effects of drive when there are competing alternatives? After several experiments with a variety of other tasks, the Iowa researchers settled on paired-associates learning. There is a distinct advantage to this learning task for testing the effect of drive on competing habits: Not only can the number of competing responses be manipulated but the strength of each competing tendency can be varied as well. In the learning of paired associates, a list of words or nonsense syllables is presented to the subject one by one. With each stimulus word is paired a response word or syllable that must be given to that stimulus and that stimulus alone. Learning tasks such as this are presented on a memory drum which displays the stimulus word first, followed a second or two later by the appearance of the response word. The task is to learn to anticipate the appearance of the response term by giving it immediately after the presentation of the stimulus. Each stimulus–response pair in a list of many pairs has one response to be learned, and the more pairs there are, the more responses there are to be acquired. In the early period of learning, the stimulus–response associations to be made are weak and errors are frequent.

Failure to make a response is one obvious type of error. Another is the remote association—giving a response that would be correct to another stimulus. It is possible to increase or decrease the frequency of remote associations by varying the degree of similarity among the stimulus and response words. The greater the associative similarity, the more remote associations may be expected. This is a competitional situation in which high drive should impair performance early in learning. A paired-associates list with little interpair similarity, on the other hand, would allow less generalization across pairs; high drive here should facilitate.

Spence, Farber, and McFann (1956) did this experiment—in fact, two of them, one with a competitional list, the other with a noncompetitional list. The competitional list was made up in the following way: Four stimulus-response pairs were selected, the response terms of which were synonyms of the stimuli—barren–fruitless, little–minute. The remaining stimulus terms in the list were synonyms of the first four stimulus terms—for example, arid and desert for barren, and petite and undersized for little. The response words to be associated with these stimuli were words with no connection—grouchy, agile, and placid. One can think of the list as being made up of groups of three stimulus–response pairs; in each group, there is one strong association pair (barren–fruitless) and two pairs each containing a stimulus synonymous with the first stimulus word and a nonrelated response (arid–grouchy and desert–leading). The first pair should be easy to learn, but the learning of the second and third pairs should suffer from the strong tendency to give the remote association fruitless to arid and desert. The performance of the anxious subject should suffer on this list. The list for the noncompetitional experiment was made up of stimulus–response pairs with high associative connection—stubborn–headstrong, tranquil–quiet, and urgent–pressing. Similarity between items was minimized. In each of these two experiments, subjects were again selected from the extremes of the distribution of scores on the MAS. Fig. 2.6 presents the results for the noncompetitional list and Fig. 2.7 for the competitional list. As Fig. 2.6 shows, low response competition

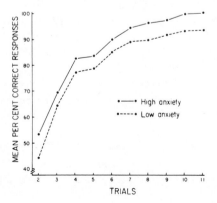

FIG. 2.6. The learning of noncompetitional paired associates by high and low anxiety subjects. Each pair of stimulus and response terms was strongly associated, and interpair similarity was small. (From Spence, et al., 1956.)

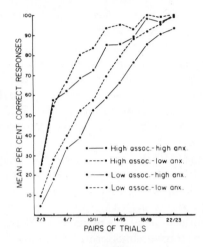

FIG. 2.7.   The learning of competitional paired associates by high and low anxiety subjects. The critical pairs of stimulus and response terms in the list were associatively unrelated, and there was high interpair similarity. (From Spence, et al., 1956.)

gave the anxious subjects a distinct advantage, and they were consistently superior to the low anxiety group. The next figure, presenting the results of the competitional task, is a more complex one, because we are concerned with the performance of high and low anxiety subjects in the learning of two kinds of items. There were the stimulus–response pairs with strong associative connections and pairs with weak association between stimuli and responses, whose stimuli would tend to elicit competing responses. The anxious subjects performed more poorly than the low-anxiety subjects on both kinds of items, although early in learning there was a slight (though nonsignificant) tendency for the anxious subjects to outperform the low-anxiety group. The theory predicts a significant difference since the high-association pairs presumably involve only a small degree of response competition. On the competitive pairs, it appears that the anxious group is consistently inferior, although this difference was not significant either. Spence, Farber, and McFann did find, however, that the anxious group required a significantly greater number of trials to learn the entire list. This is, in fact, the general finding from studies of anxiety in learning tasks in which there is a high degree of response competition: Anxious subjects tend to perform more poorly even when correct responses somewhat dominate incorrect ones. The early performance deficit and later facilitation that should follow from high anxiety according to the theory is not often found.

L⌀vaas (1960) repeated an earlier experiment by Spence, Taylor, and Ketchel (1956), one very similar to the Spence, Farber, and McFann study. Instead of the MAS as the measure of D, however, L⌀vaas manipulated drive by inducing muscular tension. Could the hard squeezing of a hand dynamometer produce an increase in D? This is exactly what L⌀vaas proposed. The effort required in exerting strong pressure on the dynamometer should be directly reflected in drive level. The tense person has higher drive, which is of course just what we might expect from the reasoning behind the MAS. One of the components of anxiety is muscular tension. Recall, here, the Runquist and Spence (1959) finding that level of muscular tension (their measure was muscle action potential recorded from the neck) was related to conditioning.

Løvaas's subjects had to squeeze the dynamometer on each trial of the paired associates learning task. One group squeezed hard—the tension group; the other only gripped the handle with light pressure. The paired associates list was very much like the list used by Spence, Farber, and McFann in the competitional response experiment. Some of the pairs were strongly associated, while others tended to evoke competing responses. The results are shown in Fig. 2.8. On the competing pairs, the tension group (bottom curve) did significantly worse. Their performance, as the theory would predict, was poorer than the low tension group or their own performance on the highly associated stimulus–response pairs. Very early in learning, the tension group made fewer errors than the low-tension group on the noncompetitional items.

I think there is at least one possible alternative to the drive interpretation of this experiment. Squeezing the dynamometer may have been a distraction, adversely affecting the difficult competitional pairs more than the easier noncompetitional ones. Løvaas did a clever experiment, however, one at least consistent with drive theory. His findings with a stimulus operation for defining drive reproduce closely the results of paired associates studies in which drive was response-inferred, and they deserve to be recognized.

Both the classical defense conditioning and verbal learning studies made use of S–R and R–R research designs, and the drive researchers moved from stimulus-defined to response-defined drive in a most adroit way. The differences in these research approaches is really at the heart of my purpose of reviewing these studies of anxiety and drive. Let's now take a contrasting look at the logic and the strategies of S–R and R–R research.

FIG. 2.8. The learning of competing and noncompeting paired associates in high induced muscular tension and low induced tension groups. (From Løvaas, 1960.)

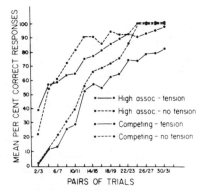

## THE LOGIC AND STRATEGY OF R–R RESEARCH

I think there was great ingenuity in the drive studies in developing a variety of operations to measure drive. The stimulus operations included UCS intensity, threat of shock, and induced muscular tension, and level of drive was response-inferred from the MAS and autonomic reactivity. There is a critical question about the drive research, as about all research in which theoretical inferences are made. How much confidence can we have that some hypothetical state, drive, is responsible for the behavioral results found in the learning situations? What confidence can we have that a stimulus manipulation—varying the level of intensity of the UCS—*caused* an (inferred) effect on drive, causing in turn a systematic effect on conditioned responses? At the simplest level, there is the undeniable fact of a regular empirical relation between variation in UCS intensity and the frequency of conditioned responses. How do you know that drive occupies a casual place in the chain?

Let us not be fooled by words. Drive is not real. It is a theoretical convenience which helps to reduce the explanation of many empirical relations to a small set of theoretical principles. Three conditions must be satisfied if we are to be confident about inferences to theoretical concepts. First, the stimulus operations must be clearly denoted. There can be no question about what was manipulated. This is purely and simply a question about the explicitness of the operational definition: The intensity of the air puff to the cornea was 2.0 lbs./sq. in. Sometimes this is a problem, although I think not in the case of these drive studies.

Second, the stimulus operations must be sufficiently understood so that we are reasonably certain that the intended effect is not confounded with other unintended and unknown ones, and the influence of any effects other than the critical one must be controlled. The more well-established a stimulus operation is in the research literature, the more confidence can be placed in its known effects. I have already suggested that the induction of muscular tension in Løvaas's experiment might have operated as a distracting or interfering stimulus, making it more difficult for subjects in the tension group to attend to the complex learning task; I am not certain that drive was manipulated. Only further studies using induced muscular tension as the independent variable and attempting to control for distraction can resolve this question. Perhaps some other distractor could be included deliberately in the design of the experiment so that its effects could be contrasted with those of dynamometer squeezing.

The third condition is a much more difficult one to satisfy. It requires the establishment of a network of relations, with several stimulus definitions of the construct and many response measures. That is, a single relationship (between UCS intensity and the frequency of CRs, for example) does not establish a construct. A number of predictions from the construct must be tested and confirmed, and these must reflect the range of the antecedent conditions implied by the construct and the response processes that the inferred state should affect. If some major implications of drive theory concern the role of motivation in conditioning and in more complex verbal learning, and if the theory specifies classes of stimulus events which influence drive, there must be several experiments testing these predictions. The range of stimulus events by which drive is varied will have to be fairly represented. Only then can there be confidence in the validity of the construct.

The conditions for converging on a response-defined construct are not in principle different, although they are concerned with response operations for inferring the intervening construct rather than with stimulus operations. The distinctions between S-R and R-R research in the procedures followed and the steps by which inferences are made are shown in Fig. 2.9. Remember that

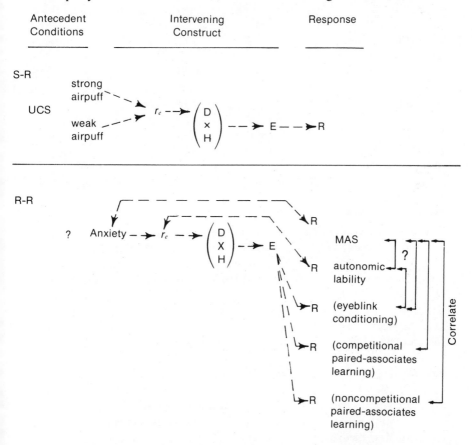

FIG. 2.9.   S-R and R-R definitions of anxiety, emotionality, and drive.

there is no difference in the theoretical problem for the two research approaches. They differ in the logic of inference and the strategy by which that logic is empirically supported. The S–R paradigm is an example from drive research similar to the one we saw earlier in the chapter. It is paired with an R–R diagram showing how anxiety is inferred and measured. The lines of inference in this figure are dashed to distinguish them from the empirical procedures of the R–R paradigm, which are at the far right.

The S–R paradigm in the upper portion of the figure is straighforward, and I shall not discuss it further except by contrast with the R–R approach. You can see the major distinction: All the operations for the R–R definition of anxiety and drive take place on the response side, and there is a question mark in place of some specified antecedent conditions. The "antecedents" of anxiety are the operations for eliciting the responses defining anxiety and the criteria for anxious and low-anxious performance. The MAS thus defines anxiety by the score on a scale—that is, by the kinds of responses a subject gives. The autonomic lability measure does, too, except that the responses elicited from the subject are quite different and they are treated quantitatively in a somewhat different way. In principle, however, these two operations are the same. The inference bridge is traced by the dashed lines from the MAS and the autonomic lability measure to anxiety and $r_e$. I have separated them at this point because it seems to me that anxiety and $r_e$ are clearly separable in anxiety–drive theory. Autonomic lability is an emotionality measure directly involving $r_e$ but not necessarily a state of anxiety. Note that there is a question mark by the link between these two sets of response operations. The relation between MAS-defined anxiety and autonomic arousal to mild stress is not satisfactorily established. Later in this chapter, we shall review a study by Hodges that suggests that anxiety–drive theory took too simple a view of this problem.

The inference steps from anxiety and $r_e$ are now familiar. D varies with the intensity of anxiety and $r_e$, and combines multiplicatively with H to produce a value of E; the results are seen in the consequent response effects in classical defense conditioning and verbal learning. Operationally, however, the MAS or the measure of autonomic lability are simply correlated with conditioning or verbal learning performance as the solid lines show, and we infer the causal link between anxiety–emotionality responses and learning. The Iowa researchers did not use correlational statistics (it is common practice not to), but the experimental statistics they did use to contrast high and low anxiety or emotionality groups are logically correlational. The more of these correlational relationships there are covering the major implications of the theory, the more certain we can be about the causal inference.

This section began by raising the question of how theoretical inferences are established as mediating bridges between stimulus operations and observed response effects, and I pointed out that the conditions that must be satisfied to affirm a stimulus-defined construct apply identically to constructs which are response-defined. However, when we make causal claims, it is clear that the stimulus definition of a concept is on much firmer ground. We can point to the observed effect of one level of stimulus variation and a different effect (or no effect) at another level: a 2 lb/sq. in. air puff produces greater eyeblink conditioning than a .25 lb/sq. in. puff. Although a certain amount of healthy caution is needed in constructing lengthy and complicated chains of causal inference, the stimulus-operations–response-effects sequence in a carefully controlled experiment clearly establishes an empirical cause–effect relation from which theoretical inferences can be made.

## Questions of R-R Inference

The inference of cause from the correlation of responses is more touchy. The critical issue concerns the meaning of the response measure, which is presumed to be the antecedent or causal variable. To repeat an earlier question, how can we be sure that the MAS is a measure of anxiety and not some other variable we can't identify? The validity of the MAS as a measure of anxiety is the key, and how do we establish that? Spence, Farber, and McFann (1956) had a fundamental answer: Predictions can be derived from anxiety–drive theory which specify particular relations between anxiety and conditioning and between anxiety and verbal learning. The successful outcome of these predictions gives support not only to the theory but to the validity of the test—the MAS. How could the predictions have been confirmed had the MAS *not* been measure of anxiety? If this question cannot be countered, the MAS and anxiety–drive theory gain strong credence.

*Construct Validity.*   A major question in R–R research, then, concerns the validity of the response operations from which inference to the construct is made, and in the anxiety–drive studies, as in much of personality research, this is a question of the validity of a personality test. It is a question of construct validity. The logic and requirements of making inferences to a construct from responses to a test were worked out by Cronbach and Meehl (1955). "Construct validation takes place," they wrote, "when an investigator believes that his instrument reflects a particular construct to which are attached certain meanings. The proposed interpretation generates specific testable hypotheses which are a means of confirming or disconfirming the claim [p. 290]." The confirmation of a single hypothesis will not be sufficient since theoretical constructs involve a number of meanings which cannot be collapsed into the test of a single hypothesis. Construct validity, then, involves the establishment of a network of laws that Cronbach and Meehl called a *nomological network.* "The laws in a nomological network may relate (a) observable properties or quantities to each other; or (b) theoretical constructs to observables; or (c) different theoretical constructs to one another. . . . A necessary condition for a construct to be scientifically admissable is that it occur in a nomological net, at least *some* of whose laws involve observables [p. 290]." Cronbach and Meehl were most emphatic that *"Unless the network makes contact with observations, and exhibits explicit, public steps of inference, construct validation cannot be claimed* [p. 291]."

Construct validation involves nothing fundamentally different from the processes of making theoretical inferences and subjecting them to tests that we have already considered. Its contribution is to make clearly explicit the fact that psychological tests are not exempt from the rigors of careful theoretical analysis and validation. The critical problem in construct validity, as in all theory-oriented research, is to converge on the construct. As a point in space is located by convergence or triangulation from independent points of reference, so a theoretical construct is established by converging on it or triangulating its position in a network of laws.

## The MAS and Construct Validity

The R–R studies with the MAS rest on the construct validity of the anxiety scale. Had the MAS not successfully predicted the response effects of drive in learning situations critical to the theory, it would have been exceedingly difficult to tell whether the anxiety part of drive theory was wrong or the MAS was inadequate as a measure of anxiety. R–R or construct validity research is especially vulnerable on this point: Negative results are ordinarily uninformative. Even in the case of a relatively successful program of research like the anxiety–drive studies, it is a perplexing problem to determine why some experiments turned out according to prediction while others did not. Not all the eyeblink conditioning studies were successful, nor have reliable anxiety effects in complex learning consistently been obtained (Katchmar, Ross, & Andrews, 1958; Saltz & Hoehn, 1957; Sarason, 1957). These predictive failures are embarrassing for the MAS and for anxiety–drive theory, and I think taken together they must suggest a weakness in the network of laws relating the response operations for drive to the learning dependent variables.

What sort of weakness? Jessor and Hammond (1957) proposed that we can understand the frailties of the MAS–drive studies as a result of a distressingly weak link between the construct of drive and the operations for assessing anxiety. Taking the MAS as a case in point, Jessor and Hammond argued that

> the test situation itself, and the kinds of test behavior it elicits, must be coordinated to the theory in exactly the same manner as the experiments aimed at validating the test. The Iowa experiments with the [MAS] were designed to fit

the paradigm required by the Hullian framework—i.e., they were designed to measure learning, to control probability of occurrence of correct responses, to control other significant sources of drive variation, etc.—in order to make inferences to that framework. The same logic requires that the [MAS] itself should likewise have been designed so that performance on it might be a basis for inferring drive independently of the outcome of subsequent experiments.... It is an artifact of tradition that theories have been utilized to derive experiments but not to derive tests [p. 162].

This is a demanding requirement, and if Jessor and Hammond are correct we shall have to admit to some laxity in establishing forceful links between personality tests and the constructs they are presumed to reflect. The Iowa investigators have been far from the only offenders. The problem of tightening the links between operations and constructs is one of providing clear, public, and repeatable steps of inference—a well-marked trail of logic— between the defining operations of a construct and the construct itself. S–R methodologists traditionally have been concerned about the adequacy of stimulus operations for making theoretical inferences, and at times, perhaps, have even been overzealous. It seems incontestable that a set of responses to a test—or any other operational procedures, for that matter—cannot be assumed to reflect some inferred state or process simply because a theorist has so designated them. By itself, confirming evidence for theoretical predictions from a test is not enough. The test needs a convincing theoretical rationale, or we face the uncomfortable prospect that some alternative interpretation may be correct. Jessor and Hammond suggested several alternatives to the anxiety–drive explanation of the MAS studies, and a number of others have been proposed in the years spanned by the anxiety–drive research. Before we consider the most prominent of these, however, we shall need to see just how the Jessor and Hammond requirement may be satisfied—and how, specifically, the MAS fails to meet it.

An investigator is required to make as strong a case as possible that the contours of the theory are reflected accurately, point by point, in measuring operations. One might think of this as duplicating a key, except that the duplicating process is carried out conceptually and not physically. The theory is the model, whose principal inflections must appear in the response measure. The "mechanics" of this accomplishment are formidable but clear: The model must prescribe the essential details of the response measure, and the response measure must duplicate them. Those essential details, said Jessor and Hammond, are the selection of the test items, the content of those items, the specific form in which the items are presented, and the nature of the choices the subject is required to make (e.g., true–false, a scaled response, or a forced choice between two or more alternatives). If these can be derived from the model and reproduced in the test, the most damaging uncertainty in making theoretical inferences from the test will be reduced. If there is a point-by-point logic connecting test and inferred state or process, there must be less of a problem with alternative interpretations of experimental findings.

How well does the MAS fare on the Jessor-Hammond criteria? The items were selected, as we saw earlier, by clinical psychologist judges, and only those which the judges agreed were symptomatic of anxiety found their way into the scale. Although the judges did agree on a large number of items, their criteria for anxiety statements must have been largely intuitive. We cannot single any item out and say, "That is an anxiety statement because...," enumerating the formal reasons for its inclusion. All we can point to is the fact of concensus among the judges. Perhaps a more critical failing is that MAS is supposed to reflect differences in emotionality and drive, and we should thus expect the explicit linking of the clinical symptoms of anxiety to the properties of the concept of drive. The relation between acknowledged symptoms of anxiety and emotionality and drive is intuitively plausible but not irrefutable. What about the specific content of the items—the symptoms or signs which, if acknowledged by the subject, allow us to infer an internal state of anxiety? What has having "the runs" once a month or more got to do with drive? The judges agreed that diarrhea is a clinical sign of anxiety, but we are back to test-theory coordination based on intuitive plausibility. There are surely several reasons, physical as well as psychological, why someone might endorse such an item.

The third of the point-by-point correspondences to be satisfied is the consistency of the form of the scale with the specifications of the theory. Jessor and Hammond asked how the level of drive is reflected in the topography of responses and whether there is any reason to believe that drive-related responses would clearly appear on self-report devices. For example, if it were true that states of anxiety or emotionality are sometimes inaccessible to awareness, or inaccesible to awareness in some people, the inference of drive level from acknowledgement of anxiety symptoms would be greatly weakened. If some highly emotional subjects could not label their internal emotionality as anxiety and link it to symptoms of worry, restlessness, or social unease they would be shown as nonanxious by the test, yet perform—if the theory is correct—like anxious subjects on learning tasks. The outcome of the test prediction would be weakened or nullified, and there would be no way of detecting the reason why.

The final requisite is related to the one we have just considered. Jessor and Hammond pointed out that "we observe or elicit responses (verbal) about other responses (nonverbal). A veridical relationship between verbal and nonverbal responses is a fundamental requirement of the chain of inference involved in the use of the [MAS] to measure drive [p. 165]." That is, we wish to make inferences about an internal state of affairs—emotionality and drive—whose relation to verbal responses is not well understood. The question is, *can* people inventory the kinds of internal processes to which the concept of drive has reference and accurately report the results? Anxiety–drive theory does not provide a very explicit answer. This issue could be avoided by asserting that drive is an inferred construct with purely mathematical properties (a "mathematical fiction") and that it does not refer to the internal processes of emotionality (Spence & Spence, 1966). I think this kind of argument begs the question of the defining operation–construct link. We could ask a further question: not only can subject report states of drive, but *will* they? To identify oneself as anxious on the MAS requires one to acknowledge some very unflattering things and disclose some very personal affairs that we ordinarily reserve for the privacy of our own concerns about ourselves or for the bathroom. To get a high score on the MAS demands claiming some socially undesirable things, and there is powerful and abundant evidence to indicate that the probability of endorsement of personality test items is directly and highly related to their social desirability (Edwards, 1957). It's clearer to put it the other way around: The more socially undesirable a personality test item is judged to be, the less likely it is to be endorsed. This general relation is so well established that were it to be shown that the MAS is affected by the tendency to give socially desirable responses, the faithfulness of the MAS in reflecting anxiety, and perhaps the very meaning of the test as well, would be seriously questioned.

## Some Theoretical Alternatives to Anxiety and Drive

The main thrust of Jessor and Hammond's argument is that an explicit, public, theory-derived relation between response operations—personality tests—and the constructs they are presumed to define must be shown. The heart of the question is whether we can establish the meaning of response measures with the same degree of certainty as stimulus operations in the definition of constructs, and so we come back again to the problem of making causal inferences to describe R–R relations. If the meaning of the "causal" response can be well anchored in a network of empirical relations *and* theoretically, we shall be less plagued by doubt that the hypothetical state of affairs bridging the gap between the R–R end terms can be easily supplanted.

The drive studies have not wanted for suggestions that anxiety–drive theory could be supplanted by other plausible, or even *more* plausible, interpretations. It seems to me that the alternative explanations of the anxiety–drive research fall into two major categories. In the first category are alternative interpretations which attack the very core of drive theory. They have in common the suggestion that the operations for varying drive—stimulus and response—vary some other process instead or some other process in addition to drive. In the second are proposals that the MAS does not reflect drive but some other variable which can equally well account for the MAS findings, or proposals that it reflects other variables besides drive. Let's take these in turn.

Does high anxiety mean simply high drive? Child (1954) proposed that it does not. His alternative to the concept of drive is an excellent example of a competing interpretation. He began by pointing out the ambiguity of the theoretical analysis of learning in competitional response situations on which the anxiety–drive prediction is based. To predict the inferiority of the anxious subject requires knowledge of the probabilities of correct and incorrect responses. Suppose the correct response was dominant in the hierarchy; then, of course, the theory would demand predicting the superiority of the anxious group. Only when there are equal probabilities of correct and incorrect responses or higher probabilities of incorrect responses is the condition for inferior learning of the anxious subjects met. A possibility that Child's criticism suggests is that anxious persons would perform more poorly during the beginning trials, when incorrect responses are more likely to vie with correct ones for dominance, and perform better on later trials when the correct response has attained dominance. This, as you recognize, is just what drive theory says. But, the early inferiority and later superiority of the anxious subjects would cancel each other out, and we should find no overall effect. Child now argued that we could think of anxiety and emotionality as a state involving disruptive internal stimulation. Being anxious means that one is bombarded with internally-produced stimuli or cues. He agreed that anxiety contributes to a state of drive, but the energizing properties of drive together with drive-produced stimuli should impel responses to the state of anxiety itself. These responses will be disruptive to task performance. As Child observed, "in complex situations, where the subject is already in conflict between various response tendencies relevant to the task, the presence of irrelevant responses made to anxiety heightens the conflict and interferes with performance to a greater extent than the increased drive improves it [p. 154]." In simple conditioning, however, competing responses to the task are not a problem, and responses to internal anxiety stimulation are going to be less disruptive. Thus, high drive should enhance conditioning. The interfering response interpretation is not necessarily restricted to anxiety defined by scores on the MAS, as Child stated it. Manipulating the level of drive could have the same effect by producing drive-stimulus-related interfering responses in the process of making subjects more fearful and emotional. Muscular tension could result in interfering responses, as I suggested about the Løvaas experiment. The stimuli of muscular contraction could have been distracting and interfering.

Child's interfering response theory predicts the same outcomes as drive theory, neatly sidestepping the problem of specifying the positions of correct and incorrect responses in the hierarchies of various stages of competitional learning—a problem that anxiety–drive theory is obliged to consider. That should be chalked up as a point in favor of interfering response theory, but otherwise we have two conceptualizations paralleling each other right down to predictions of identical outcomes. Which one is likely to turn out to be more fruitful? Since we are dealing with inferred processes whose response outcomes in conditioning and verbal learning are identical, the answer must now boil down to a matter of preference. Perhaps a better question is how anxiety–drive theory comes to suffer the embarrassment of having a rival capable of the same accomplishment.

The second category of criticisms of the anxiety–drive studies questions the MAS as a measure of anxiety. Substantial correlations are found between the MAS and measures of neurosis and maladjustment (Brackbill & Little, 1954; Eriksen & Davids, 1955; Franks, 1956). These correlations, many of them between the MAS and other scales of the MMPI from which the MAS was derived, are frequently very high, revealing a consistent pattern of response. It is hard to escape the implication that the MAS and the scales with which it so highly correlates are measuring the same thing. The concept of anxiety as emotionally based drive, however, should not entirely overlap with the concepts of maladjustment and neurosis, and it would not be unreasonable to expect the correlations between the MAS and measures of these concepts to reflect the distinctive meaning of anxiety. An experiment by Kimble and Posnick (1967) makes the point even more forcefully. Kimble and Posnick rewrote the items in the MAS to construct a scale paralleling the MAS in every major respect save the anxiety content of the items. For the item, "I have diarrhea ('the runs') once a month or more," the following substitute was written: "I am the butt of a practical joke once a month or more." For "My hands and feet are usually warm enough" they wrote, "My plans and goals are usually clear enough." What sort of correlation would you expect between the MAS and the anxietyless version? Surely, it ought to be negligible. It wasn't: In two samples of subjects, the correlations were .84 and .74. Kimble and Posnick concluded that endorsement of the items on the anxietyless scale may reflect maladjustment in that endorsement requires making some generally negative (but not anxiety-related) claims about oneself. Thus, the high correlation between the two measures suggests that the MAS overlaps with another more general variable. Whatever the specific interpretation, there is no happy alternative to the conclusion that responses to the MAS reflect other things besides the presence of anxiety which drive theory requires.

*What Does the MAS Measure?*    What is it about the MAS and the Kimble–Posnick version that causes subjects to respond to the two scales in such a remarkably similar fashion? Perhaps the common denominator is maladjustment, but there is another possibility: Subjects respond to personality test items on some other basis than the content of the items. One prominent determinant of test responses, which I briefly noted earlier, is their social desirability, and what may tie the MAS to scales measuring variables other than anxiety is the common tendency to give or not to give socially desirable responses.

Edwards (1953) had judges rate the social desirability of a large number of personality test items. They were to decide whether endorsement of each item would reflect desirably or undesirably on the endorser. He then correlated these judges' ratings with the frequency of endorsement of the items in a new sample. The correlation between the social desirability scale values and probability of endorsement was an extremely high .87. Edwards' interpretation of this finding was that the location of an item on a social desirability continuum is the best single predictor of its likelihood of being endorsed.

Edwards then constructed a measure of individual differences in the tendency to give socially desirable responses. From a large number of MMPI items, he selected those on which there was unanimous agreement among a number of judges about their social desirability or undesirability. The resulting scale reflects the tendency of a subject to give socially desirable responses, a high score indicating a strong tendency and a low score a weak one. Correlating this scale with a variety of personality tests, including the various scales of the MMPI, yielded the predictable result of high negative correlations. The greater the tendency to give socially desirable responses, the fewer socially undesirable symptoms are acknowledged on other tests. What is the correlation of the MAS with the social desirability scale? It has been found repeatedly to reach -.80 or better. Since the correlation is so high, argued Edwards, the primary determinant of responses on the MAS must be regarded as social desirability rather than anxiety. So far, Edwards's data have shown that procedures for obtaining socially desirable responses from subjects correlate highly with the MAS—so highly, in fact, that there seems to be no other conclusion but that responses on the two scales are determined by the same tendency. Is this primary determinant social desirability or is it anxiety? Or, indeed, is it some other personality variable—perhaps one called ego strength, as Block (1964) suggested from his analysis of the structure of intercorrelations on the MMPI?

The high correlations between the MAS and scales of maladjustment, neuroticism, and the tendency to give socially desirable responses must surely cast doubt on the purity of the MAS as a measure of anxiety. They cannot, of course, call into question the fact that the MAS, whatever it measures, is generally (but not always) found to be related to performance in eyeblink conditioning and in verbal learning. But there, uncomfortably, is the rub: If anxiety–drive is not the explanation of the learning findings, what is? Edwards (1957) proposed that the social desirability hypothesis could equally well account for the learning findings. The relation between the MAS and the measure of individual differences in the tendency to give socially desirable responses (the SD scale) is inverse and very high. Thus, we can expect subjects with high scores on the MAS to be low scorers on the SD scale, while low-anxious subjects will generally obtain high SD scores. Now, if the low-anxious subjects are really socially desirable subjects and the high-anxious subjects are really socially undesirable, we can make a desirability-based prediction about performance in complex learning. This is Edward's prediction.

> I believe it is possible, therefore, to describe the low group on the [MAS] as those who desire to make a good impression on others and the high group as those who are less interested in what others may think of them. I would predict that the group desiring to make a good impression on the [MAS], that is to say, those with low scores, might also desire to make a good impression in terms of their performance on the learning task. They are, in other words, perhaps more highly motivated by the desire to "look good" not only in their responses to the [MAS], but also in their performance in the learning situation itself. Surely, to be able to learn fast is, in our society, a socially desirable characteristic. If a subject has a strong tendency to give socially desirable responses in self-description, is it unreasonable to believe that he may also reveal this tendency in his behavior in a learning situation where he is aware of what would be considered socially desirable, namely to learn fast, to do his best [p. 89]?

The social-desirability–good-impression hypothesis can make the same verbal learning prediction as anxiety–drive theory, simply given the fact of a high negative correlation between the two response measures. There is, in fact, some independent support of this interpretation. Stricker (1963), in a reanalysis of a study by Brown (1960), showed a positive relation between the tendency to give socially desirable responses and delayed recall in paired associates learning. There is an infirming flaw in the social desirability hypothesis, however. While it can neatly account for competitional learning, it must also explain the results of the conditioning studies, and I do not see any plausible theoretical ground on which to argue that social desirability or desire to make a good impression (equal, remember, to low anxiety on the MAS) should be associated with poorer conditioning performance. Anxiety–drive theory is clearly superior in its ability to predict both simple and competitional learning. Still, the overlap between the MAS and social desirability (as well as the other measures we have considered) is an embarrassment. The MAS fails to display what Campbell and Fiske (1959) called discriminant validity in its high correlation with measures of conceptually different variables.

## Summing Up

How does anxiety–drive theory hold up against the criticisms and alternative interpretations we have been reviewing? It seems to me that the drive studies exemplify both excellence in the empirical analysis of a theoretical concept and some of the most plaguing problems of theory building and testing. The Iowa investigators were adept in their use of stimulus and response operations for drive, testing similar hypotheses with a variety of procedures. Their analysis of classical defense conditioning and more complex verbal learning is highly sophisticated in its emphasis on the need to specify the details of learning—the number and strengths of the habits to be acquired—and on the complex effects of drive manipulations. On the other hand, there have been several predictive failures that are not easy to account for, and the alternative interpretations to anxiety–drive theory suggest its major weakness. The link between anxiety–drive operations and the inferred state which mediates drive-related performance has a number of gaps, as we saw in Jessor and Hammond's critique. The most acute ones are between the response operations for anxiety and the construct of drive, and they highlight the problem of making unambiguous theoretical inferences from responses whose determinants are many and not well understood. This problem is reflected, empirically, in the disturbingly high correlations between the MAS and measures with which it ought to differ.

It could be said that the Iowa theorists didn't claim that anxiety *is* drive. They proposed that anxiety *contributes to* drive, separating it from drive in the inferred anxiety–emotionality–drive chain. Here, I believe, lies the great problem in this approach to the study of anxiety. By failing to build a secure bridge between the measure of anxiety and the inferred state of drive, the anxiety–drive theorists left the door wide open to any plausible competing interpretation. It was an error to make the distinction between anxiety and drive and then to give less attention to the careful theoretical analysis of anxiety and the question of its measurement than these thorny problems deserved. It was an understandable error, but it introduced a serious flaw.

Another weakness lies in the fact that relations among the various operations for drive are not well established. For example, what is the correlation between the MAS and autonomic responsiveness? Runquist and Ross (1959) found a correlation of .22 between autonomic lability and the MAS. This relationship, however, is a very weak one, and with the exception of a study by Mandler, Mandler, Kremen, and Sholiton (1961) that found a more substantial correlation, the bulk of the research on the MAS and autonomic responsiveness has shown negligible relations (Jackson & Bloomberg, 1958; Katkin, 1965). Although the failure of the MAS to relate consistently and substantially to emotionality as defined by autonomic responsiveness can be attributed in part to the extraordinary complexities of autonomic arousal, there is more to the question. If anxiety is an emotional response, involving the response-produced stimuli of internal autonomic processes, there must be substantiating empirical relations between anxiety and arousal. The MAS would be established more securely if it could be shown that scores relate to autonomic reactivity, increase under stress, and parallel increases in autonomic responsiveness to stress.

Our analysis of S–R and R–R research and review of the anxiety–drive studies raise some very general issues that will come up repeatedly in evaluating the research in the chapters to follow. I can anticipate one question that will occur to the reader. Why, if R–R research is as touchy as the anxiety–drive studies suggest, is the response definition of constructs so prevalent, especially in the area of personality? The answer is that the kinds of variables of interest in the investigation of personality are often difficult to manipulate in the laboratory. Necessary constraints on what we may do to subjects can limit laboratory investigation of the variables of personality to states of low intensity from which effects may not be observed or generalization may be precarious. Further, the kinds of variables which the study of personality encompasses are likely to have long, strongly reinforced histories, which will be resistant to change by short-lived and circumscribed manipulation in the laboratory. The response definition of constructs really cannot be avoided if we are seriously to investigate personality. A major point of this chapter, however, is that some crucial problems need to be dealt with systematically if meaningful and durable findings are to result. With each of the concepts to be examined in the remaining chapters, we shall need to judge the adequacy of the defining operations, the explicitness of the links between operations and construct, and the anchoring of the construct in a nomological network.

## BEYOND DRIVE THEORY AND THE MAS

The literature on anxiety is enormous (Spielberger, 1975a, reported finding more than 2,000 studies using the MAS alone), and the drive theory of anxiety is only one among many conceptual approaches to the problem. I chose to concentrate on the basic anxiety–drive research in this chapter for the reasons summarized in the preceding section. Critical study of this experimental program is amply rewarded by a growing clarity of understanding of a number of critical issues in the methods of psychological science that are not at all easy to see. At least, this was true for me, and I hope it will be so for the reader.

Our concern is also with anxiety—with its conceptualization, measurement, and consequences. We need to fill out our analysis a bit and bring it up to date. I want to do this by outlining certain of the approaches that recent research on anxiety has taken. The drive studies stimulated a very large amount of research. Many other psychologists picked up the MAS and set off to do anxiety studies themselves; I think they found anxiety–drive theory too narrow and restrictive in its implications. They had in mind, I suspect, the painful and crippling emotional state itself and the great potential expanse of situations in which the various effects of anxiety arousal could be seen. It was difficult to accept the self-imposed limitation of the anxiety–drive theorists

(Spence & Spence, 1966): "in our work involving the MAS we have been primarily concerned with the role of aversive motivational factors in relatively simple types of learning situations, and not with anxious individuals per se [p. 322]."

Thus, it was to have been expected that research on anxiety would branch off in some quite diverse directions, following an array of theoretical inclinations: among them, anxiety as an emotional state (Lazarus & Averill, 1972; Schachter, 1966); as the experience of helplessness deriving from the interruption of planful activity (Mandler, 1972; Mandler & Watson, 1966); as the pathological outcome of intense activation (Malmo, 1966); as proneness to react physically and psychologically to stress (Basowitz, Persky, Korchin, & Grinker, 1955; Grinker, 1966); and as a source of interfering internal responses and cognitive processes that disrupts learning and achievement in children (Sarason, Davidson, Lighthall, Waite, & Ruebush, 1960). Without disparaging the important contributions that approaches such as these have made to our understanding of anxiety, and the considerable ingenuity that methodologically distinguishes many of them, I believe the most significant acheivement of the post-Iowa research lies elsewhere. It lies in the conceptual and operational recognition of a really elemental point—as Shedletsky and Endler (1974) say, that "an appropriate assessment of the trait of anxiety must... consider both the responses that characterize anxiousness and the situations which are likely to arouse them [p. 514]." It is thus the conceptual and operational recognition of the situation–person interaction.

Anxiety is particularly unsuited to conceptualization and experimental treatment as an unvarying trait. Except in extreme form, anxiety is experienced in situations that, through learning and by generalization, have come to evoke it. To think of a chronic, unmitigated state of high drive not explicitly associated with anxiety-inducing situations just doesn't conform to clinical observation or common sense. Yet that is what the measurement of anxiety by the MAS rather implied—or perhaps to be fairer, that potential implication was not ruled out by a more explicit, situation-specific alternative. Though the anxiety–drive theorists clearly linked the arousal of drive to identifiable stimulus events in conditioning situations (refer back to Fig. 2.2), they did not make the analogous links with anxiety. They *were* aware of the issue, but I think they failed to say so convincingly until very late in the research program. As they then pointed out (Spence & Spence, 1966):

[A] problem that arises in assessing the results of studies comparing high and low anxiety groups is concerned with specification of the conditions under which the groups can be expected to differ in degree of emotional responsiveness and hence to differ in performance in the manner predicted by our theory. In this connection we have considered two alternative possibilities. One of these is that the intensity of the emotional responses ($r_e$) of high anxiety subjects tends to be greater than that of the low anxious in any and all types of experimental situations, due perhaps to the former tending to be chronically more anxious and emotionally aroused. The second possibility is that high anxiety subjects differ from the low primarily in their lower threshold for emotional arousal in response to situations perceived as having some degree of threat. If the second of these hypotheses were correct, then differences in performance due to differences in drive level would be expected to occur only in situations involving some element of stress. The evidence clearly indicates that it is not necessary to introduce stress stimuli into the situation (e.g., a noxious event or instructions designed to elicit fear or failure or some other type of psychological threat) to obtain performance differences between anxiety groups. For example, the results of the studies of complex learning . . . were all obtained under neutral, task-oriented instructional conditions and did not involve the use of noxious stimulation. . . .

Although the evidence is not unambiguous, we are inclined, because of a number of considerations, to accept the situational hypothesis rather than the chronic one. For example, a study of S. A. Mednick (1957) indicated that while experimentally naive high anxiety subjects differed from low anxiety subjects in performance on a stimulus generalization task, no differences between anxiety groups were found for subjects who had served in several prior psychological experiments. Since subjects are likely to lose their initial apprehensiveness about participating in such experiments and become quite blasé after several such experiences, these findings suggested that, in the absence of experimental conditions designed to be stressful, anxiety groups differ in emotional responsiveness only when the experimental situation is novel and thus more likely to be perceived as potentially threatening. Still other evidence favoring the situational hypothesis may be found in the results of conditioning studies. In contrast to classical aversive conditioning, no differences have been found between anxiety groups in classical reward (salivary) conditioning (Bindra, Paterson, & Strzelecki, 1955), a situation which involves neither noxious stimulation nor performance on a task which reflects some valued characteristic. Even within eyelid conditioning there is some evidence (Spence, 1964) that more satisfactory results are obtained when experimentally naive subjects are used and physical arrangements are such that they make the subjects somewhat fearful and uneasy (e.g., placement of subjects in a dimly lit room, isolation of subject from experimenter, etc.) [pp. 306–307].

## A State-Trait Analysis of Anxiety

Following the extensive and complex research of Cattell and Scheier (1961), Spielberger (1966) proposed that we need to be clear about what we mean when we describe someone—"Mr. Smith"—as anxious. Do we mean that he is anxious *at the immediate moment* or that he is prone to anxiety in many situations? That, said Spielberger, is the distinction between *state* and *trait* anxiety.

Research findings suggest that it is meaningful to distinguish between anxiety as a transitory state and as a relatively stable personality trait, and to differentiate between anxiety states, the stimulus conditions that evoke them, and the defenses that serve to avoid them. There is considerable general agreement that anxiety states... are characterized by subjective, consciously perceived feelings of apprehension and tension, accompanied by or associated with activation or arousal of the autonomic nervous system. Anxiety as a personality trait... would seem to imply a motive or acquired behavioral disposition that predisposes an individual to perceive a wide range of objectively non-dangerous circumstances as threatening, and to respond to these with...[anxiety] reactions disproportionate in intensity to the magnitude of the objective danger [pp. 16-17].

*The Measurement of Trait and State.* Trait anxiety is assessed by a scale with some close resemblances to the MAS. That was quite deliberate. Spielberger, Gorsuch, and Lushene (1970), who developed these anxiety measures, chose items highly correlated with the MAS to maximize the similarity of the trait anxiety scale to an established anxiety questionnaire. The trait anxiety scale mainly differs from the MAS in the way responses are made: there is a four-point scale instead of the true–false choice given on the MAS. Some sample items from the trait anxiety scale can be seen in the upper part of Table 2.2.

State anxiety is measured by items on which one can express his immediate feelings. There is no requirement that state responses show stabiliity over time as we would expect of trait responses, and in fact they vary considerably according to the situation. That rather suggests a question: how do we know that trait anxiety is more than just a "snapshot of a state," as Cattell (1966) picturesquely put it? The demonstration of stability in scores over time—test–retest reliability—is one basic way. We can also have some confidence in an enduring personality disposition when the measurement of the personality variable is well separated in time from the experimental procedures. States should dissipate; recurrent dispositions should persist. There are some representative state anxiety items in the lower half of Table 2.2. The respondent is typically instructed to complete the items as he felt at some specified moment—while anticipating a forthcoming shock or working on an experimental task, for example.

*A State–Trait Experiment.* Research on episodic and dispositional anxiety has studied very different experimental problems than anxiety–drive theory. This research has not been so theoretically derived and guided. It has focused on more empirical questions of the kind investigated by Hodges (1968): what are the effects of ego threat and threat of physical harm on state and trait anxiety? Hodges' study will give us a picture of the state–trait experimental analysis of anxiety. He used earlier versions of state and trait anxiety measurement, predating the scales shown in Table 2.2. We can be fairly assured of comparability, however, since the state and trait anxiety scales correlate highly with Hodges' measures.

TABLE 2.2
Representative Items from the Trait and State Anxiety Scales[a]

| Trait Items | Almost Never | Sometimes | Often | Almost Always |
|---|---|---|---|---|
| I feel that difficulties are piling up so that I cannot overcome them. | | | | |
| I worry too much over something that really doesn't matter. | | | | |
| I lack self-confidence. | | | | |
| I feel secure. | | | | |
| I take disappointments so keenly that I can't put them out of my mind. | | | | |
| I become tense and upset when I think about my present concerns. | | | | |

| State Items | Not at All | Somewhat | Moderately So | Very Much So |
|---|---|---|---|---|
| I feel calm. | | | | |
| I feel tense. | | | | |
| I feel upset. | | | | |
| I feel nervous. | | | | |
| I feel content. | | | | |

[a]From Spielberger, Gorsuch, and Lushene, 1970.

The trait anxiety was assessed some time previous to the conduct of the experiment, and subjects with scores in the extremes of the distribution were selected for later participation. In the experiment itself, subjects first quietly rested while heart rate was recorded; they filled out the state anxiety scale at the end of this interval. Next, they were given practice trials on a measure of immediate recall—repeating series of digits backward. This set the stage for the critical experimental procedures in which the digit test was given again under ego threat, threat of physical harm, or no threat conditions. The ego threat condition made subjects feel they were failing the digit test and for threat of physical harm subjects were given to believe they would receive several strong electric shocks. The state anxiety scale was taken at the end of this period as were recordings of heart rate.

Hodges found no difference between the high and low trait anxiety groups either in state anxiety or in heart rate during the rest period. The threat conditions, especially failure threat, increased state anxiety. Failure was particularly effective in raising state anxiety in the high trait anxiety group. Shock threat, however, was not any more stressful for the high than for the low trait anxiety subjects, though this was the more effective form of threat in increasing heart rate. Hodges concluded that high trait anxiety entails a special vulnerability to ego threat, and there are now many studies with supporting findings (e.g., Hodges & Spielberger, 1969; Rappaport & Katkin, 1972). As he pointed out:

> The most significant implication of the results of this study for furture research on anxiety is that in investigation of the effects of stress on state anxiety for subjects who differ in trait anxiety the type of stress must be taken into account. The response to pain or threat of pain, often used as stressors in this research area, does not seem to be related to neurotic or trait anxiety, but may be related to personality traits associated with fear of pain (Hodges & Spielberger, 1966). A-trait [trait anxiety] appears to reflect differences in dispositions to manifest A-state [state anxiety], but only in response to stress situations that contain threats to self-esteem or ego threat [p. 370].

## Persons, Situations, and Modes of Response

There is another situation–person approach to anxiety. Endler and Hunt (1966, 1969; Endler, Hunt, & Rosenstein, 1962) have developed an Inventory of Anxiousness and an analysis they regard "as a methodological framework for conducting research on anxiety" (Shedletsky & Endler, 1974, p. 514). The Inventory of Anxiousness is far more cumbersome than the state–trait measures. It consists of 11 situations, to each of which the subject indicates his modes of response on 14 different scales. One situation and a sampling of the various modes of response are shown in Table 2.3. This technique permits

TABLE 2.3

One Situation and Sample Response Modes from the Inventory of Anxiousness[a]

| "You are about to take the final examination for a course in which your status is doubtful." | | | | | |
|---|---|---|---|---|---|
| Heart beats faster | 1 | 2 | 3 | 4 | 5 |
| | Not at all | | | | Much faster |
| Get an uneasy feeling | 1 | 2 | 3 | 4 | 5 |
| | None | | | | Very strongly |
| Emotions disrupt action | 1 | 2 | 3 | 4 | 5 |
| | Not at all | | | | Very disruptive |
| Perspire | 1 | 2 | 3 | 4 | 5 |
| | Not at all | | | | Perspire much |

[a]From Endler, Hunt, and Rosenstein, 1962.

analysis of the way people characterize their own reactions to a variety of situations. We can thus see how (self-reported) anxiety responses differ from one situation to another. We can also see the patterning of anxiety responses and whatever individual consistency there may be (that is, a trait of anxiety).

Typically, the inventory is given to a large number of subjects (sometimes selected on an independent dimension—for example, socioeconomic status— and sometimes not), and the responses are subjected to analysis. The analytic technique yields terms for subjects (i.e., individual differences), situations, modes of response, and the interactions of these. Though there are individual (trait) consistencies, Endler and Hunt believe their data reveal the idiosyncratic organization of anxious responses in each person. If their data are generally representative, they suggest, the understanding of personality "might be improved by emphasizing *what kinds of responses individuals make with what intensity in various kinds of situations* [1966, p. 336; italics mine]."

## A New Perspective on the Measurement Problem

The Spielberger and Endler and Hunt concepts and measures of anxiety, though representing an important methodological advance in their respective emphases on situation–person interactions, also significantly retain features of the anxiety–drive approach. The state–trait analysis, for example, is based on drive theory. Spielberger (1975b) notes that state–trait anxiety research was "stimulated by Spence-Taylor Drive Theory and by Freud's clinical conception on anxiety. In general, the results of these studies have provided additional empirical support for Drive Theory and contribute to clarification of the nature of the anxiety as a psychological concept [p. 140]." The Inventory of Anxiousness, while theoretically distinct from anxiety-as-drive, shows the influence of the MAS in the selection of anxiety responses (Endler, Hunt, & Rosenstein, 1962). Both approaches share with the anxiety–drive research a degree of unconcern about the critical relation between concept and measurement. They are vulnerable to the same issue that plagued the MAS studies: is it anxiety that is being measured, or are competing interpretations plausible? We saw that anxiety–drive theory got into difficulty by relegating anxiety to a peripheral place in the theoretical chain and failing to give questions of measurement their due regard. The considerable theoretical and experimental sophistication of the anxiety–drive researchers was applied elsewhere.

In contemporary research on anxiety—state–trait, person–situation– mode-of-response, and some other current analyses as well—measurement is not greatly advanced over the MAS, save in the one respect of situation-specific assessment. That is an important achievement, as I have indicated, but there is still the problem of what is measured. Contemporary research on anxiety has largely sidestepped questions of measurement, accepting subjects' anxiety scale responses as factual and accurate. That has come about because current models of anxiety tend to be less formal and rigorous. They are looser constructs, more reliant on a characterization of the experience of anxiety, and in consequence their specifications for measurement must be less detailed. The state–trait and person–situation–mode-of-response concepts do prescribe situational measurement, but they otherwise rely on the respondent's ability and willingness to report on his experience of anxiety.

Our review of the Jessor and Hammond criteria for the link between personality tests and constructs made clear the need for theoretical derivation of the details of response measures. In effect, the theoretical concept must anticipate the way in which people cognitively represent the personality characteristic to themselves and the way in which that representation may be elicited. We have long known of the potential difficulties that face such a task. A compelling analysis of the evidence on introspective report by Nisbett and Wilson (1977) strongly suggests that people often cannot report on the reasons for their own choices, actions, feelings, and preferences. It raises the serious issue that self-perception and self-attribution are less likely to be based on accurate assessment of cognitive processes than on a priori personal theories. As Nisbett and Wilson say:

> People often cannot report accurately on the effects of particular stimuli on higher order, inference-based responses. Indeed, sometimes they cannot report on the existence of their responses, and sometimes cannot even report that an inferential process of any kind has occured. The accuracy of subjective reports is so poor as to suggest that any introspective access that may exist is not sufficient to produce generally correct or reliable reports.... Subjective reports about higher mental processes are sometimes correct, but even the instances of correct report are not due to direct introspective awareness. Instead, they are due to the incidentally correct employment of a priori causal theories [p. 233].

The evidence that we are unaware of much of our mental life is considerable and widely arrayed. It comes from studies of perceptual encoding, cognitive dissonance, self-attribution, subliminal perception, and insightful problem solving. A more searching review would certainly reveal yet further research indicating that choices, feelings, and actions are often poorly accounted for. What people *do* report are plausible theories or reasons for choosing, feeling, or acting that are usually applied after the fact. We almost always *feel* that we know why we did or felt something, but that is because our a priori theories *are* plausible.

What happens when a person fills out a personality questionnaire like the MAS? If this sort of self-perception and self-attribution fits into the body of evidence reviewed by Nisbett and Wilson, as it probably does, there should be frequent misattributions of symptoms. Mistaken denial or acknowledgment should occur when items refer to feelings and behavior that are not distinctly tied to identifiable stimulus events that are likely to cause them. Example: "I am not at all confident of myself." Items that seek admission of symptoms that run counter to personal theories of self will also tend to elicit inaccurate responses. In this category will be items that are strongly socially undesirable. Example: "At times I feel that I am going to crack up." The accuracy of self-description will be adversely affected when items refer to experiences that are remote in time or unspecified as to time. Asking about distant or timeless feelings and behavior is really asking for the intrusion of personal theories of causation. Thus, one might deny most anxiety symptoms on a questionnaire because he genuinely does not believe himself to be anxious. One could have plausible reasons for occasional upset stomachs and diarrhea—"the flu" or unusual foods that one happened to eat—and other symptoms would also get believable explanations or simply recede into a gray, unnoticed background. One might endorse many items and not be a very anxious person from holding the general theory of himself as tense and nervous. In completing personality questionnaires, if people are sometimes inaccurate about themselves and sometimes accurate, or if some people are mostly inaccurate and others mostly accurate, measurement must badly suffer. Our ability to predict from measures of personality concepts will be impaired, and our confidence in R–R relationships must be weakened by the possibility of alternative interpretations.

Of the three anxiety scales we have considered, the MAS seems to be the most vulnerable to the introspective problem. Its items do not ask about specific experiences of recent origin. Instead, they are general and nonspecific, and vague qualifiers are used for frequency and time of occurrence (e.g., "at times," "often"). The measurement of state anxiety in the State–Trait Anxiety Scale is an improvement in calling for judgments of feelings in the situation in which they have just been experienced. The stimuli responsible for tense and anxious feelings will still be salient and distinctly remembered, and personal theories about how one reacts to anxiety-producing situations will have had less time to be consulted. The Trait Anxiety Scale, patterned as it is after the MAS, is likely to have the same susceptibility to introspective inaccuracy. Because the Inventory of Anxiousness specifies particular situations in which anxiety may be experienced, responses may give a closer approximation to the way people would actually react. The remoteness-in-time problem is still present, however, and there is still room for the play of personal theories (e.g., "Exams make me nervous."). It is not clear whether the Inventory of Anxiousness is intended as a *predictive* measure of anxiety in specific situations or simply as a measure of self-attribution in specific situations. If its purpose is to study situational variation in self-report, the potential inaccuracy of personal theories will not create a serious problem that might exist for a scale intended to predict behavior in anxiety-inducing situations.

The two newer scales do seem to be more likely to encourage accurate self-perception. The State Anxiety Scale, especially, takes important advantage of what people potentially *can* tell about feelings of tension and anxiety, and the Inventory of Anxiousness may also reflect more accurate self-attribution from its reference to situations. Not one of the three scales, however, is free of the general problem. It is still necessary for a particular construct of anxiety to prescribe the critical details of the measuring instrument—to specify the conditions under which people can report symptoms of anxiety, the items, the format of the test. Personal theories may be very sensitive expressions of some personality constructs. They may badly stand in the way of measuring other constructs. Anxiety, I think, probably falls in the latter category.

Despite the problem of self-awareness and these critical comments, there is surely an enduring and substantial body of findings. The MAS does predict classical defense conditioning and complex verbal learning, and there are important extensions and applications of this research. The work of Spielberger (1966) on the relations of anxiety–drive theory and the MAS to learning and college achievement suggests the generality of the construct and the MAS. The state–trait and person–situation–mode-of-response approaches are promising. As Chapter 8 points out, the study of situation-person interaction marks the end of an era in personality psychology that was all too occupied by a fruitless person–*or*–situation debate. It is unfortunate that fruitful and creative research should be marred by uncertainty over the meaning of measuring instruments: Uncertainty detracts.

# 3 Conflict

## ABSTRACT

*The study of conflict is the study of behavior impelled by opposing tendencies that are of approximately equal strength. This chapter is concerned principally with one form of conflict that produces greater misery and is less amenable to solution than others—the approach–avoidance conflict. We review the theoretical and experimental analysis of approach–avoidance conflict developed by Miller. The theory is based on four assumptions about approach and avoidance behavior: (1) how the tendency to approach a goal becomes stronger as the goal is neared; (2) how the tendency to avoid a feared situation becomes stronger as the situation is neared; (3) how the tendency to avoid has a steeper gradient than the tendency to approach; and (4) how increases in motivation affect the strengths of approach and avoidance. We consider some of the experimental studies testing deductions from the theory with animals in simple, well-controlled situations and with humans in more complex clinical and life situations. The implications of conflict theory for the understanding of neurosis, psychotherapy, and alcohol and drug dependence are discussed.*

*Some critical questions arise in conflict theory and research concerning the relative intensities of approach and avoidance, whether their gradients intersect, and whether the approach gradient can ever be steeper than the gradient of avoidance. In the last section of the chapter, we take up experimental studies of conflict in sport parachutists and the cognitive, performance, and physiological effects of strong desire competing with intense fear.*

## INTRODUCTION

This and the next chapter are concerned with two great themes in personality—those of conflict and stress and the processes, which we have come to characterize as coping and avoiding, by which people struggle with conflict and stress. The two themes are related but not overlapping: Stable conflict situations are stressful and lead to both psychological and physiological expressions of stress. Although not all stress is produced by conflict situations, conflict is an important stressor, and it is perhaps the most important psychological source of stress.

We can differentiate conflict and stress by noting that the study of conflict is the study of *situations* and the kinds of behavioral outcomes they produce: The investigation of stress focuses on *responses*—the psychological and physiological effects of exposure to stressors. Conflict is thus *stimulus defined*: We manipulate situations, creating, say, an approach–avoidance conflict, and we examine the effects on the person's (or animal's) behavior of those experimental manipulations. The definition of stress is typically in terms of its consequences: Stress is *response defined*. Two quotations will help to make this distinction clearer. The approach taken in the experimental analysis of conflict can be seen in an analogy drawn by Neal Miller (1959):

> For example, suppose we want to know whether polarized light or radio waves can be stimuli for bees. There is no way to decide the matter from a priori considerations of the physical energies involved. The only thing that we can do is to set up a discrimination experiment to determine whether or not physically specified changes in the polarization of light, or the onset of radio waves, can be correlated with changes in the animal's behavior. It is conceivable that electrical recordings from end organs, sensory nerves, or sensory projection areas could be substituted for the learned response. But I doubt whether most of us would want to accept such results if they were consistently contradicted by discrimination experiments. Similarly, as a first approximation, we might substitute for the learned response an innate reaction, but I doubt if we would want to call the event a stimulus if, in an exhaustive series of experiments we found it impossible to make any learned response contingent on it [pp. 239–240].

The difference between this sort of procedure—systematically varying the stimulus features of a situation and observing the behavioral results—and the way stress is investigated is highlighted by Lazarus (1966):

> It soon becomes clear that stress cannot be defined exclusively by situations because the capacity of any situation to produce stress reactions depends on characteristics of the individual. Similarly, stress reactions in an individual do not provide adequate grounds for defining the situation associated with it as a stress, except for that individual or individuals like him. An observation of Janis

(1958) is typical and relevant. He found that the intensity of preoperative fear in patients anticipating surgery was not correlated very substantially with the objective seriousness of the operation. *The important role of personality factors in producing stress reactions requires that we define stress in terms of transactions between individuals and situations, rather than of either one in isolation....* The approach is ... at first circular in that the stress stimulus is defined by the reaction, and the stress reaction is, in turn, defined by its relationship with the stress stimulus [p. 5].

This is not a hard and fast distinction, although as a rough guide it does pretty well in distinguishing stress from conflict research. There are occasions when we may observe a given behavior and infer conflict, as the clinician routinely does and as Murray (1954) did in an attempt to apply the experimental analysis of conflict to psychotherapy. We shall encounter that study later in this chapter. We may choose to study certain kinds of stress *situations*, investigating, perhaps, the effects of natural variations in them—the passage of time, for example, and the approaching imminence of a stressful situation, as Epstein and Fenz (Epstein, 1962) undertook in the study of novice sport parachutists. This research, in fact, lies almost exactly at the junction of the problems of conflict and stress, and it may be viewed from either perspective.

Conflict and stress can produce enormously heightened emotionality and great misery, and the psychological and physiological tolls can be extreme. For that reason, psychologists cannot expose human subjects to strong and painful conflict situations contrived in the laboratory. That leaves us with limited possibilities—largely, to study conflict as we encounter it clinically in people with nuerotic symptoms or to investigate experimentally-produced conflict in animals. Miller (1959) argues that we may reasonably assume that the basic principles of learning and motivation (and of conflict behavior) apply to human and infrahuman species. Then:

For certain (but not all) problems it may be desirable to work out the laws first in more rigorously controlled experimental situations with animals. Although these laws will have to be checked later at the human level, it will be easier to check them once they have been precisely formulated so that one knows exactly what to look for than it would to discover them in the complex human situations which are less subject to experimental simplification and control. Furthermore, one's confidence in the conclusions from the less-controlled clinical situation is increased if the same relationship is found also in the better-controlled animal experiments [p. 204].

There is litte hesitancy in accepting this sort of reasoning in the study of disease and disease-producing agents—for example, the *experimental* investigation of cancer-producing substances—and medicine often proceeds in a way exactly analogous to the strategy Miller proposes. Why should we not accept the rationale in the study of psychological problems?

The problem of stress again differs. Because stress has traditionally been response defined, many of its investigators have chosen to study stress in naturalistic situations—Janis' (1958) research on patients facing surgery is an excellent case in point. But as before, the distinction between conflict and stress research must not be overdrawn. Some psychologists have experimentally manipulated stress in animals, as Brady, Porter, Conrad, and Mason (1958) did in a famous study of ulcer development in "executive" monkeys, the intent being to produce a well-controlled experimental analogue of stress and an important stress response that might later be applied to the challenging problem of stress-produced ulcers in humans.

With these distinctions between conflict and stress in mind, we can now turn to the experimental study of conflict. Some great and classic figures in psychology have dealt with conflict—Pavlov, Prince, James, Lewin. Lewin (1931), in fact, presented a formal analysis of conflict that provided a model for the sytematic conflict theory of Miller (1944, 1959), whose research will mainly occupy us. And, of course, there is Freud and the rich clinical look into neurotic conflict that he provided. Miller was strongly influenced by psychoanalysis (he underwent a psychoanalysis with Heinz Hartman in the mid-1930s), but he chose to reject the mentalistic concepts and exclusively clinical focus of the Freudian system and to develop instead an analysis of conflict behavior founded on basic principles of learning. As we shall see, however, Miller has been sensitive to the question of applying the experimental analysis of conflict to complex human situations.


## A THEORY OF CONFLICT BEHAVIOR

Miller (1959) begins by making four assumptions. Let's take the first two of them, which form a pair.

1. *"The tendency to approach a goal is stronger the nearer the subject is to it. . . .*
2. *"The tendency to avoid a feared stimulus is stronger the nearer the subject is to it* [p. 205]."

These assumptions respectively postulate a gradient of approach and a gradient of avoidance, and they are graphically illustrated in Fig. 3.1. Although the reasons for these two assumptions are not immediately obvious, a couple of real-life examples will help to show that the assumptions make sense. What do you observe about the approach of two lovers who have been separated for a time? There is really no question about the increase in the

FIG. 3.1. The gradients of approach (A) and avoidance (B), showing the increasing strength of the tendencies to approach or to avoid a desired or feared goal as the goal is neared. The steeper slope of the gradient of avoidance is taken up in Miller's third assumption (see text).

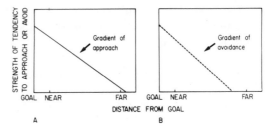

strength of approach as they come closer to each other. A boy on his way home from school with a report card the he knows will displease his parents dawdles, and the closer he gets to home the slower he goes.

There is a formal basis for the approach and avoidance gradient assumptions in a hypothesis proposed by Hull (1932)—the *goal gradient* hypothesis. It is well known that the closer in time that reinforcement follows the response, the more the response is strengthened. Immediate rewards (or punishments) are more effective than delayed ones. Hull's hypothesis was that responses made in close proximity to the goal are strengthened more than responses made earlier in the sequence, since the earlier responses are more remote from the reward. The stronger a response is, the stronger will be the tendency to make it, the greater will be its magnitude or intensity. The specific responses made by a hungry rat as it approaches the goal box in a straight alleyway will be strengthened in proportion to their nearness to the goal and to reward. Avoidance follows the same rule: Those responses made in the presence of or near to a feared goal will be strengthened more than responses more distant in time (or in space). We can represent the hypothesis by a gradient rising toward the goal. It is only for convenience that the gradients of approach and avoidance are shown by straight lines: Curves continuously increasing toward the goal would do equally well.

As Fig. 3.1 shows, in describing approach and avoidance situations graphically we plot strength of the tendency to respond against distance from the goal. Distance may be time until the occurrence of the goal event ( a feared and forthcoming examinination!) or it may be spatial distance. Traversing physical space in moving toward or away from a goal changes the stimulus situation, bringing the person or animal into proximity to new cues that signify greater nearness to or distance from the goal. Space itself is not a stimulus, nor is time; the passage of time also changes the stimulus situation, but it does so by arousing anticipatory thoughts about or implicit responses toward the goal. One can move spatially toward or away from a goal; time can simply bring a desired or feared goal closer. We might thus expect that the nature of approach or avoidance behavior could differ depending on whether spatial movement is required or time must pass. There are few data on this question, and it needs both naturalistic/clinical observation and experimental analysis.

The first two assumptions help to explain the behavior of dawdling children and rats in runways. So far so good. Let's go on to Miller's (1959) third assumption.

3. *"The strength of avoidance increases more rapidly with nearness than does that of approach.* In other words, the gradient of avoidance is *steeper* than that of approach [p. 205]."

## Why Is the Avoidance Gradient Steeper?

One of the most painful conflicts is that in which the same goal (i.e., the same *situation*, the same *person*, or the same *response* that one might make) is both desired *and* feared. This is the approach–avoidance conflict, and Dollard and Miller (1950) argue that it is the basic conflict in neurosis. People in approach–avoidance conflicts characteristically vacillate, cannot seem to make up their minds, start toward the goal and then stop. And they are miserable. Here is Herzog, the hero of Saul Bellow's (1964) novel, nearly undone by the disastrous breakup of his second marriage. Should he now marry Ramona?

> In the crowds of Grand Central Station, Herzog in spite of all his efforts to do what was best could not remain rational. He felt it all slipping away from him in the subterranean roar of engines, voices, and feet in the galleries with lights like drops of fat in yellow broth and the strong suffocating fragrance of underground New York. His collar grew wet and the sweat ran from his armpits down his ribs as he bought the ticket, and then he picked up a copy of the *Times*, and was about to get a bar of Cadbury's Caramello, but he denied himself that, thinking of the money he had spent on new clothes which would not fit if he ate carboydrates. It would give the victory to the other side to let himself grow fat, jowly, sullen, with broad hips and a belly, and breathing hard. Ramona wouldn't like it either, and what Ramona liked mattered considerably. He seriously considered marrying her, notwithstanding that he seemed, just now, to be buying a ticket to escape from her. But this was in her best interests too, if he was so confused—both visionary and muddy as he felt now, feverish, damaged, angry, quarrelsome and shaky. He was going to phone her shop, but in his change there was only one nickel left, no dimes. He would have to break a bill, and he didn't want candy or gum. Then he thought of wiring her and saw that he would seem weak if sent a telegram [pp. 33–34].

*Because* of this observation about people in conflict—the simultaneous inability to reach the goal or to successfully avoid it—Miller reasoned that distant avoidance responses must be strengthened more weakly than approach responses at the same distance from the goal. Thus, with the intensity of avoidance dropping off more sharply than approach, we would have the basis for intersecting gradients if, close to the goal, avoidance was stronger than approach. The vacillation and indecision of people in conflict occur, Miller argued, at the point of intersection of the two gradients. At any point farther than that from the goal approach is stronger than avoidance, and we see movement toward the goal. But at the critical point of intersection, approach and avoidance tendencies are equal, and an enduring situation of misery and irresolute and unsuccessful efforts at conflict resolution is the outcome. The person cannot approach more closely because his fear now dominates his desire. The only possible way that Miller could see to deduce such indecisiveness and misery was through the assumption of the steeper avoidance gradient. That assumption was later augmented by two further assumptions essentially proposing that fear, as a *learned* drive, differs from such approach drives as hunger in being more dependent than physiologically-based drives on situational cues. Thus, fear-producing stimuli at a distance from a feared goal will more weakly evoke avoidance responses and will result in a weaker drive arousal. A steeper avoidance gradient follows. Miller was strongly encouraged in the making of the third assumption by the results of an experiment of Brown's (1940), which appeared to provide confirming evidence. I say *appeared* because the experiment had a bad, inadvertent flaw that Maher and Nuttall (1962) discovered much later. We shall return to the Brown study and Maher and Nuttall's and to the question of intersecting gradients later in the chapter; for the moment, we can let the assumption stand. In Fig. 3.2, an approach–avoidance conflict of the kind we have been discussing is graphically presented.

Maher (1966) makes a nice point about the deductions that may be made from the third assumption. Going part way and stopping is not a deduction from the assumption, although it is explained by it; it is the *observation* that dictated the assumption. However, what happens when a person (or an experimental animal) is placed in a conflict situation *beyond* the point at which avoidance has become stronger than approach? According to the

FIG. 3.2. Conflict between the tendencies to approach and to avoid the same goal. At a distance from the goal (the Far point), there is a stronger tendency to approach than to avoid; near to the goal and beyond the presumed point of intersection of the gradients, avoidance is stronger than approach. Approach behavior should be observed far from the goal, while avoidance will be the dominant tendency close to the goal. Going part way and stopping followed by smaller, partial approach and avoidance responses around the intersection of the gradients will be observed. (From Miller, 1959.)

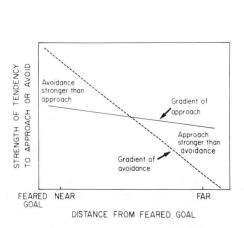

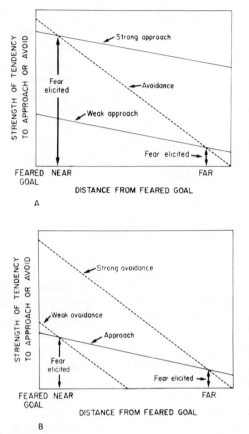

FIG. 3.3.   The effect of increasing the strength of the approach tendency (A), which increases the intensity of fear. In (B) is seen the fear reduction that follows from increasing the strength of the tendency to avoid. (From Miller, 1959.)

assumption, he should retreat to the region in which the strengths of approach and avoidance are equal. This is a *deduction* from the third assumption, and a test of it will provide important evidence about whether the assumption is tenable.

4. "*The strength of tendencies to approach or avoid varies directly with the strength of the drive upon which they are based.* In other words, an increase in drive raises the *height* of the entire gradient [Miller, 1959, p. 205]."

This last assumption concerns the effects of increasing the motives (drives) to approach or to avoid. Fig.3.3 shows what occurs when the strength of the motives to approach A or to avoid B is increased. The first might happen when well-meaning friends urge a person in conflict to try to reach a desired-but-feared goal. They succeed in raising his desire by pointing out all the appealing features of the goal and pressuring him to attempt it, but the effect, while bringing him closer, is only to increase his fear and to intensify the conflict. When fear is increased (Fig. 3.3B), the result is that the person remains farther from the goal and at that point experiences *less* fear. A person plans a winter vacation trip, but is afraid of flying. A friend uninformed of this conflict tells the person of a recent bad experience—rough trip, bumpy landing, mechanical difficulties with the aircraft—and dreadfully increases the person's fear. The person now ceases planning and postpones the trip, and the fear diminishes.

## Tests of Some Basic Deductions

The strategy followed in testing deductions from the four assumptions evolved quite early in the research. That strategy was to design simple experiments using animals, in which the deductions could be tested without complication. One of the most important simplifications that was introduced was that deductions concerning approach and avoidance behavior could be investigated *separately* in *different* groups of animals. This is a startling simplification, and on first exposure one feels a good deal of resistance to it. The objection is that the experience of *conflict* is more than the desire for or fear of a goal alone. It is not an intuitively obvious idea that the principles explaining the behavior of approach and those explaining avoidance can be directly and simply combined to yield an explanation of conflicting approach–avoidance tendencies in the same organism: Conflict *feels* different! The *feeling* comes from competing tendencies to respond that are approximately equal in strength, and it is deducible from the combination of approach and avoidance principles.

As a first approximation, Miller proposed, the laws of approach and avoidance behavior needed to be worked out; then, these laws could be combined and applied to the understanding of conflicting motives. Experiments by Miller and his students sought to relate strengths of the tendencies to approach or to avoid to increased hunger, intensity of shock, and distance from the goal. These experiments were with rats, and they came to rely on one technique for measuring the strength of the tendency to respond—the partially restrained animal's strength of pull. The relation between response strength and pulling strength was defined as follows: "Within the limits of the animal's capacity to pull, the strength of the response tendency is positively related to the strength of pull exerted by an animal temporarily restrained [Miller, 1959, p. 209]."

Miller (1944) describes the technique as Brown (1940) used it to study the gradients of approach and avoidance:

> In the study of the approach gradient Brown trained a group of hungry albino rats to run down an alley to secure food at a point made distinctive by the presence of a light. During these trials, the animals wore a little harness attached to a cord which moved so easily that it was not a hindrance. After they had

learned to run down the alley to approach food, some of the animals were restrained for one second [*sic*: 5 sec.] at a point near the goal and others at a point far from the goal. During this restraint, they pulled against a calibrated spring attached to a marker tracing on a polygraph so that the average force of their pull could be computed. . . . It was found that the animals restrained near the goal of food pulled reliably harder than those restrained farther away. This test verified the first assumtion, that of an approach gradient.

In an investigation of the avoidance gradient Brown gave a different group of animals a brief electric shock at the same end of the alley. After receiving two shocks the animals, when placed in that end of the alley *without shock*, showed a marked tendency to avoid it. Brown restrained half of them near the place they were avoiding and the other half far from this place. The rats pulled harder when restrained near than when restrained far, thus verifying the second assumption, that of an avoidance gradient [p. 435].

With an unusual but quite believable technique for measuring response strength, and having established gradients of approach and avoidance, Brown next conducted the critical experiment in the series of conflict studies. In this experiment, he varied the intesities of approach and of avoidance, and he varied the distance from the goal at which the animals were tested. Each animal in the experiment was first trained to run down a straight alley for food. Following this training, the rats were broken up into four groups: strong and weak approach groups that were tested respectively under 46 hours and 1 hour of food deprivation, and strong and weak avoidance groups given one high or low intensity shock in the goalbox. The animals in both avoidance groups and those in the strong approach group were given two tests for strength of pull five minutes apart; once at a location in the alley near to the goalbox. where they had been shocked or fed and once at a point far from the goalbox. We need to note an important matter of procedure: In the repeated tests, the order of testing was counterbalanced so that half the animals were first tested at the near location and then at far, and the other half were tested in the reverse order. Thus, the order of testing itself, which is of no interest to us, could have no effect on strength of pull. Testing the animals twice with only a short interval between did have an effect, however—one which may alter the interpretation of the experiment. We shall return to this question later in the chapter.

Fig. 3.4 shows the results, and given the assumptions that Brown and Miller made, they appear to lend strong support to the concept of intersecting gradients. If approach–avoidance conflicts *in the same organism* are governed by the same laws that independently determine approach or avoidance behavior, we have a powerful explanation of this kind of conflict behavior. Miller, Brown, & Lipofsky (see Miller, 1944) performed this experiment with rats, first training hungry animals to run a straight alley for food in the goalbox and then shocking them there. The strengths of approach

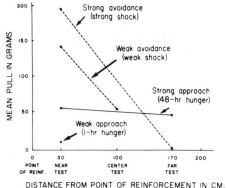

FIG. 3.4.   The results of Brown's experiment. Three of the four groups of animals (strong approach, strong avoidance, weak avoidance) were tested twice following training trials, once at the near point and once at the far testing point. The weak avoidance group was tested at 100 cm rather than 170 cm in the likelihood that no pulls would be recorded because of minimal tendencies to avoid at the greater distance (i.e., the gradient would have dropped to zero before this distance was reached). The weak approach group was tested only at 30 cm for a similar reason: 1 hr. food deprivation would not be enough to produce measurable pulls beyond 30 cm. Note the steeper gradient obtained from the two avoidance groups. (From Miller, 1959.)

and avoidance were varied by testing some animals with strong hunger and others with low, and some with strong and others weak shocks. The animals were restrained in the pull harness and tested without shock. As Miller (1944) describes the findings,

> The characteristic behavior was to approach part way and then stop. The place at which the animals stopped was determined by the relative strength of the two drives. Stronger hunger or weaker shock caused the animals to come nearer to the goal before stopping [p. 437].

The results of the Brown and Miller, Brown, and Lipofsky experiments gave impressive support to the deductions made from the theory of conflict behavior, and there were other experiments. In all, Miller (1959) reports, 11 specific deductions were made, and 10 of them were subjected to experimental test. For example, deductions 7 and 8 concerned the greater strength of pull of approach-and-avoidance–trained animals restrained near the goal than distant from it. One deduction was not directly tested—that predicting increased avoidance of the goal (remaining at a greater distance) with increases in the number of avoidance training trials—but a parallel deduction about approach behavior was confirmed, and it seems likely that the avoidance prediction would be fulfilled. The evidence from these simple experiments is compelling.

## Extensions and Applications of the Theory

The theory of conflict has some important implications for psychotherapy and for the behavioral and social effects of alcohol and drug usage. First, let's consider psychotherapy.

*Conflict and Neurosis.* The key to neurosis—its central feature—is conflict, and where we see persisting neurotic conflict it is likely to be of the approach–avoidance type. Although the specific symptoms differ, most people come to psychotherapy because they are the victims of strong, competing drives and incompatible tendencies to respond—fear or anxiety on the one hand and powerful desires to approach on the other. An important effect of anxiety is that thoughts that greatly increase it tend to be avoided. If this avoidance is successful in reducing anxiety, it will be repeated when the anxiety-producing thoughts occur again. Reduction of fear reinforces the responses associated with fear reduction. This is the behavior theorist's analysis of repression, and because repression has interfered with thinking about the goals that the patient is so impelled toward and so fears, neurotic conflicts are unconscious and thus inexplicable by the patient himself.

*The Inadvisability of Increasing Motivation to Approach.* Because the patient is unable to think directly about the conflict, and because of the nature of the approach–avoidance conflict itself, it will do little good to urge the patient to get over his inhibitions and try to accomplish that which he cannot. We saw that earlier in the chapter in the discussion of the assumption of intersecting gradients. Psychotherapists who attack the problem of treating neurosis by attempting to motivate patients to approach the goals they fear are probably going to intensify conflict and greatly increase their patients' fears. The end result, if the therapist persists, may be to drive the patient out of psychotherapy—an unfortunate resolution of a conflict between the therapist's insistence and the patient's fear.

*The "Negative Therapeutic Effect."* Lowering the gradient of avoidance, on the other hand, will not entail such great increases in fear, although some increment must be expected as Fig. 3.3B shows. Weaker avoidance brings the patient nearer the goal, and the amount of fear he experiences is, paradoxically, increased. This is called the *negative therapeutic effect*. As the patient's fears of important goals are partially extinguished with the help of the therapist's reassurance and discrimination training, he is able to approach more closely, and in so doing he is exposed to a greater intensity of fear. A temporary reappearance of symptoms may be the result, but with the help of the theory of conflict behavior the therapist knows that the rearousal of symptoms is indeed temporary, and that with the further extinction of fear, symptoms will abate and complete approach will be possible. A case reported by Goldstein and Palmer (1963) vividly shows the negative therapeutic effect. The patient is a young woman in treatment for a sexual conflict.

At first she was quite loquacious, reciting much of... [her] history with many brief intellectual insights. She attributed much of her problem to the fact that she was "Daddy's little girl," saying that she had never really grown up. She began to dress in a more adult fashion, using more cosmetics and wearing revealing blouses or knit dresses that emphasized her shapely figure. Her walk and mannerisms became markedly seductive. She made many slips of speech, particulary referring to her father as her husband or vice versa. Once she slipped and said "Daddy" instead of doctor in addressing her therapist. When these slips were called to her attention, and it was suggested that she confused her husband, father and therapist, she would either smile sweetly and remain silent or attempt to make a joke of it, "Oh you and your psychology!" After several months she reported that her sexual relations with her husband had improved markedly. "I'm so sexy every night that poor Bobby just can't keep up with me." She interpreted this change in her feelings to mean that her main problems had been resolved. She had about decided to stop treatment, but changed her mind, saying, "I guess you've just become a habit with me." Shortly thereafter she became increasingly silent and obviously depressed. Whereas previously she had always been prompt for her appointments now she was frequently late and several times cancelled the appointment. It was suggested to her that her resistance might be the result of some feelings she might have regarding the therapist. She hotly denied this interpretation and became increasingly angry at the therapist, saying that she felt that he was pressuring her into something, to the extent that she felt as if she were being raped. Attempts to get her to explore these feelings further met with stormy silence. Finally, in tears, she admitted that she had recently had several dreams wherein she imagined the therapist making love to her. Following this revelation she had another brief amnesic period which lasted one day. She wandered the streets not remembering who she was, and finally found herself standing in front of the clinic [p. 77].

*Conflict and Displacement.*    So far in our analysis, we have represented conflict by gradients of increasing strength of approach and avoidance as the goal is neared. Distance from the goal in space or time has been the critical dimension. Suppose that instead of distance from the goal we used a dimension of stimulus similarity. Thus, as stimuli increasingly resemble those of the goal situation, we should expect tendencies to approach or to avoid to become stronger. The process responsible is *generalization*: The more similar a given stimulus to the original stimulus to which the response was acquired, the more likely it will be to evoke the response. This idea is not very different from the distance notion. We noted earlier that spatial or temporal distance is not itself a cue; rather, it is the change in the stimulus situation that increasing proximity to the goal brings. Small children in the first year or so of school sometimes make the mistake of addressing their teachers as "Mother," an error made understandable by the concept of displacement. In the absence of the person to whom the goal response is directed, the response is displaced to the most similar person present.

The response to the goal stimulus may be prevented by conflict—stronger avoidance than approach—and displacement will then occur to stimuli that are partly dissimilar to the original. Stimuli that are too similar will tend to arouse the fear preventing the approach response; stimuli too different will not arouse approach itself. Miller (1948) confirmed a series of deductions concerning displacement, and Murray and Berkun (1955) combined the models of conflict and displacement in a single conflict/displacement theory. In an experimental test, they showed the displacement of approach responses of rats exposed to a hunger–fear conflict in a straight alleyway. The animals approached closer to the goalbox in alleys that differed from the original.

Psychotherapy gives us an opportunity to apply conflict/displacement theory. Murray (1954) studied the displacement of anger in a psychotherapy patient in whom an anger–fear conflict was a major problem. This patient was initially unable to express the strong hostility he felt toward his mother, but with the therapist's permissiveness and reassurance he began to overcome his fear-based inhibition. As he began to think about and express his anger, however, his fear became stronger, and his hostile words for his mother were blocked. Fig. 3.5 shows what happened to his hostile statements over the course of his psychotherapy. The sixth hour seems to have been a crisis point. The relatively mild hostility expressed toward his mother appears to have intensified his conflict, and we see two resulting effects: almost complete retreat from the direct expression of hostility toward his mother and the *displacement* of hostility to another target—his aunt. By the tenth hour, it appears, the anger toward his aunt had also become too fearful, and there is a further displacement to the more remote targets represented by the category of "others." As Murray comments, "Mother, aunt, and others form a meaningful gradient of generalization [p. 307]." Later in this brief psychotherapy he was able to express the anger felt toward his mother, and by this time the hostile statements were louder and stronger. The therapist, evidently, had been successful in reducing avoidance to a point at which a much greater hostile "approach" could take place. Murray also reported a reciprocal relation between hostility inhibition and the appearance of anxiety-reducing defenses. At those points in the treatment where the patient

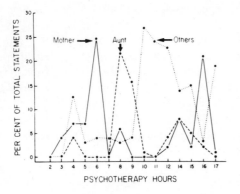

FIG. 3.5. Hostile statements concerning mother, aunt, and others as percentages of the total number of statements made in each psychotherapy hour. (From Murray & Berkun, 1955.)

was inhibited in the expression of anger, he made many more physical complaints and remote, intellectualized statements.

*The Effects of Alcohol and Barbiturates.*    The overuse of alcohol and drugs represents a social problem of major proportions. Drinking and drug-taking are as severely problematical as they are not only because of what they cause people to do but because they are extremely resistant to treatment. Conflict theory has something to say about that, and it also entails a hypothesis about why people drink and take drugs (at least certain of them) in the first place.

The hypothesis is that alcohol and drugs (the barbiturates, especially) reduce fear-motivated avoidance and have little if any effect on approach. We do things when we have been drinking that we would not do sober: anger, blatant sexuality, recklessness, and tearful emotionality that would never be seen when we're sober come out under drink. They do so because alcohol reduces the fear that normally inhibits this kind of behavior. The same effect occurs with barbiturate drugs, and because of this it is common practice to administer a barbiturate dose to patients about to undergo surgery; their fear is greatly reduced. One of the barbiturate anesthetic drugs, sodium amobarbital or amytal as it is known, was extensively used during World War II in the treatment of neuroses resulting from the stress of combat (Grinker & Spiegel, 1945). The reduction of fear under amytal enabled the recovery of traumatic memories that had been repressed, thus making possible the extinction of fear in psychotherapy.

An experiment by Conger (1951), a student of Miller, provided the basic data on the fear-reducing efforts of alcohol. Hungry rats were trained to run a straight alley for food and were then shocked in the goalbox. The intensity of the shock was just sufficient to prevent the animal from approaching the goalbox. Rats tested in the alley after injections of alcohol more often returned to the goalbox for food than rats that were injected with a placebo (saline). In another experiment in the series, Conger used the strength-of-pull technique to show that injections of alcohol had little effect on the strength of approach of hungry rats restrained in the alley, while there was a considerable decrease in pulling strength under alcohol by rats that had been shocked in the goalbox. Note that the avoidance animals were pulling in a direction *away* from the feared goalbox. Finally, Conger tested the abilities of animals to discriminate while drunk or sober. The discrimination of avoiding the desired-but-feared goalbox when sober and approaching food in the goalbox when drunk was acquired more readily than learning to avoid in the drunken state and approaching while sober. Thus, the states of sobriety and drunkenness were discriminable by the animals. It was the intensity of fear-based inhibition that contributed to ready avoidance when sober and the dominance of approach once avoidance had been reduced by alcohol that made these discriminations different.

The effectiveness of alcohol in reducing fear should result in its repeated use under conditions of chronic conflict. This is the second part of the hypothesis—the reinforcement of drinking as a response to fear and conflict. There are some data from a classic experiment of Masserman and Yum (1946). Cats subjected to a strong hunger–fear conflict that produced the symptoms we call experimental neurosis came to develop a preference for a five percent alcohol-in-milk solution once its fear-reducing effects had been experienced. Normally, cats will not choose the adulterated milk over plain milk; after the conflict was established, was it the alcohol that was adultered by the milk? Following successful "therapy" for the conflict and extinction of fear, the preference for plain milk returned.

These studies of the effects of alcohol and drugs leave some important questions unanswered. Is the nature of the drive motivating approach important? Do the fear-reducing effects of alcohol or drugs affect some kinds of responses more than others—that is, are some conflict situations affected more than others? Is the effect of alcohol or drugs the result of their weakening the most recently acquired habit (remember that in all of these studies approach training was carried out first, followed by acquisition of the avoidance response)? Is it fear reduction that yields the effects or impairment of the organism's ability to discriminate the cues signalling the fearful situation? Miller's (1961) summary of an extensive series of experiments on the effects of sodium amytal makes clear that the specific drive and approach–avoidance situation appear to be unimportant and that when we pit the hypothesis of fear reduction against competing alternatives in each case the answer favors fear reduction.

There are two further points to be made about the alcohol/drug hypothesis. Alcohol and drugs should come to be used habitually to the degree that they are successful in reducing fear. If fear reduction is only partial, the closer approach to the goal that follows will be accompanied by an increase in the intensity of fear experienced. Dollard and Miller (1950) proposed that drinking under these conditions should not be acquired as a response to fear-based inhibition. I am ignoring here the addictive effects of alcohol and barbiturate drugs to make the specific point to be derived from the hypothesis.

It is possible that even in cases where fear is too intense to permit the attainment of the goal, drinking or drug use will still be reinforced. Suppose that drinking decreases avoidance but not below approach. The person moves closer to the goal, and his fear and misery increase. He drinks more, to the extent of stupor or sleep, and he is unlikely to remember his strong fear the next day. The result, then, may be the reinforcement of extremely heavy drinking in a sequential process of partial fear reduction followed by effective removal from heightened conflict.

Dollard and Miller also observed that the use of alcohol or drugs to cope with conflict situations would be of little more than temporary benefit.

Because of immediate and powerful effects on fear, the person comes to depend on alcohol or drugs rather than dealing more directly with his fear and the problem of its extinction. Drinking and drug-taking abolish inhibitions and not repression: The feared goal is attained but thinking about it and why it is fearful are not facilitated. Indeed, it seems probable that by the time a sufficient amount of alcohol or drug has been consumed to produce an effective reduction of fear, thinking and memory have been impaired. This means that there will be little generalization of fear reduction to the sober or nondrugged state, and without the extinction of fear the conflict continues unaltered (*except when drunk or drugged*). One of the experiments reported in Miller's review of drug/conflict studies was directed to this problem. An approach–avoidance (hunger–fear-of-shock) conflict was created in rats. Half of them were then tested on extinction trials (without shock) under amytal and half with injections of saline. Two further test days followed during which the extinction trials were continued without the drug. The fear-reducing effects of amytal did not transfer to the sessions without the drug, and the conclusion appears to be that while alcohol and barbiturates do reduce fear, the experience of reaching the goal while drunk or drugged does not result in any observable extinction of fear.


## Do the Gradients Intersect?


We return to a problem mentioned earlier in the chapter—the flaw in Brown's experiment. I hinted then at a major implication of that flaw for the assumption that the gradient of avoidance is steeper than that of approach. Maher and Nuttall (1962) carefully reviewed the details of Brown's experiment and noted the possibility that testing the animals twice, once at the near and once at the far point, might have had a different effect on the avoidance than on the approach groups. Near the goal, the pulls of the avoidance animals far exceeded those of the approach-trained rats, while at the far testing point they pulled little or not at all. Indeed, of the 20 animals in this group, 16 had zero pull scores at the far point. Maher and Nuttal suggested that the weaker average strength of pull in the far test might have resulted from the fatigue of the animals tested first at the near point. A careful replication of the experiment that provided for examination of the effects of *sequence of testing* revealed what they had suspected—the animals tested at the far point first pulled harder than those given their first avoidance test near to the goal. Brown's averaging of the near and far test first subgroups made the mean strength of pull at the far point lower than it should have been, thus creating an avoidance gradient of unwarranted steepness.

Maher and his students unearthed two other problems with conflict theory and the deductions made from it. It is clear from the theory that approach behavior in conflict situations should be proportional to the space to be traversed before the point of intersection of the gradients is reached. Introducing animals to the conflict runway at different distances from the goalbox (that is, with a variably-placed start box) should result in runs of lengths varying with the location of the start box. Maher and Noblin (1963) found, instead, that rats tend to run a fixed distance from the point of introduction to the alley. They suggest that it is not distance from the goal or the changes in cues that closer approach to the goal brings that increasingly arouse fear but the *approach response itself*. The approach response—here, running—becomes a conditioned stimulus for fear. Thus, for accurate prediction of conflict behavior we need to know what stimuli, internal as well as external, are cues for fear.

The second problem concerns the kind of behavior observed when organisms in conflict—rats or people—find themselves at a point in distance or time at which nearness has made the intensity of fear unbearable. Conflict theory is clear about what we *should* observe in this "avoidance zone" of conflict situations: retreat to the point at which approach is slightly stronger than avoidance. The key word is *retreat*. In fact, that is not what always happens. Experiments by Trapold, Miller, and Coons (1960) and by Taylor and Maher (1959) revealed that rats were as likely to run *toward* the goal as away from it when placed in the conflict situation close to the goal. Lester and Crowne (1970) found much the same result in people. Although our chief interest was in studying obedience, the situation gave us an opportunity to introduce people to a manifestly intense conflict at distant (approach zone) and close (avoidance zone) points.

College girls who reported strong fear of and aversion to cockroaches were our subjects. On the pretext of studying the effects of handling on maze learning, these subjects were instructed to pick up, place in a T-maze, and retrieve giant South American cockroaches (they were about four inches long!). Protestations were met with increasing insistence on obedience up to the point of, "You have no choice; you must continue [with the task assigned you]." Refusal at this point meant the subject had successfully resisted the obedience demands. Half the subjects were introduced to this situation at a point many feet distant from the glass enclosure containing the cockroaches, and for half the roaches were suddenly encountered up close. About 44 percent of the girls fully complied with the experimenter's obedience demands (to no detriment, I should note); for our present purpose what matters is that the point of introduction to the conflict situation made no difference. In highly fearful girls, sudden exposure to the avoidance zone produced no greater retreat than that observed among equally fearful girls introduced at the distant point. The experience of finding oneself in the dentist's office about to undergo a frightening procedure is an anecdotal case in point:

Although one's fear is so strong that thoughts of fleeing become insistent, we usually go through with it.

Maher (1966) suggests that in the avoidance zone, where one immediately is is intolerable, and the organism attempts to escape from where it is. That escape may lie in the direction of the goal as well as away from it. Whether the escape consists of retreat, a reckless and desperate plunge toward the goal, or freezing in fear may depend quite exactly on the specific response punished. Fowler and Miller (1963) gave shock to the forepaws to one group of animals in an approach-avoidance conflict; in another group the hindpaws were shocked. The forepaw–shock group yielded the conflict results we should expect: the more intense the shock the more they slowed and stopped. Shock to the hindpaws, however, made the animal run *faster toward* the goal, and the more intense the shock the faster they ran. It helps in understanding this result to note that two consequences may follow running toward the goal for the hindpaw–shock group—termination of the shock and the food reward. If this is what the animal experiences, the response of dashing for the feared goal should be reinforced. Thus, conflict behavior may only make sense when we have the details of the response–punishment history.

Finally, we should note that in many important human conflict situations there are strong pressures to go through with it; there were such pressures for our obedience subjects, there are social pressures and common sense that impel us to remain in the dentist's office, and as we shall shortly see, there are pressures to cause people who are (and should be) very afraid to take their first parachute jumps out of airplanes.

## Avoidance-Approach Conflict

It has been traditional to assume that approach is stronger than avoidance in the "far" zone of conflict. If this were not so, there would be little or no motivation to approach the feared goal, and conflict would not exist. Losco and Epstein (1977) have challenged this assumption, presenting data to show that approach gradients occasionally can be steeper than gradients of avoidance. This seems an odd situation, but it is far from an impossible one. The person in conflict remains at great distance from the feared goal, successfully avoiding it, until events beyond his control bring him closer. Now, approach is stronger than avoidance, and he moves quickly toward the goal. His behavior will seem strange, unpredictable, and "completely out of character," as Losco and Epstein say, because of his previous history of absolute avoidance. "An example of such a case," Losco and Epstein note, "is the shy, inhibited 'model' boy who, faced with a temptation that he had previously succeeded in avoiding, commits a bizarre crime of passion. It is just such ego-alien behavior that can be accounted for by avoidance–approach conflict [p. 367]." This conflict situation should have further analysis. Our understanding of impulsive crimes of violence that appear wholly out of keeping with the perpetrator's past behavior might well profit.

## A Proposal of Parallel Gradients

The spuriously steep avoidance gradient that Maher and Nuttall discovered in Brown's experiment and the gradients obtained in some other experiments (cf. Rigby, 1954) have led Maher (1966) to propose that approach and avoidance gradients do not intersect. Instead, in approach–avoidance conflicts the gradients are parallel with approach consistently stronger than avoidance. A diagram of a conflict situation will now look like that of Fig. 3.6. Why doesn't the rat or person in such a situation go all the way to the goal? The answer is that as the gradients rise toward the goal their *relative values* become closer, and at some point there is a *"functional equilibrium"*—the intensity of desire for the goal is indistinguishable from fear of it. We then see the characteristic vacillation misery that occur when approach and avoidance are equivalent.

It may help to make the point clearer to think of plotting the ages of two people. As small children, they are two and four; the age of the older is double that of the younger. At 20 and 22, the absolute difference is the same but the relative difference has greatly diminished. On our scale of strength of tendency to approach or to avoid, the point is reached at which 20 and 22 or 40 and 42 just don't seem different.

Why must the approach tendency be stronger than the tendency to avoid? This is a necessary assumption since a higher avoidance gradient would keep the person so far from the goal that the tendency to approach would be aroused only in exceptional situations.

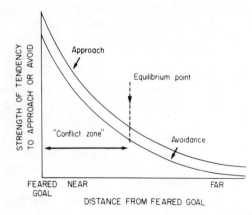

FIG. 3.6.   A proposal of parallel gradients in approach-avoidance conflict situations. (Adapted from Maher, 1966.)

Maher's parallel gradients proposal has the virtue of involving fewer assumptions than the original Miller version of intersecting gradients. It fits most of the data, and it entails one most important implication: Approach–avoidance conflict must be studied in the same organism. We could not know much about the equilibrium point of parallel gradients in separately-trained approach and avoidance groups. On the other hand, Miller has put together a highly persuasive case for intersecting gradients. The large number of experiments, their ingenuity, and the extensions of the theory make it plausible indeed to assume a steeper gradient of avoidance. We clearly need conflict studies in which the gradients are carefully mapped; it would be desirable to measure the strength of tendencies to approach or to avoid at several points rather than at near and far extremes.

## THE STUDY OF AN ACUTE CONFLICT:
## THE SPORT PARACHUTIST

The investigation of conflict in clinical situations may provide some rich and provocative data about approach and avoidance behavior, and we may find suggestive concordance with experimental studies, as Murray showed. But the conflicts we encounter in disturbed people are far from evident. It may be very difficult to establish what the conflict is about, its source, and the specific response–reward–punishment history that would enable us to explain the conflict symptoms of the patient and to treat the relevant fears. How advantageous it would be to study people in immediate situations of conflict in which there is no long, buried history of conflict learning and behavior to contend with. Epstein and Fenz (1962) found just such a conflict in novice parachute jumpers. There has to be strong motivation to approach (to achieve mastery of something difficult and dangerous, to seek thrills, perhaps to gain admiration and recognition), and there must unquestionably be intense fear. An extensive and fruitful research program had its beginning in a fortunate happenstance—Fenz himself was a sport parachutist.

Epstein and Fenz start by adopting most of the basic assumptions of the Miller conflict theory, but there is one major departure that has several consequences. Instead of measuring the strength of tendencies to approach or to avoid—that is, response strength—they suggest measuring the strength of drive. Epstein (1962) notes that high and persisting states of drive arousal have three effects.

1. They produce symptoms of tension and perhaps psychosomatic symptoms as a result of chronic autonomic activation, and we also see the person's performance falling off, sometimes to the point of going to pieces under stress.

2. There are effects traceable to the motivating aspect of the drive state. We observe preoccupation with drive-related stimuli that may with high and prolonged drive arousal become obsessive or compulsive symptoms and hallucinatory activity. Concentration and the ability to perform capably must obviously be impaired. In a classic study, subjects who voluntarily submitted to semistarvation became obsessed with food and food-related objects—pots and pans, menus, magazine advertisements for foods that became pinups (Franklin, Schiele, Brozek, & Keys, 1948). We often see people in conflict endlessly preoccupied with conflict-related thoughts.

3. Persisting states of high drive tend to foster responses that either reduce drive arousal or inhibit the further increase of drive. We tend to avoid thinking about things that make us afraid.

## The Measurement of Drive and Conflict

These three effects suggest a number of different possibilities for measuring drive and thus measuring the strengths of approach and avoidance in conflict situations. From the effects of prolonged activation we might derive such measures as the height of arousal of the autonomic nervous system, the appearance of somatic symptoms, or deficit in the ability to engage in some performance. We might study approach and avoidance behavior at a time when the goal is remote and when the passage of time has brought it close. As the strength of the avoidance motive overwhelms approach, drive-inhibiting responses ought to begin to make their appearance. Epstein and Fenz used three of these measures—autonomic arousal, deficits in performance, and drive (fear) inhibiting responses in their studies of skydivers.

Each jumper rated his feelings of approach ("looking forward to the jump, wanting to go ahead, being thrilled by the prospect of jumping") and his avoidance feelings ("wanting to turn back and call the jump off, questioning why you ever let yourself get into jumping, fear") at times before, during, and after the jump. An approach–avoidance conflict is strongly suggested by these ratings, as Fig. 3.7 shows. From the time of boarding the plane until after the tap on the shoulder that is the signal to jump, avoidance is stronger than approach. Epstein (1962) comments that

> This is a somewhat peculiar finding, as the parachutists, after all, do jump. Apparently, they are jumping on psychological momentum rather than because of their immediate desire. The momentum consists of commitment and the difficulty in reversing the decision once in the aircraft [p. 179].

Some very clever procedures were used to assess the various facets of drive. Jumpers and nonjumping control subjects were presented with lists of words; to each word, a measure of the reactivity of the autonomic nervous system

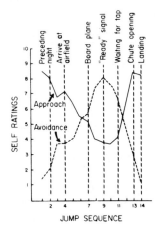
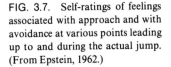

**FIG. 3.7.** Self-ratings of feelings associated with approach and with avoidance at various points leading up to and during the actual jump. (From Epstein, 1962.)

was taken. Change in the electrical resistance of the skin (partly a function of increased sweat gland activity) provides an excellent index of the momentary arousal of the autonomic nervous system. Skin conductance (the reciprocal of resistance) responses were taken to words that would evoke anxiety ("killed", "injury"), neutral words, and words of low ("sky"), medium ("fall"), and high ("ripcord") relevance to parachute jumping. This word association test was given to the novice jumpers two weeks before the date of the jump, and on the jump day itself. Figure 3.8 shows the results: a strong autonomic response to the anxiety words on the day of the jump, a clear gradient of responses to the parachute-relevant words on the jump day, and a much weaker anxiety-word response and a lower gradient two weeks earlier. The control subjects produced no gradient at all to the parachute-jumping words. Thus, for the parachutists, the greater the degree of relevance of the words to parachute jumping, the greater was the autonomic response, and the imminence of the conflict situation raised the height of the gradient.

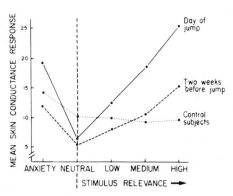
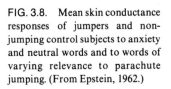

**FIG. 3.8.** Mean skin conductance responses of jumpers and non-jumping control subjects to anxiety and neutral words and to words of varying relevance to parachute jumping. (From Epstein, 1962.)

## Cognitive and Performance Effects

Actual performance deficits were occasionally seen. Fenz and Epstein (1969) described the response of a jumper whose main chute did not open: "He waited the prescribed time before pulling his reserve chute—and then, 'wanting to be sure,' waited a while longer. He waited until it was almost too late [p. 58]." Such observations of near disasters were not very frequent, however, and might occur at times when they would be difficult to detect. The investigators thus sought other ways in which performance or cognitive deficits might be manifested. One test involved a specially constructed set of pictures varying in degree of relevance to parachute jumping to which the subject was instructed to tell a story. This technique is patterned after the Thematic Apperception Test (TAT), widely used clinically in personality assessment. The stories to the TAT-like pictures were rated for approach themes and for avoidance (fear) themes. Stories told on the day of the jump showed a marked increase in approach themes at each level of relevance, a finding contrary to Epstein's prediction which was that there would be an increase in approach to low relevant cards and a decrease to high relevant ones. Fear responses were greatly diminished to the high relevant cards, sometimes to the point of outright denial, but appeared instead to cards irrelevant to parachute jumping—that is, fear appeared to be displaced. The denial of fear on high relevant cards at times strained credibility (Epstein, 1962): "He is not afraid at all; just looks that way because of the wind that is blowing in his face. He will have a wonderful jump. It will be great, just great [p. 178]!" Thus, the cards seemed to elicit stories indicative of the ways in which the subject dealt with his fear—by displacement to stimuli more distant, more remote from parachute jumping, and by denial. We should note that fear-inhibiting responses are adaptive only to the degree that they enable one to modulate the intensity of his fear, to keep it within endurable bounds. They are maladaptive and may be thought of as contributing to a performance or cognitive deficit when they interfere with accurate perception of the situation. Along this same line, Epstein reports that on the jump day there were frequent misperceptions of the anxiety words (hearing "tilled" for "killed"), a phenomenon called perceptual defense and related to the process of repression. Did the subject *actually hear* "tilled" instead of "killed"? Epstein is convinced that there was, indeed, a perceptual deficit since the skin conductance response to the misperceived words was like that to the neutral words.

## The Inverted V Gradient

The final data of the Epstein and Fenz studies that we shall consider appear in Fig. 3.9, and what is of particular note there is the one odd gradient, the

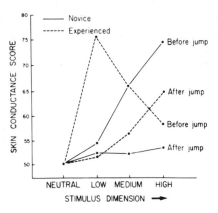

FIG. 3.9. Skin conductance responses of novice (1 previous jump) and experienced (100 + jumps) skydivers to words varying in relevance to parachute jumping. Each subject was tested twice—before jumping and afterward. Skin conductance responses are expressed as a deviation from the mean response to the neutral words. (Adapted from Epstein, 1962.)

inverted V. Its discovery was pure happenstance—the result of a novice jumper who didn't show up. Epstein (1962) describes what happened:

> Fenz filled in the time by testing a highly experienced jumper. Unlike the inexperienced jumpers, all of whom had produced monotonic GSR [skin conductance response] gradients, the experienced jumper produced an inverted v-shaped curve. At first we suspected that the falling off at the upper end of the dimension was a matter of the unreliability of the test, and were more than a little disappointed at having our perfect record of prediction spoiled [p. 181].

Testing other experienced jumpers, however, confirmed the reliability of the inverted V gradient, and it also appeared in other measures of activation in the experienced jumpers. The inverted V gradient seems to mean that arousal and fear peaked *earlier* for the experienced than for the novice jumper— that is, the conflict had become *anticipatory*. Thus, as one gains experience in a conflict situation, fear is aroused earlier in the sequence of events, and it is maximally aroused by stimuli of less immediate relevance to the conflict. The inverted V suggests, as Fenz and Epstein (1969) put it, an "early warning system" by which anxiety is controlled. There are some important implications for the understanding of neurotic conflict in the finding of the inverted V. The cues that arouse fear and produce avoidance may well be fairly remote from the original source of the conflict. The conflict has "moved backward" as the person has repeatedly experienced it, and the effect will be to keep him at a greater distance from the goal.

## A Final Comment

These studies of sport parachutists give some important clues as to how people handle approach–avoidance conflicts; they are especially informative about the processes by which intense fear is inhibited. The Epstein and Fenz data clearly portray the strength of approach–avoidance conflict for the skydiver, and the widespread effects of that conflict on both bodily and psychological processes. We have treated them from the standpoint of conflict, but they are also expressive of stress. As we shall see in the next chapter, stress involves the perception of threat and the anticipation of harm (surely there for the skydiver), and responses to stress include physiological arousal, the experience of such emotions as fear, processes of coping or avoiding, and the impairment of thinking and action.

# 4 Stress, Coping, and Avoiding

## ABSTRACT

*The concept of stress did not originate in psychology. It came to psychology by way of medicine through the important work on stress and adaptation by Selye. The* general adaptation syndrome, *which describes what happens when the body is subjected to* any stressful assault, became a model for psychological stress.

*In this chapter we review the general adaptation syndrome and then develop a psychological model of stress, modifying and extending the general adaptation syndrome with concepts appropriate to a behavioral analysis. We consider clinical and experimental studies of stress that illustrate four important points about psychological stress: (1) stress cannot be defined by the intensity of the stressor alone; (2) coping with or avoiding stress is determined by cognitive processes of appraisal of threat; (3) people react to stress distinctively—there are many different patterns of stress response; and (4) stimulus factors in stressful situations are important determinants of the appraisal of threat, coping, or avoiding. One of these factors is uncertainty about the occurrence of harm; another has to do with the effects of the stressed person's own behavior in combatting the stressor.*

## INTRODUCTION

The concept of stress originated in engineering, where it refers to the forces acting on an object. The application of stress produces strain in the object. Stress was brought into biology and medicine and into psychology because the analogy to phsyiological and psychological processes gave promise of helping to understand a variety of disturbances in functioning that previously had been the province of other concepts. The concept of stress came to unify much of our thinking in biology and medicine and in psychology about problems involving sudden and serious perturbations of the normal ebb and flow of bodily processes and of psychological equilibrium, by noxious stimuli, emotional arousal, and anxiety.

The Canadian endocrinologist, Hans Selye (1950, 1956), whose research on stress began during the 1920s, introduced the concept to deal with the discovery that *any* sort of damage or assault to the body produces a *common* reaction, whatever its specific effects may be. In using stress in this way, Selye abandoned the direct engineering analogy (stress—a stimulus—results in strain—a response) to use stress to describe the processes set in motion by stress-producing agents—"stressors." Despite some serious terminological confusions in the literature on stress (see Lazarus, 1966), most investigators have followed Selye in dropping the engineering convention.

## WHAT IS STRESS?

In current usage, stress is not a stimulus, nor is it the organism's response. Although stress is employed by some writers as an intervening construct between stimuli and responses, referring to a set of physical or psychological processes, the position taken by Lazarus (1966) is the most comfortably adopted. Stress, he says, is not a "stimulus, response, or intervening variable, but rather a collective term for an area of study [p. 27]."

Our concern is with psychological stress, and we shall delve only briefly into physiological processes. Because Selye's studies and analysis of physiological stress have so powerfully affected the study of psychological stress, it will help to consider what happens when the body is subjected to injury. Selye (cf. 1956) has given a name to the sequence of processes. It is the *general adaptation syndrome.* The immediate reaction of the body to injury (or to invasion by disease-producing agents, excessive cold or extreme heat—or to events that produce strong and persistent emotional arousal) is one that Selye characterizes as a reaction of *alarm.* There is a brief period of shock during which there is a momentary decrement in the body's defensive processes. A sub-phase of *counter-shock* follows during which there is a sharp increase in stress responses. If the stress persists, a stage of *resistance* succeeds the alarm reaction, and we see heightened defensive responses, especially at the site of injury or damage by disease. Finally, with long-persisting stress, the body's ability to resist begins to fail and is eventually drastically reduced. This is the stage of *exhaustion,* and its consequences for the organism are severe. This sequence of events is shown in Fig. 4.1. The dashed line in this figure

FIG. 4.1. The sequence of events in the general adaptation syndrome. The alarm reaction is the two-stage response of bodily systems to a noxious (injurious) stimulus: an initial shock followed by mobilization of the body's defensive resources. These defensive responses are heightened during the stage of resistance, and if the stress is not overcome they become exhausted during the final stage. The solid line depicts the stages of reaction to some initial stressor, while the dashed line shows the course of response to a new stress piled on top of the old one. (Adapted from Selye, 1950.)

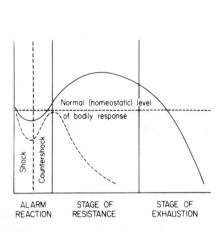

shows the weak response to a new stressor with which the body must cope before it has successsfully resolved the previous stress.

What are the defensive responses of the body? They involve an area deep within the brain called the *hypothalamus* that lies between the midbrain (controlling such vital processes as respiration, heart contraction, and arousal) and higher brain structures. They further involve two important glands in the endocrine system, the *pituitary* gland or *hypophysis,* connected to the hypothalamus, and the *adrenal* glands, situated on the upper tip or pole of each kidney. The relation between the pituitary and adrenal glands is so critical and intimate that we refer to it as the *adrenal-pituitary axis.* In Fig. 4.2A we see the location of the hypothalamus and hypophysis in the brain, and Fig. 4.2B shows the connections between them. Figure 4.3 gives the location of the adrenal glands along with the other major glands in the endocrine system.

FIG. 4.2. A. The location of hypothalamus and hypophysis in relation to some other major brain areas. B. The relation of anterior and posterior hypothalamic areas to the hypophysis. Stippling between hypothalamus and posterior pituitary indicates a direct neural link, which does not exist for the anterior pituitary. There, the link is vascular.

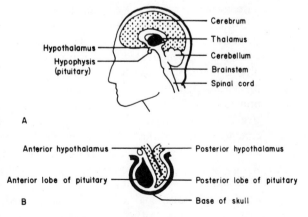

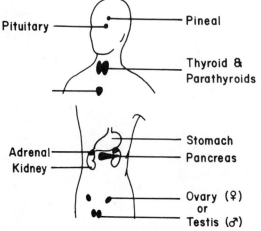

Pituitary

Pineal

Thyroid & Parathyroids

Adrenal
Kidney

Stomach
Pancreas

Ovary (♀)
or
Testis (♂)

FIG. 4.3. The location of the major glands in the endocrine system.

## Two Systems: Short-Acting and Long-Acting

To understand the workings of the adrenal-pituitary axis and its control by the hypothalamus, it is easiest to begin with the end organ in the system, the adrenal glands. The adrenals are divided into two major parts: a central core, the *medulla,* and an outer surface, the adrenal *cortex.* Both medulla and cortex secrete biochemical substances that powerfully affect other organs of the body. Their secretions, however, are quite different. The adrenal medulla secretes adrenalin and noradrenalin, the effect of which is to ready the body for emergency action: increased rate and force of beat of the heart, bronchial dilation in the lungs, release into the bloodstream of glucose stored in the liver for muscular exertion, and increased sweating, to name just a few of the widespread influences of these substances. The adrenal medulla is under the direct control of the sympathetic division of the autonomic nervous system, which is regulated by the hypothalamus. It is separate and distinct from the adrenal-pituitary axis. We might call it a *short-acting* system; its effects are felt in a matter of less than a second to a minute or so and are of relatively short duration. Of course, if the danger continues the sympathetic system will continue to be activated, and more adrenalin will be discharged into the bloodstream. You have felt the effects of the short-acting system if you have had a sudden fright—a near accident, say, while driving a car. Because of the immediate influence of these adrenal medulla secretions on the heart and sweat glands, we frequently use increased heart rate or blood pressure and changes in the electrical resistance of the skin (the skin conductance response) as measures of emotional arousal and reaction to an imminent threat.

The general adaptation syndrome involves a *long-action system,* the hypothalamically controlled adrenal-pituitary axis. The resulting secretions are those of the adrenal cortex, and they are called *corticosteroids.* There are two major types of corticosteriod hormones—*mineralocorticoids* that function in the regulation of mineral (especially salt) metabolism in the body; and *glucocorticoids* that regulate glucose and also protein and fat metabolism. These adrenal cortical secretions are involved in directly opposite ways in the body's reaction to injury and disease. The mineralo-corticoids are responsible for the inflammation following injury or disease; this proinflammatory effect results in the growth of tissues that protect against further damage, and it is a critical part of the processes of recovery and healing.

Of greater importance to our understanding of stress and resistance to stress are the glucocorticoids. They have the puzzling property of *decreasing* inflammation and resistance to infection; they are *anti-inflammatory* in their effects on body tissues. While mineralocorticoid secretion is thought to be regulated principally by the concentration of sodium and potassium in extracellular body fluids, the glucocorticoids are controlled by the pituitary and, in turn, by the hypothalamus. A close inspection of Fig. 4.2B reveals the continuous stippling between hypothalamus and the posterior portion of the pituitary. That is meant to indicate a *direct neural linkage.* Such a direct neural link does not exist between hypothalamus and the anterior pituitary; the hypothalamus controls the activity of the anterior pituitary by secreting a biochemical substance called a *releasing factor.* This releasing factor is transported to the anterior pituitary via a network of blood vessels. The anterior pituitary responds by releasing another specialized substance— adrenocorticotropic hormone (ACTH). ACTH is carried in the blood stream to the adrenal cortex, where the response is glucocorticoid secretion. Glucocorticoids powerfully affect the metabolism of fatty acids. One physiologist (Guyton, 1966) suggests that "...the glucocorticoids cause rapid mobilization of amino acids and fats from their cellular stores, making these available both for energy and for synthesis of other compounds needed by the different tissues of the body [p. 1059]." There are other effects as well: the suppression of processes that help in resisting infection and some additional ones. Gray (1971) brings them together in the following hypothesis: "Under prolonged stress, then, there is a massive shutdown of those bodily activities which are directed towards growth, reproduction, and even resistance to existing infection, in favour of mechanisms which promote readiness for immediate high-energy action [p. 61]."

Our knowledge of these processes is far from complete, but it appears that the long-acting system may sacrifice other bodily needs to aid the body in combatting internal dangers from disease or injury and also dangers of another sort—those that involve the perception of threat, for which the physical resources for strong action may be required. Note that I said *"perception of threat."* It is tremendously important to recognize here a point made at the beginning of the last chapter: What is threatening and stressful for one person is not necessarily so for another. We may see a person reacting to a minor occurrence with the level of arousal and stress response that a grave

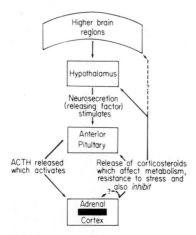

FIG. 4.4.   The control of adreno-cortical secretion by the hypothalamus. Note two significant details: the release of ACTH by the anterior pituitary, and the negative feedback process by which adrenocortical secretion inhibits further ACTH release.

emergency would call for; if persistent and protracted, this kind of extreme stress response may have serious results, both psychological and physical.

These adrenal-pituitary processes are diagrammed in Fig. 4.4, but note that we have covered only the left half of the diagram. In the right half of the figure, we see a *negative feedback* process: The release of adrenocortical secretions into the bloodstream produces an effect that inhibits hypothalamic secretion of the releasing factor and may also act directly on the anterior pituitary. Thus, like the household thermostat that reacts to the increased warmth in the house by shutting down the furnace, the adrenal-pituitary axis has a control mechanism to limit the activity of the system. Prolonged stress, however, will recycle it, and further corticosteroid production will be the result. If the defensive measures taken to combat the stressor are not successful, the eventual outcome is the stage of exhaustion. At this point, defensive resources (physical and psychological) are so depleted that effective resistance is no longer possible. At this serious juncture, the defensive struggles themselves may become destructive, further exhausting and depleting resources and impairing the body's ability to take restorative action, indeed even to resist infection.

Our understanding of stress as a psychological phenomenon has been enormously enhanced by the concepts of the general adaptation syndrome. It has provided a way of thinking about the sequence of events in stress—stages of stress response—and it has influenced the way we think about the countermeasures to threat—psychological defenses. The general adaptation syndrome has also helped us to recognize the indissoluble relation between psychological and bodily processes that we see vividly exemplified by psychosomatic disorders.

Psychological research on stress has profited from the inclusion of somatic responses as one expression of exposure to stress in three important ways. First, somatic responses may alter a person's psychological processes, most importantly his appraisals of threat and the alternatives before him. The pounding of one's heart and feeling weak in the knees may increase the experience of threat and give one a feeling of helplessness that might not have developed in the absence of those bodily reactions. Second, somatic responses represent important indices by which we may record the occurrence of stress. Third, these responses are involved in the production of psychosomatic disorders, as our discussion of the general adaptation syndrome and the long-acting system may have suggested. Thus, although we now turn to psychological stress, it is imporant to remember that we cannot really divorce psychological processes from somatic ones. We can choose a psychological or somatic focus for the purposes of a particular investigation, but in the fullest sense, to the understand stress we need to assess and understand both sets of processes and how they interact.

## THE PSYCHOLOGY OF STRESS

The general adaptation syndrome has provided us with a model for psychological stress. In place of a physically damaging stressor (injury or infection), we have a potentially harmful stimulus situation. The psycho-logical counterpart of the body's immunodefensive system may be broadly identified as a set of cognitive processes by which threat is appraised and measures of action or defense are devised. There are stress responses that, like the mobilization of the body's defensive resources in the general adaptation syndrome, attempt to deal with the harmful situation. We shouldn't stretch the parallels too far. In reactions to psychological stress we may see responses that are adaptive attempts to deal with the threatening situation—*coping responses*—but we may also see clearly inadequate and maladaptive *avoiding* responses for which there is no direct analogy in the general adaptation syndrome. To fill out the model we need to approach stress as a psychological problem with concepts relevant to the behavioral strategies we observe and the cognitive processes that direct them.

A scheme for thinking about psychological stress is presented in Fig. 4.5. On the input side, there is a stimulus situation. It becomes a source of threat (that is, entailing the prospect of harm) through an initial cognitive process, the *primary appraisal* of threat. How one reacts to a threatening situation comes about as a result of *secondary appraisal*. Finally, the results of those appraisals—how much will I be harmed by this situation? and what do I think and what shall I do about it?—are expressed in behavior (coping or avoiding), in affective responses, and in bodily reactions.

We shall review some studies of stress that illuminate four key points:

1. The intensity of the stressor is itself not sufficient to define psychological stress and to enable us to predict how a person will respond.

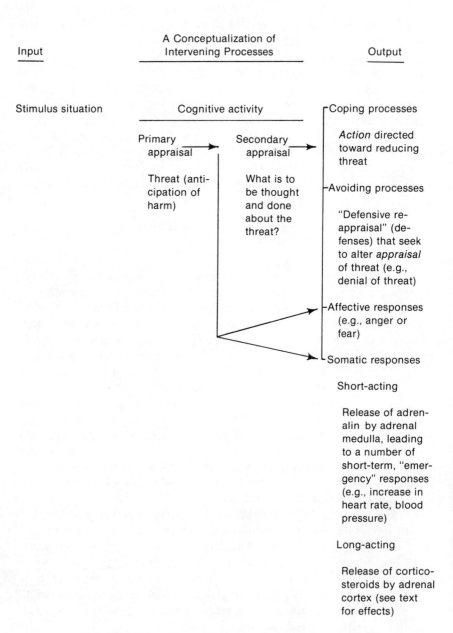

FIG. 4.5.   The sequence of events in psychological stress.

2. The processes of coping or avoiding represent strategies by which the encounter with threat is dealt with and are determined by primary and secondary appraisals and the factors that affect those appraisals.

3. Different *patterns* of response to threat are observed; we see great diversity in the ways people cope with or avoid stress.

4. There are important factors in the stimulus situation that affect appraisals of threat, coping and avoiding. One of these has to do with the *anticipation* of harm; i.e., how long beforehand does one know that harm may come. Another concerns the outcome of one's behavior in relieving stressful conditions.

Let's begin by examining some case study data. They come from interviews of patients about to undergo surgery that were conducted by Janis (1958) as part of a quite extraordinary investigation of psychological stress. The summaries of the two interviews that follow vividly illustrate the first three points above.

Interview Case H-1

Mrs. C., a 31-year-old housewife, was in a chronic state of fear before the operation. On two occasions she became so agitated that she attempted to leave the hospital in order to avoid having the operation (hernia repair). She consented to remain only after considerable coaxing and reassurance on the part of the nursing staff.

Throughout the week following the operation she expressed a high degree of relief about the fact that everything had worked out well and she felt that her fears had been unjustified. Nevertheless she continued to display symptoms of acute emotional disturbance. On her first postoperative day she felt elated for a few hours but, later on, began to feel extremely worried and wept frequently because, as she put it, "I felt like a tractor had run into me and made chopped meat of me." During the following five days her uncontrollable crying spells persisted, occurring mainly when she was alone in her room, thinking about the operation. Each night she felt very tense and suffered from insomnia:

I can't sleep nights. I've seen and heard so many things here, it bothers me. I get upset when the other patients shriek. I'd be more calm at home.

This patient was generally cooperative, extremely grateful, and warmly affectionate toward all the nurses and physicians; but she became very apprehensive whenever any of them came into her room to administer routine treatments. She was reluctant to conform with demands that might result in pain or discomfort. For example, when the nurses asked her to stand up for the first time (on the second postoperative day), she managed to conform, but she described her subjective experience as follows:

I felt terrified. I had a cold sweat all over my body. I didn't think I could stand it. I thought my stomach would fall on the floor.... But I did what they told me; I just tried to stand it....

Mrs. C. described herself as a "nervous person," constantly worried about her own health, her children's welfare, and her family finances. She reported that ever since the experience of protracted labor in giving birth to her first child eleven years earlier, she had been afraid of coming to a hospital for any sort of treatment and had avoided doctors as much as possible. Throughout her entire adult life she had experienced intense fear in connection with crossing streets, which seemed to be linked with strong self-punitive impulses. This phobic reaction originated, according to the patient, at the age of ten when she made a suicide attempt on the street in front of her house:

I was badly beaten by my mother one day and I felt there was no use going on living. So I threw myself under a car and I was run over but not badly hurt.... I've been afraid of crossing streets ever since then, and I worry about my children crossing streets because of it [pp. 240–244].

Interview Case L-6

Mr. G., a 56-year-old business man, consistently impressed the hospital staff as one of the most cheerful, carefree, and cooperative patients who had ever been hospitalized for surgery. Following his operation (partial thyroidectomy), this man became so resistant, tense, and hostile that he was scarcely recognizable as the same person.

In a very relaxed, sociable mood during the preoperative interview, the patient denied having any feelings of fear:

When they told me last night that the operation was definitely scheduled, I had no reaction, no fear at all.... I feel the same way about it now.... Having this operation is like a vacation for me.

Detailed questioning about his feelings revealed only that he felt a slight degree of concern about the possible long-range effects of having too much thyroid tissue removed, but he maintained that he had no "real" concern about this because of his absolute confidence in the doctor's ability to take proper care of him....

Enthusiastically, he praised the hospital staff several times during the preoperative interview. His comment about the nurses, for example, was:

The nurses? They're 100 percent good.... Of course, they could stand another nurse on this floor when they have a full house like this. But those girls really do a wonderful job—busy every minute, always on the job.

Following the operation, those who were in daily contact with him were surprised to discover that he had become very quarrelsome and irritable. On a number of occasions, he displayed extreme anger and overt resistance to routine postoperative treatments....

In the postoperative interview, five days after the operation, the patient recounted, with much heated affect, one grievance after another against the nurses and ward attendants. The following is a sample of the innumerable incidents which he reported as having enraged him:

Instead of fresh orange juice, they gave me canned juices and broth that tasted like a mixture of piss and quinine.... When the nurses tried to kick my wife and son out last night, I argued with them and with the supervisor so much that it made me sick, I got so excited and upset. . . . The nurses give me all kinds of goddamn excuses about not keeping my diet, always saying "it's not on the chart." . . . If I wasn't knocked out from my operation yesterday [when the nurse sassed me], I would have knocked her down on the floor, I really mean it!

Before the operation he had asserted "this is one of the very best hospitals in the world," but after the operation his attitude was markedly changed, colored by the alleged mistreatment he had suffered: "If any of my friends said they were going to come here I'd tell them not to—I'd warn them about the nurses here." . . .

Although he freely admitted having experienced apprehensiveness about his physical condition since the operation, the patient consistently maintained that prior to the operation he had felt no concern whatsoever. Of particular interest for the present discussion is the fact that this patient readily admitted having been worried about his health and about medical treatment at various times in the past. Approximately eight months earlier, he had undergone an operation similar to the present one. At that time, however, he had experienced considerable fear beforehand, and he was deeply impressed by the fact that after the operation he had experienced very little pain and had actually enjoyed the indulgent care, attention, and sociability that characterized the convalescent period, which he referred to as a "real vacation." . . . Apparently the favorable memory of the antecedent operation played a major role in determining the low level of anticipatory fear before the present operation. The contrasting preoperative emotional reactions to the two very similar operations, only eight months apart, show quite clearly that such reactions can be extremely variable. After his first operation, he had been friendly with the entire staff of his ward; whereas after the second operation, his hostility was so overt that he became exceptionally disliked by essentially the same personnel [pp. 269–270].

These two patients certainly differ in their reactions to the stress of impending surgery and its aftermath. On the basis of the interviews with them and with a number of other patients, and from a large-sample survey of people who had undergone surgery, Janis proposed that the principal difference lies in the degree of anticipatory fear experienced. Coping responses before the operation and the patient's reactions postoperatively both reflect the intensity of initial fear. The apprehension experienced before a threatening event may be called, said Janis, the "work of worrying." Some fear is appropriate and adaptive because it enables the person to anticipate the threat (e.g., the realistic dangers of surgery, the postoperative discomfort that may be experienced) and to prepare for it mentally and with plans of action where action is possible. Mrs. C. and Mr. G. were at the extremes of preoperative fear. Mrs. C. and patients like her became overwhelmed by fear, felt extremely threatened and vulnerable, and tended to show avoidance rather than coping reactions. Postoperatively, these highly fearful patients were likely to be anxious and emotional.

Patients like Mr. G. failed to carry out the work of worrying and were unprepared for the stress of postoperative discomfort. The sudden and unanticipated occurrence of discomfort left them feeling helpless and terribly vulnerable; fear and anger directed toward the hospital staff who had failed to protect them were often seen in these patients.

## Experimental Studies of Stress

We now take up a series of studies attempting to examine stress under the more controlled conditions of the laboratory. Mainly, the studies we shall consider were conducted by Lazarus and a large group of collaborators—students and associates—at the University of California at Berkeley. Three principal objectives guided this program.

1. The investigators set out to create a situation that would be stressful in some degree for most subjects in order to observe the various facets of stress response—the cognitive activity of appraisal, coping and avoiding responses, and physiological reactions.

2. They sought to identify personality characteristics associated with variations in the primary appraisal of threat and the effects of primary appraisal on stress responses.

3. The third objective was the most ambitious—to *manipulate* cognitive activity by providing subjects with ready-made appraisals of threat so that the effects of cognitive activity could be investigated without reliance on inference from subjects' responses (e.g., self-report of threat).

The stressor in these studies was a film. In the early experiments, and anthropological film was used; it shows a crude, primitive, and starkly painful circumcision rite (a subincision of the penis made by cutting with an instrument made of rock along its ventral surface) carried out on several young adolescent boys. The operation is part of the ritual of becoming a man in an aboriginal Australian society. Because of its distinctiveness (as some writers [Aas, 1958; Schwartz, 1956] have suggested, it is singularly effective in arousing castration fear), the investigators switched to another film in later experiments. This one, an industrial training film, vividly depicts some dreadful workshop accidents—severe laceration of fingers by one worker, the loss of a finger by another, and the fatal impaling of a bystander by a piece of lumber flung from a circular saw. The viewer can see the last two accidents coming, and there is a high degree of stressful anticipation. The use of motion picture films as a means of threatening subjects was an inventive experimental manipulation. No deception need be practiced on the subject, the stressor is standard from subject to subject and not variable in the way that experimenter-induced threat can sometimes be, and films can achieve an extraordinary realism and arouse a high degree of emotionality.

The first experiment in the series was a frank fishing expedition. Lazarus, Speisman, Mordkoff, and Davison (1962) set out to establish the viability of this stress-inducing technique, to assess a variety of psychological and physiological responses that might reveal the stressful impact of the film, and to investigate those personality characteristics associated with differing stress responses. Subjects were evaluated on a number of personality scales, and two measures of autonomic arousal, skin resistance and heart rate, were recorded as they watched two films—a control film *(Corn Farming in Iowa)* first, followed on a second occasion by *Subincision.* There were some questions for each subject to answer about his reactions to each film and a list of adjectives by which to describe the feelings (mood) aroused.

Some very complicated cluster analysis techniques were used to reduce the large number of variables derived from the autonomic and psychological measures to those that best represented the subjects' reactions to the "benign stimulation" of the control film and the change in their responses to the stressful *Subincision.* We see the effects of the two films on one measure of autonomic arousal in Fig. 4.6, and Fig. 4.7 shows autonomic responses to each of the operations in the stress film. The effects are dramatic: Subjects tend to relax during the control film, showing levels of autonomic activity

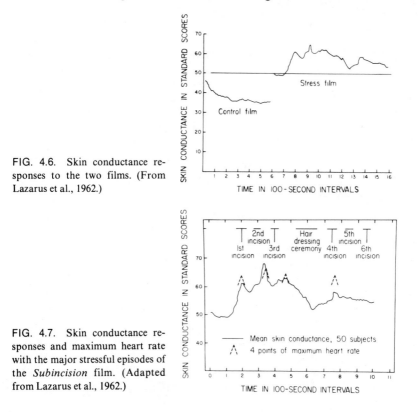

FIG. 4.6.  Skin conductance responses to the two films. (From Lazarus et al., 1962.)

FIG. 4.7.  Skin conductance responses and maximum heart rate with the major stressful episodes of the *Subincision* film. (Adapted from Lazarus et al., 1962.)

that fall below a control baseline period, and autonomic activity rises sharply to the stress film. During the stress film itself, both measures of autonomic response peak during the most disturbing scenes and fall during episodes that are not threatening (e.g., a hair-dressing ceremony).

Not every subject responded in this way to the two films. Indeed, some showed a minimal autonomic response to the stressor. An analysis of personality characteristics revealed by the personality scales the subjects had taken suggested the following portrait to Lazarus et al. (1962):

> Those who show little autonomic reactivity under the stressor condition (Group 1) may be described as confident, poised, and socially adroit. They are also self-seeking, self-centered, and think well of themselves. Such persons are prone to impulsive and spontaneous acts: they are socially outgoing rather than introspective, more verbally fluent, and interpersonally forceful and socially ascendant. With this combination of personality characteristics, such persons could well be less moved by empathetic feelings about the plight of the boys in the *Subincision* film, and more apt to express themselves directly in physical action and verbalization rather than by internal physiological response [p. 23].

The subjects who did show a strong autonomic response present a quite different personality picture:

> Those who reacted to the stressor condition with marked autonomic effects (Group 2) might be described as independent, self-reliant, forceful, responsible and stable, conscientious, concerned with rectitude and integrity, and gifted with maturity and foresight. This description is based on the CPI [California Psychological Inventory] scales of socialization and achievement via indepen-dence, with the Block Ec [Ego Control] scale added. Assuming the Ec scale to indicate socially correct control of impulse rather than rigid overcontrol, we emerge with a set of qualities which might well lead to a sense of personal affront at the crude victimization of the boys in the *Subincision* film [p. 23].

These personality-related differences in autonomic reactions to the stressor were constructed from the patterns of high and low scores on the various personality scales shown by reactive and less reactive subjects. Among the validity data on these scales (drawn from the Minnesota Multiphasic Personality Inventory [MMPI] and the California Psychological Inventory [CPI]) are clinical descriptions of high and low scorers based on many individual cases and lists of adjectives judged to be characteristic. Despite the clinical usefulness of the MMPI and CPI, a considerable degree of caution is needed lest we accept these personality portraits too uncritically. Only a few of the MMPI and CPI scales were used; the clinical descriptions are really profiles based on the outstanding characteristics of *groups* of subjects from which individuals may deviate considerably; and there is the problem of the social desirability response style that we took up in Chapter 2 in connection with the Manifest Anxiety Scale. Even if these personality descriptions did turn out to characterize accurately those who autonomically react to a stressor like *Subincision* and those who don't, we would still not know about the cognitive processes of the personality groups involved in the appraisal of threat. How did the nonreactors do it?

*The Short-Circuiting of Threat.* Clinical evidence and some other personality characteristics involved in stress appraisals and response to stress suggested a possible answer and an experimental approach to the problem. In several studies it was found that subjects identified by personality scales as tending to use the ego defenses of repression and denial differed in their threat responses to the subincision film from subjects with a more "sensitizing," threat-responsive pattern on the personality tests. In six experiments, subjects high on repression–denial reported much less distress to the film than subjects with high sensitization scores. Both groups, however, showed equivalent autonomic reactions (see Weinstein, Averill, Opton, & Lazarus, 1968). Thus, *denial* appeared to provide a partially successful defense against the threat posed by *Subincision*. By denying (for example, not attending to the signs of pain shown by the native boys or by altering one's appraisal of the operations so they pose less of a vicarious threat as one views them) the experience of threat might he minimized. Is that what the nonreactors in the first experiment more successfully accomplished?

A more decisive test of the effect of defensive appraisals on stress responses would be provided by *manipulating* subjects' cognitions about the threat—that is, giving them a defense by which to "short-circuit" the development of a stress response. This process of short-circuiting the appraisal of threat was studied in several experiments. One by Lazarus, Opton, Nomikos, and Rankin (1965) is representative. In each of three experimental conditions, subjects heard a brief tape-recorded orientation to the workshop accident film. The orientation for subjects in the control condition was:

> We have been conducting a series of investigations on the effects of motion picture films on physiological and psychological reactions. The short film you are going to see is a portrayal of two woodworking shop accidents. In one a worker runs the tips of his fingers through a ripsaw. In the other, a worker loses a finger. These incidents are used by the shop foreman to give the men a lesson in safety practices [p. 624].

The two other conditions involved the short-circuiting of threat. The short-circuiting process in one condition was denial, and the orientation was patterned after clinical observations of this ego defense. The critical part of it persuasively argued that the threat was really not a threat:

> The short film you are going to see now was designed to frighten industrial employees into faithfully using safety devices. You will see the portrayal of two woodworking shop accidents, one in which the worker runs the tips of his

fingers through a ripsaw, the other in which another worker loses a finger. As you watch the film, remember that the people you see are actors, and none of them is actually injured. While every effort was made to give the impression of reality, it is all completely faked.

One's awareness of fakery is enhanced by the poor acting ability of the participants. In order to give the impression of bleeding, red dye is squeezed from the palm of the hand, and where necessary, a finger is made to appear missing by properly concealing it, and by effective photographic work. The accidents are both staged because it would have been almost impossible to have made such a film based on real life incidents. Everything is done to make you believe that the fictitious events are real [p. 624].

The short-circuiting process in the third condition was intellectualization, and it, too, was modeled on clinical observations of defense. Intellectualization involves a detached emotional attitude toward threat. One focuses on a selected aspect of the situation, or on analyzing and understanding it. Those, like police and physicians, who have to deal with human disasters or with severe disease and injury must make use of intellectualization to a fair degree to insure some degree of personal comfort. The intellectualization orientation toward the film played on the themes of detachment and an objective, scientific analysis.

The short film you are going to see deals with an effort to train men in the use of safety devices. In doing so, two woodworking shop accidents are presented. In one a worker runs the tips of his fingers through a ripsaw, and in the other, a worker loses a finger. The events portrayed are interesting to analyze, and we may view them from the point of view of the socio- and psychological dynamics of the situation.

A shop foreman is endeavoring to train the men in the use of safety devices. The pattern found here is typical of what might be observed in industry, which has been greatly concerned with accidents and their prevention. In the film you will see a foreman giving detailed explanations of the way in which the safety devices work. When the first accident occurs, he capitalizes on it, using it as an object lesson to the rest of the men, showing them what might have been done to prevent it, demonstrating the mechanical features of the guards on the machine, and explaining in detail how they work.

In order to bring home the point, he remembers an experience of Armand, one of the older shop workers, an experience which has had a great influence in leading Armand to respect and use the proper safety devices. In using the past episode, he calls upon Armand, whom he knows will give him support in this matter, to tell his story, which is presented in the flashback. Armand's story reveals the value of direct experience with object lessons in influencing behavior.

As you watch the film, you may reflect upon the psychodynamics revealed by the interchanges between the people, and be analytical about the devices used by the foreman to influence the men in the shop, that is, the psychological processes

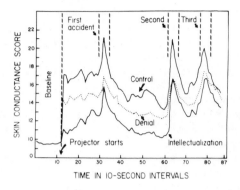

FIG. 4.8. Skin conductance responses to the stressful episodes of the accident film of subjects in the various orientation conditions. (Adapted from Lazarus et al., 1965.)

that are involved. This frame of reference is of course used by the psychological scientist as he observes, analyzes and understands these processes [pp. 624–625].

The effects of the orientation conditions were determined from the autonomic responses of subjects. Figure 4.8 shows the results for the skin conductance response. The two short-circuiting orientations made subjects significantly less emotionally aroused than the control subjects by the first two accidents. There is a third accident in the film, not mentioned in any of the three orientations, and the ego-defensive orientations did not protect against this unexpected threat. Lazarus et al. make a key point about the effectiveness of the threat manipulations in noting that it was not simply the subjects' verbal responses that the orientation messages succeeded in altering. By changing the cognitions involved in the primary appraisal of threat, emotional reactions were substantially diminished.

The purpose of the short-circuiting studies was to show that the response to threat is a function of cognitions about threat—that is, that the cognitive processes of appraisal determine whether threat is perceived and how severe a threat it is. These experiments were very successful in creating, experimentally, close analogues of important ego defenses by which people in stressful situations attempt to avoid threat. There are certainly stressful situations in which short-circuiting may have the effect of making a person feel less fearful and more comfortable without closing off at the same time possibilities for realistic and approporiate action. Sitting in the dentist's chair and waiting for the inevitable injection of local anesthetic is one such situation in which many people undoubtedly have short-circuiting cognitions. Here, denial, intellectualization, or other defensive processes can avert needless worry and apprehension. There are, indeed, more drastic circumstances, as in the following excerpt from Hamburg, Hamburg, and DeGoza (1953), in which defensive appraisals have an ego-protective, adaptive value.

This may be illustrated by the case of Patient B., who died 2 weeks after injury. Although she preferred not to think about the circumstances and nature of her injury and avoided the subject whenever possible, she remembered it clearly. However, within a few days she developed the attitude that she was not seriously ill at all, but practically well. She then recalled having been afraid of dying immediately after her injury, particularly when she first went to the operating room, but said that when she had survived this ordeal she knew that she would be all right; she felt there was no doubt that she was now practically well, that she would require little further care and would soon be back to a normal family life. She asserted that she was not helpless, but to a considerable extent could care for herself. She talked rather lightly and comfortably for the most part. She felt that she would be sufficiently improved in a few days that she would be able to go home and take care of her children. The fact that this patient made such statements calmly and deliberately while she lay helplessly on a Stryker frame— a charred remnant of a woman—had a powerful impact on all observers [p. 9].

Short-circuiting appraisals are not always adaptive, however. When one deceives oneself about threats toward which some action is needed and is possible, defensive appraisals may be seriously maladaptive. Fear and emotional arousal may be minimized, but there is also the short-circuiting of secondary appraisal. The question, "What do I think and do about this threat?" may not even get asked. One of Janis' (1958) surgery cases provides a telling example. This is the case of a middle-aged man who failed to respond to increasingly severe symptoms of lung disease for more than a year. He finally acceded to surgery after considerable family pressure. His responses in the preoperative interview were compelling evidence of his use of denial.

He doubted that his illness was serious, asserting that he could probably get along quite well without the operation but that, since everyone said he should have it, he was willing to give it a try. During the interview, the patient made many joking, facetious remarks, and behaved in such a way as to give the interviewer an impression of forced gaiety. When asked the standard series of questions about his expectations and feelings concerning the impending operation, he responded in a stereotyped manner, mechanically shrugged his shoulders, grinned, and remarked: "What's the use of worrying? I've got nothing to worry about" [p. 260].

This patient died of advanced lung cancer 11 months after the surgery. As Janis notes, "in a very real sense, his denial reactions cost him his life [p. 261]."

The processes of secondary appraisal are concerned with the cognitions leading to coping with threat once a situation has been appraised as threatening. There is an important research literature on coping behavior that we shall touch on briefly in the context of two questions—the anticipation of threat and the effects of uncertainty.

*Anticipation and Uncertainty.*   Which is more stressful: to be suddenly exposed to threat with little warning, or to anticipate the threat, to know it is coming beforehand? Some of the research on stress suggests that long anticipation is more stressful, but there is also the point made by Janis: Worrying, if not carried to an extreme, accomplishes some necessary "work" in helping a person facing threat to prepare for it. This question of the relative impact of "surprise versus suspense" was investigated by Nomikos, Opton, Averill, and Lazarus (1968) using the same stress film procedure as in the previous studies. The anticipation interval was varied by cutting out of the workshop accident film nearly all of the scenes leading up to the first two accidents. These scenes were then spliced into a second copy of the film to create a suspenseful version in which the anticipation intervals were three to six times as long. Both autonomic and self-report measures of stress response were taken. The skin conductance measure of autonomic arousal showed a clear difference in reaction to the two versions of the film; long anticipation was more stressful, and most of the increases in threat-induced arousal occurred during the anticipation intervals. The self-report measures did not discriminate between long and short anticipation, although they did reveal an increase in disturbance over that experienced by subjects during the innocuous control film, *Corn Farming in Iowa.* Perhaps the insensitivity of self-report of stress was due to the fact that these ratings were not taken during the anticipation and accident scenes themselves as were the autonomic measures; perhaps subjects could not make the kinds of distinctions necessary to reveal a difference in their reactions on the rating scales provided.

With some suggestive evidence that under conditions of vicarious threat long anticipation is more stressful, two more experiments were undertaken to explore stress anticipation further. These studies used the direct threat of a forthcoming electric shock. The first of them varied the anticipation interval, and in the second experiment the uncertainty of the shock or the time when it would occur were varied. Folkins (1970) threatened several groups of subjects with electric shock; each group had a different anticipation interval, ranging from 5 seconds to 20 minutes. His measures were both autonomic (skin conductance and heart rate) and psychological. Among the latter procedures was a post-stress questionnaire and interview to assess the kinds of coping/avoiding responses used by the subject in anticipation of the shock.

The various anticipation intervals produced clear differences in autonomic reaction. Stress response was least at the very short interval (5 seconds), rising to a maximum at 1 minute. Smaller autonomic reactions were shown by the 3- and 5-minute groups, and there was a slightly greater response by the 20-minute-anticipation group. These results suggest that the full import of the threat is just not assimilated when the anticipatory interval is very short. Given some minimal period of time, however, subjects appreciate that it is coming and show reactions of arousal and anxiety. Something quite different appears to happen when the waiting period is longer: With time to prepare, subjects engage in processes of cognitive reappraisal, finding ways of reassuring themselves and coping with the impending shock. As one subject said, "I tried to figure out which of the attachments could be the shock electrodes. Although I was by no means ready to quit the experiment, I recalled the sentence in the instructions about how I could quit any time I wanted to [p. 176]." The greater response by the 20-minute group is a bit difficult to explain. Twenty minutes *is* a long time to sit still, as the experimental procedure required, and perhaps that in itself contributed to arousal responses. Or, alternatively, the long interval may have magnified subjects' expectancies about the severity of the shock: If it's that far off, it must be pretty awful indeed!

Theoretically, the cognitive processes of appraisal are responsible for the perception of impending harm, and secondary appraisals (or reappraisals) of the threat are responsible for the ways in which we cope with or try to avoid it. Thus, we ought to find that cognitive activity during the anticipation interval varies in the ways just suggested. At short intervals, there is not enough time to work out coping responses, and defensive (avoidant) thoughts predominate; with greater time, subjects should develop reappraisals that cope more effectively with the expected harmful event. Folkins's data appear to bear this out. The post-stress questionnaire/interviews were rated by judges for the kinds of coping or avoiding processes that characterized subjects' responses. There were a large number of them, but they group into three major categories—coping, defense, and ego failure. Coping responses occurred more frequently at both the very short and the longer anticipation intervals (but not at 20 minutes), while panicky, ego failure reactions predominated at the short intervals of 30 seconds and 1 minute. One subject's regressive response was: "I felt insecure. Then I felt indignant that the experimenter is able to take advantage of such an unknowing and unaware person as I [p. 176]." Another subject's response bordered on the delusional: "Jesus may happen baby. I heard that today. I was thinking Jesus was happening to me a little bit [p. 176]."

One additional finding would have provided dramatic evidence for the mediating role of cognitive appraisal and reappraisal in responses to stress. That finding would have been a relationship between the type of coping or avoiding response of the *individual* subject and his autonomic response to stress. No such correlations between the coping/avoiding categories and stress response were obtained. As Folkins notes, however:

> although the exact relationship between cognitive activity and stress reaction postulated by a cognitive theory analysis is not fully clarified by these data, they do at least offer support for the idea of a functional, and probably complex, relationship between anticipation time, cognitive activity, and degree of stress reaction [p. 183].

A plausible hypothesis, then, is that with time one can carry out the work of worrying, thinking, or acting in ways that help to cope with the impending harm. Not everyone does that, of course, as the Janis interviews reveal, and there are stress situations that can impose the most extreme demands on coping. Lazarus (1966) concludes from his extensive review of the stress literature that:

> *More adaptive and reality-oriented forms of coping are most likely when the threat is comparatively mild; under severe threat, pathological extremes become more prominent....*
> *In short, high degrees of threat encourage primitive, inadequate solutions* to it [pp. 162, 164; italics in the original].

The longer the anticipation interval, the more one can prepare for the stressful event. But suppose the occurrence of the threat is uncertain—there is only some *probability* that it will happen, say a 50% chance. How does that compare with the stressfulness of a waiting interval that is of uncertain duration? One knows the harm is unavoidable but does not know when it will arrive.

In a complex experiment, Monat, Averill, and Lazarus (1972) again threatened subjects with electric shock. There were two sets of conditions. In one, the shock threat was *time-locked*: The shock might or might not happen depending on the specific condition the subject was in (100% or only 50% probable), but if it did it would come at the end of a fixed interval. In the other, the *time* at which a shock would be delivered was uncertain; the subject could expect a shock at any time from 0 to 6 minutes. Shocks were actually delivered in this experiment (they were not in Folkins's), and the shock in this condition was administered after 3 minutes.

We can look at two principal measures—autonomic responses over the waiting interval and a measure of "attention deployment." The latter was derived from ratings by each subject of the amount of time he spent during the waiting intervals of each of the three shock-threat trials thinking shock-relevant or avoidant thoughts ("I thought about things not related to this experiment such as exams, movies, songs, dates, sex, etc. [p. 239]"). This measure, then, reflected the subject's vigilant anticipation of the shock or his defensive attempts to avoid it.

The heart rate data shown in Fig. 4.9 during the anticipation interval show the effects of the time-locked and time-uncertain conditions. The pattern is one of an initial increase in arousal, a period of decline, and increase again as the time for shock approaches for the two time-locked conditions (and for a third time-locked condition in which shock was not given on any of the three trials). The one deviation from this profile is the time-uncertain condition.

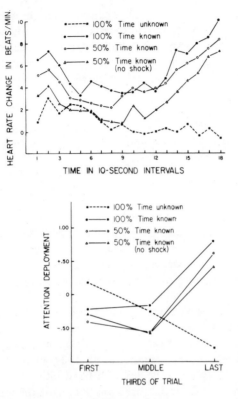

FIG. 4.9.   Heart rate during 3-minute anticipation period. There are four conditions of uncertainty about the shock. (Adapted from Monat, Averill, and Lazarus, 1972.)

FIG. 4.10.   Attention deployment during 3-minute period waiting for electric shock. The score is number of task-relevant thoughts minus task-irrelevant thoughts. (Adapted from Monat, Averill, and Lazarus, 1972.)

Here, following the initial increase, there was a steady drop in heart rate over the anticipation interval. Figure 4.10 shows the attention deployment results; again, the distinctive condition is the time-uncertain one.

These results suggest that the initial uncertainty about *when* a threat will occur is no less disturbing than certain knowledge that it will happen at a definite time or uncertainty about whether it will happen at all. Thereafter, however, while the time-known conditions produce comparable patterns of increasing arousal as the end of the interval approaches, time-uncertainty seems to be associated with a decrease in stress response. Monat, Averill, and Lazarus proposed that the process by which stress relief occurs may be inferred from the attention deployment measure. Lower scores mean that the subject was more engaged in shock- or situation-avoidant thoughts, and as we see in Figure 4.11, time uncertainty resulted in increasing attention elsewhere. If cognitive appraisal is the causative variable, it was the very success of these avoidant thoughts that promoted the drop in emotional arousal. Monat, Averill, and Lazarus are careful to note that we need to be cautious in accepting this conclusion, and it would appear that an experiment *manipulating* attention deployment in a manner analogous to the short-circuiting studies is called for.

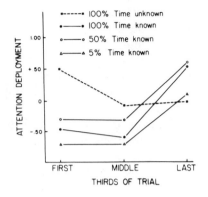

FIG. 4.11.   Attention deployment during 3-minute period waiting for electric shock. The score is the same as in the preceding figure. (Adapted from Monat, Averill, and Lazarus, 1972.)

The Folkins and Monat, Averill, and Lazarus studies on anticipation interval and uncertainty are both excellent examples of the achievements of experimental stress research, and at the same time exemplify the major problem of this research area. These studies suggestively point to the role of cognitive processes in mediating stress response, and they implicate the temporal and event-certainty aspects of the stress situation in the kinds of coping or avoiding activity that people will call forth to deal with an impending threat. At the same time, they highlight the problem posed by the great individual differences we find in stress response. Subjects, no less than the people we observe around us, have well-established repertoires of thinking and acting in stressful circumstances, and the cognitive appraisals and coping/avoiding responses we see in experimental studies of stress reflect those pre-existing individual differences as well as our experimental manipulations. The effect is to weaken the power of experiments: If some subjects have strong tendencies to vigilant coping, for example, conditions of time-uncertainty are going to produce much less avoidance-based stress relief. We return here to a point made at the beginning of the last chapter: Stress, inevitably, is defined by the individual's response. While we may seek experimental stressors that will *tend* to arouse some degree of stress response in every subject, what we find is that *some* subjects react strongly and others hardly or not at all. The weaker the experimental manipulation, the more difficult it is to find experimental effects. There is a partial answer to this problem to be found in the use of fear survey questionnaires to preselect subjects for some special degree of sensitivity to the sort of stressor to be applied in an experiment (cf. Geer, 1965). Stress research could also profit from more careful development of techniques for assessing the cognitive processes of appraisal and reappraisal of threat and for taking such measures at times of peak threat. But even with refinements such as these, stress research will continue its intimate involvement with individual differences. That is all right, of course, because individual differences are one of the hallmarks of the study of personality.

*Uncontrollability: The Learning of Helplessness.*   The final experiments to be covered are from a different research program, a ten-year inquiry into the ways in which people and animals learn to become helpless in the face of stress, reported in a provocative book, *Helplessness,* by Seligman (1975). He begins by making a case for the importance of the distinction between learning that one's responses are instrumental in achieving an outcome—the relief of stressful or traumatic circumstances—and learning that the stressful situation is uncontrollable. He calls the latter *response independence,* and what happens when an organism is confronted with response independence is helplessness.

Actually, three things happen when organisms are subjected to uncontrollable traumatic stimuli.

1. A *motivational deficit* develops. Seligman argues that we learn *expectations* about response contingencies. When an animal or person acquires the expectation that there is nothing possible to be done to relieve stress, the motivation to attempt control is badly diminished and, Seligman points out, "when an organism learns that it is helpless in one situation, much of its adaptive behavioral repertoire may be undermined [p. 36]." The organism's behavior changes from overt fearfulness to passivity.

2. The organism's subsequent learning displays the effects of *cognitive interference*—a specific instance, Seligman thinks, of proactive interference (a disruptive effect of prior on subsequent learning). Learning that an outcome is utterly unaffected by any response in one's repertoire makes the later learning of coping responses more difficult. This also involves the learning of an expectation ("There's nothing I can do," or whatever the cognitive equivalent of that may be in an animal) and is closely related to the motivational deficit. Even when the person or animal has experiences of success in relieving stress, prior exposure to uncontrollability interferes with the ability to recognize that success.

3. *Emotional disturbance* develops. Stress and trauma produce heightened emotionality—fear. As control over stressful stimuli is learned, fear diminishes. An animal in the early stages of avoidance learning is manifestly fearful, but as it successfully acquires the avoidance response, fear declines, and it may finally develop what appears as an almost blasé unconcern. Experienced parachutists have little fear at precisely those critical moments that produce panic in the novice. Uncontrollability results in initial fear, which later gives way to depression. Seligman makes an interesting point about fear and about another emotional state, frustration.

> Fear and frustration can be viewed as motivators that have evolved in order to fuel coping and that are set off by trauma. The initial responses to control a trauma are elicited by this fear. Once trauma is under control, fear has little use, and it decreases. As long as the subject is uncertain whether or not he can

control trauma, fear is still useful, since it maintains the search for a response that will work. Once the subject is certain that trauma is uncontrollable, fear decreases—it is worse than useless since it costs the subject great energy in a hopeless situation. Depression then ensues [p. 55].

The most compelling experiments were done by Seligman, his colleagues, and students with dogs using an experimental design that Seligman characterizes as the *triadic design*. The basic features are these: one group of animals is exposed to stress, but the stressor is *controllable*—the animals can learn to make some response that will enable escape. A second group receives every stressful stimulus administered to the first group but can do nothing to escape. A third is unexposed to the stressful stimuli. The test comes when the three groups are trained on a different, *avoidance* learning task—that is, the animals have to learn a response that prevents the stressful stimulus from occurring.

The stress situation for groups 1 and 2 involved placing each dog in a hammock-like restraint and administering moderately severe electric shocks. The dogs in the first group could escape the shocks by learning to press a panel with the nose. Every shock received in this group, in exactly the same temporal pattern, was administered to the dogs in the second group, but for these dogs the shocks were uncontrollable. This group was thus *yoked* to the first group with respect to the stressful stimuli. The dogs in group 3 were not shocked in the hammock. After a twenty-four hour interlude, each dog was trained in an avoidance shuttlebox. There was a signal (the dimming of a light), shortly followed by electric shock. The dog learned, at first, to *escape* the shock by leaping over a barrier into an adjoining compartment. When the light dimmed there, shock again occurred and escape then had to be back to the first compartment. The animal learned that the dimming of the light was a warning of shock to come and acquired a shock *avoidance* response—it leaped the barrier before shock onset. I should say that the group 1 (controllable stress) and group 3 (no prior stress) dogs readily learned the avoidance response, but the group 2 (uncontrollable stress) dogs did not. Indeed, six of the eight animals in this group in one experiment wholly failed to learn even the escape response. Here is Seligman's description of a group 2 dog.

A dog that had first been given inescapable shock showed a strikingly different pattern [from the group 1 and group 3 dogs]. This dog's first reactions to shock in the shuttlebox were much the same as those of a naive dog: It ran around frantically for about thirty seconds. But then it stopped moving; to our surprise, it lay down and quietly whined. After one minute of this we turned the shock off; the dog had failed to cross the barrier and had not escaped from shock. On the next trial, the dog did it again; at first it struggled a bit and then, after a few seconds, it seemed to give up and to accept the shock passively. On all succeeding trials, the dog failed to escape. This is the paradigmatic learned-helplessness finding [p. 22]. . . .

Outside the shuttlebox, too, helpless dogs act differently from non-helpless dogs. When an experimenter goes to the home cage and attempts to remove a non-helpless dog, it does not comply eagerly: It barks, runs to the back of the cage, and resists handling. In contrast, helpless dogs seem to wilt; they passively sink to the bottom of the cage, occasionally even rolling over and adopting a submissive posture; they do not resist [p. 25].

The principal implications of these striking findings have been reproduced in man, and indeed in many other species. Seligman argues that exposure to severe uncontrollable stress can lead in man to symptoms of depression and with very severe uncontrollable stress to physically giving up altogether—to death.

Compare the description of the helpless dog to the following, a report of a man's experience of severe depression (Reid, 1910).

I was seized with an unspeakable physical weariness. There was a tired feeling in the muscles unlike anything I had ever experienced. A peculiar sensation appeared to travel up my spine to my brain. I had an indescribable nervous feeling. My nerves seemed like live wires charged with electricity. My nights were sleepless. I lay with dry, staring eyes gazing into space. I had a fear that some terrible calamity was about to happen. I grew afraid to be left alone. The most trivial duty became a formidable task. Finally mental and physical exercises became impossible; the tired muscles refused to respond, my "thinking apparatus" refused to work, ambition was gone. My general feeling might be summed up in the familiar saying "What's the use." I had tried so hard to make something of myself, but the struggle seemed useless. Life seemed utterly futile [pp. 612–613].

We may touch briefly on cure and prevention. Seligman's experiments have shown that helplessness may be unlearned by ensuring the learning of new response–relief contingencies, forcing the helpless dog, if necessary, by dragging it with a leash to move from the shocked compartment to the safe one. Prevention of helplessness can come from experiences in the control of stress, as you may have imagined.

The Seligman experiments bring us back to the theme with which this chapter began—the general adaptation syndrome. There appear to be important parallels between the stages of the general adaptation syndrome and the behavioral course of dogs that have learned to be helpless. There is an initial period during which we seem to see a collapsed version of the stages of alarm and resistance: The soon-to-be helpless dog struggles frantically in reaction to the shock. This alarm-resistance stage rather quickly gives way to the disappearance of any active effort to escape. The dog experiences pain, all right, but its psychological resources to cope—further active struggle, perception of an escape route, indeed even the motivational state (fear) that would mobilize these efforts—are depleted, exhausted. I think that this phenomenon—the depletion of an organism's coping resources—suggests the unity of stress response that is one of the chief claims of the general adaptation syndrome. What was it that Reid said? "Finally mental and physical exercises became impossible, the tired muscles refused to respond, my 'thinking apparatus' refused to work, ambition was gone [p. 613]."

To be sure, the general adaptation syndrome as a conceptual model cannot account for the complex details of the cognitive processing that goes on when the existence of stressors is appraised and defensive or protective action is evolved. But as a general scheme to understand stress, it has shown great utility, enabling us to approach a broad range of stress-relevant problems in both the physiological and psychological realms.

## A Summary Appraisal

What we have covered in this chapter is only a small fraction of a vast and growing research literature. Lazarus (1966) makes its extensiveness very clear:

> Experimenters and field observers have studied a very wide variety of conditions as sources of stress reaction. In field observation, these have included such conditions as exposure to severe cold or heat, physical exertion, dental surgery, extensive airplane flights, isolation produced by shipwreck, living in a strange environment, space flight, loss of a limb, military combat, being a mental patient, engaging in a therapeutic interview, engaging in an auto race, anticipating a surgical operation, and facing imminent death from cancer or coronary infarction. This list is by no means exhaustive but only illustrative of the great range of stress conditions that have been studied.
>
> In the experimental laboratory, we find stress reactions produced by plunging the arm into icy water and doing mental work, exposing subjects to heat, cold, noise, and increased demands for speed in a skilled performance, showing disturbing movies, threatening a subject with failure or social rejection, accusing a subject of pathological perceptual distortion, requiring a psychiatric patient to face an ambiguous interview, insulting and degrading a subject, forcing a subject to lie in a lie-detection situation, frightening a subject by making him think he may be electrocuted, and producing sensory derivation. Here too the list is so extensive that only a small proportion of the studies is noted [pp. 392–393; references in the original omitted].

In one chapter I could not hope to review such an extensive and diversified area, and my choice was to focus on a few selected investigations that seemed to me to speak more clearly than others to three principal questions: observational and experimental methods in stress research, the cognitive processes involved in response to stress, and the outlines of a conceptual model of stress.

# 5 The Repression Hypothesis

## ABSTRACT

*Events of painful significance that create intense anxiety, said Freud, may be banished from awareness by the defensive process of repression. The inability to think certain thoughts, to remember certain painful experiences, or to experience certain feelings, Freud believed, has its basis in early childhood and may extend into adult life. Psychologists took up the investigation of repression, seeking ways to test this radical process of memory loss experimentally. The experimental study of repression faces some severe demands in creating the conditions for the process to occur. There are four major conditions to fulfill: (1) arousal of sufficiently intense anxiety; (2) provision of time and opportunity to repress; (3) a controlled test of the occurrence of repression; and (4) in the ideal experiment, relief from anxiety to allow the return of the repressed.*

*Studies of repression fall into three major categories: (1) studies of the recall of completed and incompleted tasks; (2) studies of learning and motivated forgetting; and (3) individual difference studies. The chapter ends with a brief analysis of alternatives to the concept of repression. A balanced and fair conclusion, however, is that the repression hypothesis, though still not experimentally verified, is viable, suggestive, and in need of further experiment.*

## INTRODUCTION

Not every experience we have, nor every memory committed to storage, can be retrieved when their remembrance is called for. Some experiences are forgotten, and there is an extensive body of theory and research on the psychology of retention, storage, and forgetting. Early in his writings Freud (cf. Breuer & Freud, 1895) proposed a more radical and extraordinary possibility—that some experiences are inaccessible to awareness because of their association with anxiety—and he came to regard this idea as a cornerstone to the whole foundation of psychoanalysis (Freud, 1914). Ideas and experiences are denied access to consciousness by what Freud called mechanisms of defense, the most fundamental of which he termed repression. He characterized (1937) the processes of repression and defense by means of a compelling analogy.

> The ego makes use of various procedures for fulfilling its task, which to put it in general terms, is to avoid danger, anxiety, and unpleasure. We call these procedures *"mechanisms of defence."* . . .
>
> It was from one of those mechanisms, repression, that the study of neurotic processes took its whole start. There was never any doubt that repression was not the only procedure which the ego could employ for its purposes. Nevertheless, repression is something quite peculiar and is more sharply differentiated from the other mechanisms than these are from one another. I should like to make this relation to the other mechanisms clear by an analogy, though I know that in these matters analogies never carry us very far.
>
> Let us imagine what might have happened to a book at a time when books were not printed in editions but written out individually. We will suppose that a book of this kind contained statements which in later times were regarded as undesirable—as, for instance, according to Robert Eisler (1929), the writings of Flavius Josephus must have contained passages about Jesus Christ which were offensive to later Christendom. At the present day, the only defensive mechanism to which the official censorship could resort would be to confiscate and destroy every copy of the whole edition. At that time, however, various methods were used for making the book innocuous. One way would be for the offending passages to be thickly crossed through so that they were illegible. In that case they could not be transcribed, and the next copyist of the book would produce a text which was unexceptionable but which had gaps in certain passages and so might be unintelligible in them. Another way, however, if the authorities were not satisfied with this, but wanted also to conceal any indication that the text had been mutilated, would be for them to proceed to distort the text. Single words would be left out or replaced by others, and new sentences interpolated. Best of all, the whole passage would be erased and a new one which said exactly the opposite put in its place. The next transcriber could then produce a text that aroused no suspicion but which was falsified. It no longer contained what the author wanted to say; and it is highly probable that the corrections had not been made in the direction of truth.
>
> If the analogy is not pursued too strictly, we may say that repression has the same relation to the other methods of defence as omission has to distortion of the text, and we may discover in the different forms of this falsification parallels to the variety of ways in which the ego is altered [pp. 235–237].

The analogy suggests that there are a number of possible ways by which the awareness of profoundly disturbing ideas, thoughts, and memories may be tampered with. The variety of defensive processes that psychoanalytic theory has proposed and that have come to be widely accepted in psychiatry and in clinical and personality psychology is actually quite considerable, including projection, reaction formation, and several other means of distorting consciousness. The most central process for averting anxiety, however, is repression.

In the experimental study of defensive processes, which was inaugurated by psychologists in the 1920s and has been seriously pursued since, repression is the most thoroughly investigated. Psychologists seem to have recognized that repression is the cornerstone for the understanding of unconscious processes, and they also became intrigued with the essential feature of the concept of repression—that memory and perceptual processes may be powerfully influenced by the avoidance of pain. So, we shall do as Freud originally did and as personality psychology has done—we focus attention on repression to understand the nature of defense.

## THE CONCEPT OF REPRESSION

From his clinical study of neurotic patients, Freud believed he found evidence for two phases of repression: *primal repression,* or by a more explicit term, *infantile amnesia;* and *repression proper,* the afterexpulsion of ideas and experiences. Although psychologists have not usually made the formal distinction between primal repression and repression proper, there is a difference between them. Primal repression refers to a denial of entry to consciousness (Freud, 1915) of impulses to commit acts that have been threatened by strong punishment and have come to evoke intense anxiety. Primal repression, then, is a development of early childhood as the Freudians view it; the punishments and threats of punishment for forbidden actions, if sufficiently severe, result both in the inhibition of the impulse and any awareness of it. There is no longer any awareness of having been made violently angry, say, and no possibility of recalling it afterwards—hence the term infantile amnesia.

The angry impulse, however, is not destroyed. Freud proposed (1915) that it "develops with less interference and more profusely if it is withdrawn by repression from conscious influence. It proliferates in the dark, as it were, and takes on extreme forms of expression...[p. 149]." Behavioristic psychologists who viewed repression as a learned response suggested that a repressed impulse persists because repression cannot prevent the occurrence of situations which instigate it; when there are cues to anger the impulse is rearoused, and the process of inhibition and repression must be renewed.

Because of primal repression, the psychoanalytic hypothesis goes, we do not remember certain painful details of early childhood, particularly those experiences with strongly motivated urges for which the fear of loss of love accompanied whatever punishment was threatened. Whether we think of Freud's metaphor or in the terms of instigating stimuli and inhibited responses, we should be clear that primal repression does not successfully block forbidden impulses; in fact, it creates that conditions for repression proper.

Repression proper, or simply repression, as we commonly refer to it, is the derivative of primal repression. The inability to think certain thoughts, to remember certain painful experiences, or to experience certain feelings may extend into adulthood and, in extreme form, may become one of the crippling features of neurosis. The basis for all subsequent repressions, Freud believed, is laid down in the primal repressions of early childhood. He proposed that primal repression and the repressions of later childhood and adulthood are the price of socialization. Those ideas and feelings that are associated with— are cognates of—the experiences that underwent primal repression are also dangerous precisely because of their associative connection with the anxious experiences of childhood. These associated ideas, then, must also be expelled from consciousness. A small child's momentary and episodic feelings of hatred of a sibling may eventually come, Freud thought, to the repression of awareness of any experience of anger as an adult if the threat of punishment and loss of love was sufficiently fearful.

So, repression proper refers to the process by which ideas and feelings associated with psychologically painful experiences of early childhood, and the memory of those experiences, are excluded from consciousness and continue to be rendered inaccessible to awareness. Repression, as Freud thought of it, takes the themes of infantile amnesia and generalizes them. The specifically dangerous impulses of a small child—principally developing childish eroticism and anger (or worse yet, rage)—that out of fear were denied awareness are in later childhood and adulthood vastly generalized. The scheme of primal repression leading to repression proper really deals with a *developmental sequence*. In effect, the threatened and anxious child must learn *how* to repress and to extend his infantile amnesia to later experiences that are associatively connected with its themes. Repression proper is immediately motivated by the experience of anxiety—an anticipatory feeling that great harm is imminent. The great harm is the recurrence of childhood states of helplessness, separation, and overwhelming fear.

## The Reactions of Psychologists to Psycholanalytic Concepts

Freud lectured on the origins and development of psychoanalysis at Clark University in 1910 and strongly provoked the interest of American psychologists. Although many experimental psychologists disdained the strange, provocative inferences Freud drew from the behavior of his patients and the theory that was built from them, there were others who saw in psychoanalysis a system of concepts worthy of serious study—that is to say, *experimental,* as well as strictly psycho-, analysis. Some American psychologists, indeed, were powerfully drawn to psychoanalysis. During the 1920s and 1930s, a number of distinguished psychologists underwent personal psychoanalyses for reasons of personal distress or to learn, intimately, the details of the theory and the processes of psychoanalytic therapy by undergoing the didactic analysis which training in psychoanalysis requires. A symposium in the *Journal of Abnormal and Social Psychology* (1940) was devoted to the accounts of psychologists who had been analyzed; in addition to characterizing their own analyses, these psychologists also struggled with the problem of the relation between psychoanalysis and psychology.

Few psychologists took psychoanalysis indifferently or neutrally; they were drawn to it for a variety of reasons and became caught up in the theory, the compelling experience of psychoanalysis, or both, or they were repelled by it and became hostile and adamant critics. To the former group, the concepts of the theory and the richness and complexity of its conceptualizations of behavior were appealing, and some of these psychologists set about the serious business of attempting to reconcile the insightfulness and the intricacy of psychoanalysis with the more disciplined, experimentally-based analysis of the processes of behavior acquisition, maintenance, and change that characterized (and still do characterize) North American learning theory. These psychologists took certain of the concepts of psychoanalysis and sought to recast them in the theoretical and experimental framework of learning theory (see, for example, Dollard & Miller, 1950, for the most ambitious, provocative, and successful of these attempts), and it was out of these efforts that one major group of experimental studies of repression emerged.

The concept of repression (that is, repression proper) made good sense to behavioristic psychologists from the 1930s on. After all, it was perfectly reasonable to assume that covert processes obey the same laws as overt responses, and those responses associated with punishment, of course, tend not to be repeated. The same thing, they reasoned, should be true of thoughts. You should remember that many of these psychologists were reared in a tradition which regarded thinking as a covert response. The notion of amnesia for important ideas, feelings, and memories was openly received by a number of psychologists engaged in the experimental investigation of memory and forgetting; the phenomenon of repression, if it could be experimentally confirmed, would be striking evidence that forgetting can be an active process motivated by the avoidance of anticipated pain.

Another group of psychologists approached the problem of repression from a different, less behavioristic, perspective. As one of them, Rosenzweig (1952) wrote:

there has been slowly struggling into existence a new experimental psychology which, in its fullest expression, is individual-centered. Such experimentation abandons the stimulus–response standpoint of behaviorism and recognizes that the stimulus is defined in the response of the subject, and that, conversely, the response is itself a stimulus which elicits further responses, including the selection of stimuli. This general approach is a result of many influences including, among others, European phenomenology, Gestalt psychology, psychoanalysis, and the projective methods. . . . In this . . . approach the environmental stimulus has its place, but the central position of the individual in selecting his stimuli and in organizing his universe of responses is paramount [p. 339].

The tack taken by these investigators in the experimental study of repression was profoundly influenced by an ingenious experiment of Zeigarnik (1927) on the role of tension (a motivational concept of Lewin's) in memory. Before we consider Zeigarnik's experiment and its modifications for the study of repression, however, we need to pause here to take up the requirements for the experimental analysis of repression.

## THE CONDITIONS FOR REPRESSION

To observe the absence from awareness of experiences associated with anxiety, several conditions must be met, and an experimental test of the occurrence of repression must also make use of controls which will enable us to rule out plausible alternatives (recall our discussion of the flawed repression experiment in Chapter 1). The following list of these requirements—establishing the conditions for repression to occur and the necessary controls—represents the very minimum we would have to do to observe the phenomenon in the laboratory.

1. Repression is dependent on the arousal of anxiety, and thus to observe it we must make subjects fearful and anxious. How anxious, and in what way? Some of the very early studies of repression by psychologists assumed simply that the unpleasantness of experiences would cause them to be repressed, but the minimal degree of discomfort involved in the recall of events that are just plainly unpleasant and some other serious problems with these studies make them irrelevant to the concept of repression.

In a careful and well-reasoned analysis of Freud's views on repression, Madison (1961) makes two key points about the condition of anxious arousal that must be met for repression to happen:

the *intensity* of the anxiety aroused is a factor in repression. Freud never made any quantitative statement on this point but a check of some of his cases shows them to be involved in rather drastic threat situations compared with what is seen in attempted laboratory analogues of repression. Consider these examples:

Katharina was a girl of eighteen whose uncle [sic: father. See Breuer & Freud, 1895, p. 134n] had tried to seduce her at fourteen. She later (age sixteen) saw him seduce her cousin and she betrayed him to his wife [her mother]. The uncle [her father] angrily threatened her. . . .

Elizabeth R., a very moral girl, found herself in love with her sister's husband. The sister died, leaving her free to marry her brother-in-law. . . .

Frau P.'s problems centered around an incestuous relationship with her older brother from childhood to age eleven. . . .

Dora was an eighteen-year-old girl in love with Herr K., a married man with children. Herr K.'s wife simultaneously was mistress to her own father. Herr K. tried to seduce Dora. . . .

When one recalls that these manifest conditions are signal–anxiety states that have profoundly traumatic meanings stemming from overwhelming infantile and childhood experiences,[1] it is clear that anxiety in clinical repression is a very intense motivational state—so extreme in fact as to raise the question whether artificial production of such states in laboratory research is possible. . . .

Anxiety, of course, is only one facet of the motivational side of repression. Simply unbearable anxiety or tension will not, in itself, lead to repression:

Let us take the case in which an instinctual stimulus such as hunger remains unsatisfied. It then becomes imperative and can be allayed by nothing but the action that satisfies it; it keeps up a constant tension of need. Nothing in the nature of a repression seems in this case to come remotely into question.

Thus repression certainly does not arise in cases where the tension produced by a lack of satisfaction of an instinctual impulse is raised to an unbearable degree. [1915. . . ., p. 147.]

For effective repression, not only must there be a state of high tension, but the tension must be associated with a threat to one's self-esteem [pp. 120–121].

More than just a momentary state of anxiousness is required if Freud is correct; the anxiety must be that desperate sort of feeling that one has terribly failed himself—failed to live up to his ego ideal. Now clearly, we cannot create anything that even approximates the anxiety, guilt, and loss of self-esteem in the examples of Freud's cases that Madison gives. Although these cases may seem rather extreme, the occurrence of repression as it is encountered clinically does involve intense states of anxiety. But is it actually necessary to create such intensities of anxiety in order to cause repression to occur? You may remember Lewin's forceful contrast of Aristotelian and Galilean thinking in Chapter 1. As another part of that general argument, Lewin (1935) was sharply critical of the idea that experiments must deal with events in all their full-blown strength and complexity.

Approximation to life conditions is often demanded of, for example, the psychology of will. By this is usually meant that it should investigate those cases,

---

[1] At the time of the traumatic events, Dora was 18, Katharina between 14 and 18.

impossible to produce experimentally, in which the most important decisions of life are made. . . . It is a requirement which, if transferred to physics, would mean that it would be incorrect to study hydrodynamics in the laboratory; one must rather investigate the largest rivers in the world [p. 21].

The analysts, in their insistence that repression can only be systematically revealed in the special conditions of psychoanalysis, may have crawled way out on an Aristotelian limb and thus deserve Lewin's scornful answer. But even if a sophisticated understanding of the nature of experiment makes it unnecessary for us to create the awesome intensity of clinical anxiety—we need, instead, to abstract the dynamic features of the process in its situational contexts to reproduce in an experiment—it is *still* a question of how much anxiety is required to trigger repression and what sort of threat is needed. We shall see what kinds of anxious and threatening situations psychologists have created to study repression as we review the major experiments, and we finally need to judge how successfully this condition has been met.

To conclude this first requirement, the repression experiment will need a control group of subjects not threatened and made anxious against which to compare the recall of the anxious group.

2. The second condition to be met is provision of the opportunity for repression to occur. This seems an obvious consideration, one that necessarily would be left to the subject once he has been made anxious. There are, however, two problems to be avoided. First, the experimental procedures must clearly ensure that the subject perceives the threat *and* the experiences associated with it (material to be learned and remembered, for example) that are predicted to fall to repression's scalpel. As one experimental psychologist (Sears, 1936), a close and sophisticated student of repression, put it:

> Apparent memory loss resulting from a failure of the original experience to be perceived might well be called a pseudo-amnesia, since there is in such cases no memory to be forgotten. The term amnesia [and the term repression also] is applied only because the patient is known to have been in contact with certain activities of the environment and it is assumed that he should have perceived and remembered them [p. 235].

Inadequate exposure or learning of the material to be repressed would automatically rule out repression as an explanation.

The second problem entailed in this condition is that the subject must be left free to repress. The time interval between anxious arousal and exposure of the material to be repressed and the test of recall must be sufficiently long to allow the process to occur. If it is too short or if there are strong cues for the subject implying that he *must* remember and would be a stupid, hopeless idiot if he could not, repression may well be interfered with. Quite early, Freud (1894) observed that the process of repression has a time course; his patients gave evidence of having struggled to achieve repression. It is also important to remember the limits on threat and anxiety arousal that will inevitably face a laboratory experiment—limits that will make any amnesia we observe less complete and drastic than clinical repression.

3. We require, next, a test of the occurrence of repression. The subjects must be asked to recall, reproduce, or reveal the experiences, learned material, or thoughts and feelings specifically associated with the earlier experience of threat and anxiety. It is critical here, if the experiences subject to repression are socially undesirable and would, if disclosed, result in embarrassment and discomfort, that the experiment provide adequate controls for response suppression or withholding or incentives of sufficient magnitude to overcome the embarrassment. The hypothetical repression experiment in Chapter 1 is a case in point: The subject angered in an experiment may well decide to suppress the expression of his angry feelings out of uncertainty about how he would be judged by the psychologist, and that sort of choice is not repression.

4. The final condition is one infrequently met in experimental studies of repression. It has to do with the recovery from the amnesia. Repression is generally only partially successful, and the repressed memories, thoughts, or feelings often intrude momentarily and incompletely into awareness. There are great pressures to remember, after all: Exposure to stimulus situations which provide strong cues for recall and the discomfort of having "blank spots" in one's memory and thought processes are two examples of the sorts of things which make repression typically a fallible defense. We see, then, what Freud (1896) called the "return of the repressed": the partial breakthrough into consciousness of the anxious memories and thoughts, usually in disguised form. When the disguise is inadequate, as it sometimes is, anxiety is keenly felt.

The return of the repressed may be seen in more complete form when the threat and anxiety motivating repression are alleviated. Psychotherapy provides this special condition, and indeed, Freudians argue, it is only under the benign conditions of psychoanalysis that we can hope to see the course of repression come full circle. But that may be an Aristotelian mistake; some psychologists have argued that the truly adequate repression experiment will provide a "therapy" for relief of anxiety and a post-test for the return of the "forgotten" material. There are a few of these experiments, and we shall take special notice of them.

A fifth condition might be argued for—that what is repressed should continue to exercise control over behavior. If it simply disappears, repression is a very uninteresting process. Thus, there should be notable gaps in the repressed person's behavior and an impairment in his cognitive processes and social behavior. There is no experimental study of repression that meets this condition, and it is fair to say that we are not ready to impose it.

## ZEIGARNIK'S EXPERIMENT AND REPRESSION

The experiment that Zeigarnik (1927) presented as her doctoral dissertation became influential in its own right as an intriguing demonstration of the effects of motivational forces on remembering and forgetting, but it had an even greater import for the study of motivated forgetting—repression. There is a story that the experiment was suggested by a rather extraordinary waiter that Lewin and his students (Zeigarnik was one of them) observed. He kept no written record of the bills at the tables he was serving, managing all the while to keep each person's check straight. When questioned *after* a party had left, however, he was quite unable to remember what the orders and amounts had been. The general proposition that these observations suggest is that incompleted tasks are remembered more readily than completed ones. Lewin (cf. 1935) thought that an unfinished task set up a tension system causing persistence in memory; with completion of the task tension subsides, and forgetting takes place.

Zeigarnik gave a large number of children and adults a whole series of tasks to perform—simple puzzles, clay modeling, etc.—and interrupted performance on half of them at a point where the subjects were fully absorbed; the other tasks were allowed to be carried out to completion. After a brief delay, the subjects were asked to recall the tasks they had worked on. Zeigarnik's finding was that the unfinished tasks were recalled better than the completed ones. The ratio of incompleted ($I$) to completed ($C$) tasks recalled ($I/C$) was 1.6 (recalling both equally would give an $I/C$ ratio of 1.0).

This doesn't sound very much like repression, but some observations made by Zeigarnik and later picked up and elaborated by Rosenzweig (1943; Rosenzweig & Mason, 1934) led to a clever twist in the experimental procedure—a twist that turned the incompleted tasks technique, for Rosenzweig and other psychologists to follow, into a test of repression. A few of Zeigarnik's subjects recalled completed tasks better than the unfinished ones, and she noted that these subjects believed that the interruptions on the incompleted tasks meant that they had failed them. The painful experience of failure and the wounding of self-esteem resulting from that caused these subjects to repress the recollection of the incompleted tasks and they thus recalled more completed ones. Zeigarnik herself used the term repression for the inferior recall of the interrupted tasks.

### Rosenzweig's Experiments

The experimental twist was Rosenzweig's invention. It consisted simply of an attempt to make all subjects believe that completion meant success on a task while interruption signified failure. In the first of two major experiements, Rosenzweig and Mason's subjects were children—all residents of a home for crippled children (a fact which we shall have to consider later)—and the experiment was presented to them as a test of their ability to do puzzles. The child who did best, they were told, would win a prize. Each child worked for three-quarters of an hour on a set of simple jigsaw puzzles, and each child was allowed to complete half and was "failed" on half. The request for recall of all the tasks was then made.

Rather than calculating the proportion of completed to incomplete *tasks* recalled, as Zeigarnik had done, Rosenzweig and Mason determined for each child a recall difference score: the percentage of completed relative to unfinished tasks recalled. Of the 40 children, 16 had positive recall difference scores—they remembered more completed than incompleted tasks—13 recalled more incompleted than completed ones, and 9 children recalled an equal proportion of both. The remaining two children recalled no tasks at all. Only 16 children could be thought of as having repressed the memory of the "failed" puzzles, but Rosenweig and Mason were able to show that they differed from the other children in two important ways. They were higher in mental age, and they were rated by their teachers as higher in "pride" ("desire to stand well with the group, and pleasure in one's own achievement [p. 257]"). Rosenzweig and Mason's (1934) conclusion is clearly put:

> It would seem to be that, given an individual of sufficient intellectual maturity and a commensurate measure of pride, experiences that are unpleasant because they wound self-respect—perhaps it should be added in a *social* situation—are, other things being equal, less apt to be remembered than experiences that are gratifying to the ego. This is in keeping with the Freudian theory of repression.
>
> In our experiment, at the most 16 of the 40 subjects satisfied these conditions. The 11 very young subjects with neutral recall difference scores seem to have been indifferent to the test situation, so that there was no basis for preferring C's [completed tasks] or X's [incompleted ones] in recall. Their low average mental age and pride rating bear out this interpretation. The group of 13 subjects with the negative recall difference scores [favoring the unfinished tasks] had a higher mental age and pride rating, but they were presumably not enough wounded for repression to operate. . . . It is as if they took a more objective attitude toward the test, regarding the puzzles as so many external obstacles to be overcome. Their need for mastery of the environment was aroused, but failure to satisfy it did not wound their egos or arouse feelings of inferiority [pp. 258–259].

Thus, sorted out on the two individual difference variables, mental age and rated pride, the children who failed to remember incompleted tasks relative to completed ones were those we would expect to be most readily threatened. In response to later criticisms, Rosenzweig (1952) pointed out that the higher mental age and pride of the children whose recall favored the completed tasks was not to be taken as an indication of greater maturity.

> Repression is surely not an indication of maturity. It is, rather, an immature mechanism of ego defense. The only point to which my original study was directed in its bearing on repression concerned the stage at which the ego of the

child might be sufficiently developed to be wounded by experiences of failure in the particular competition involved. . . . The very young children were not old enough to be affected by their failures and so would not repress them. Those approaching puberty, on the other hand, were already "mature" enough to be vulnerable and hence were concerned about failure and, in some instances, resorted to repression *as an inadequate mechanism of ego defense.* The fact that these children were physically crippled probably meant that their egos would be weaker and later to mature in any sense of ego strength, and so might more frequently employ repression. . . [p. 342].

Rozenzweig and Mason's data on recall differences and their relations to mental age and pride, though suggestive of a repression-like process, were not critical evidence. As we noted in Chapter 2, R–R relationships are more vulnerable to alternative explanations than the experimental manipulations of S–R research, especially at an early point in a program of research before a network of related findings is established. Further, the mental age and pride differences were not large, the ratings of pride were very probably of questionable reliability, and the results were not tested for significance (as was frequently the case at that time before tests of significance were well developed and widely understood).

The inference of repression would be on surer ground if it could be demonstrated in an experiment in which failure and threat to self-esteem were manipulated, contrasting a failed and threatened experimental group with a control group which would recall the tasks worked on under less ego-assaultive conditions. Rosenzweig (1943) did that experiment, this time with college students as subjects. Two groups of subjects were given jigsaw puzzles, and as before half the puzzles were interrupted. In one group, the control or "informal" group as Rosenzweig called it, each subject was led to believe that the experimenter was gathering data about the tasks themselves and that his own individual performance was not under scrutiny. In the experimental group, the puzzles were presented as an intelligence test, and it was made very clear that failure to complete a puzzle within the time limit would result in no score for that task. Again, when work on the puzzles had finished, subjects were asked to remember the tasks they had worked on. The number of subjects in each group showing the three possible recall patterns can be seen in Table 5.1.

TABLE 5.1
Recall of Completed Versus Incompleted Tasks in
Rosenweig's 1943 Experiment

| | *Recall Pattern* | | |
| --- | --- | --- | --- |
| *Group* | *Completed >* *Incompleted* | *Incompleted >* *Completed* | *Completed =* *Incompleted* |
| Experimental | 16 | 9 | 5 |
| Control | 7 | 19 | 4 |

A majority of subjects in the stressed experimental group showed the "repression" pattern of greater recall of the completed tasks; in the control group, the Zeigarnik effect was found as we would expect, and in both groups a small number of subjects showed no preference in recall. Rosenzweig also calculated a recall index—a percentage measure of the tasks recalled in two groups:

$$\text{Recall Index} \doteq 100 \left( \frac{\text{Completed} - \text{Incompleted}}{\text{Completed} + \text{Incompleted}} \right)$$

The mean index score for the experimental group was +2.95 (more completed than incompleted tasks recalled gives a score greater than 1), while in the control group the mean was –7.65. To Rosenzweig, these results suggested two tendencies in recall. In the control group, interruption of the puzzles set up in most subjects a *need persistive* tendency, one in which the tension aroused by the incompleted problem is responsible for a persisting need to continue with it and thus to remember it; in the experimental group, the dominant tendency was *ego defensive*, an attempt to avert loss of self-esteem by not remembering failures.

## Some Criticisms and Alternative Experiments

These results added weight to the earlier ones of Rosenzweig and Mason, and the evidence for an experimental demonstration of repression appeared to be much stronger. Criticisms of these experiments were not long in coming, however. In two major experiments, Alper (1946, 1948) and Glixman (1949) each used the interrupted tasks technique to approach the problem of repression in somewhat different ways. Alper's chief disagreement with Rosenzweig was over the role of individual differences—personality characteristic of the individual subject—in the selective recall experiment. Not by any means did every subject in Rosenzweig's experimental group repress; in fact, a bare majority favored completed over incompleted tasks if the number of subjects showing the "repression" pattern is compared to the number of subjects *not showing* it (16 subjects recalled more completed than incompleted tasks, while 14 subjects did not show this recall pattern.). Alper argued that the tendency to repress ego-hurtful experiences is a function of the way the individual interprets the task and recall situation. An especially vulnerable person might experience the task-oriented control group situation as personally threatening, feel as if *he* were being examined, and thus interpret interruption as failure. Rosenzweig's seven control subjects who remembered more completed than incompleted tasks might have been just such individuals, she suggested. Since individual personality characteristics will determine the pattern of selective recall, there should not be a mean difference in the recall of completed versus incompleted tasks in *either* the control or experimental groups. This is what Alper found with 10 subjects who performed the tasks (anagrams) in both conditions. In addition to the interrupted tasks, these 10 subjects were exhaustively studied by a variety of clinical procedures—interviews, projective tests, and some other assessment techniques—and Alper then looked for correlations between the assessments of individual personality and the recall of completed versus incompleted tasks in the test and task-oriented situations.

She found two major patterns of recall. The first pattern was one of remembering more incompleted tasks in the informal, non-test situation and more completed tasks in the "intelligence test" situation. The second pattern was just the reverse of this—recalling more completed tasks in the informal situation and more incompleted ones under stress. According to the clinical assessments, the first recall pattern was associated with ego *strength* and a high ability to cope with failure, while the second pattern was associated with ego *weakness* and vulnerability to failure. This seems an odd reversal and not at all what the repression hypothesis would predict. Alper (1952), in fact, denied that the concept of repression could be applied to her experiment, Rosenzweig's studies, or the experiment of Glixman that we shall consider in a moment.

> The Freudian terminology would be both inappropriate and misleading in the present context since: (1) the ego-threat induced in the experimental situation is not, and should not be, intense enough to constitute the basic conditions for Freudian "repression"; and (2) selective recall, as studied by the interrupted-task technique, involves both selective forgetting of the unpleasant and selective forgetting of the pleasant. To stress only the former, as the term "repression" does, is to neglect an important pattern of behavior [p. 86].

Thus, rather than invoking a process of repression to account for the selective recall of completed tasks following failure in her group of *strong ego* subjects—an interpretation which would make little sense—Alper proposed that it is one of the marks of a strong ego person to defend self-esteem when "objectively" threatened, and one way to do this is to focus attention (recollection) on successes rather than failures.

The Alper and Rosenzweig studies appear to be in sharp disagreement, although Alper attempted to reconcile them by arguing that it is individual personality characteristics, not experimental or control *situations*, that result in differences in selective recall. Neither her experiment nor Rosenzweig's— nor, indeed, Glixman's —revealed a reliable group difference in the recall of completed versus incompleted tasks in either the control or experimental situations. In presenting this argument, Alper was attempting to affirm or to prove the null hypothesis (the hypothesis of no difference between treatments, or here, recall of tasks), and as psychologists familiar with the logic of scientific inference know, proof of the null hypothesis would require seeing *every* instance. I believe that the experiments *are* in disagreement and that two of the reasons have to do with the tasks that Alper gave her subjects. They were anagrams, and there were a number of different solutions to each of them, a fact of which Alper's subjects were aware. As Glixman (1949) suggested, "Alper's 'completed activities' did not produce 'feelings of completion' [p. 292]." Although the *experimenter's* criterion of a completed task was one successful anagram solution, the *subject* may have experienced a feeling of incompletion from the awareness that other solutions were possible. Thus, in her experiment completed and incompleted tasks were not clearly differentiated. The other reason for the divergence of Alper's results stems from the same source—the nature of the tasks—and it was originally suggested by Osgood (1953). According to Lewin's (1935) theory, tension associated with an activity tends to spread to "neighboring" or associated activities; the more similar these are to the original activity, the greater will be the spread of tension. The intrinsic similarity of Alper's anagrams to one another would tend to result in the "spread" of feelings of completion, incompletion, and failure, and the tension associated with those feelings, from one task to another, and the effect of that would be to weaken the appearance of any recall difference betweeen completed and incompleted tasks.

Glixman (1949) was unhappy with the discrepancies in the Rosenzweig and Alper experiments, and he believed also (cf. 1948) that both of them gave an undue and exaggerated importance to "the individual as an individual." His experiment was an attempt to create neutral (informal) and stress situations and to study their effects on the recall of completed and unfinished tasks. This sounds remarkably like the purpose of the second of Rosenzweig's experiments, but there is a difference in emphasis. Glizman sought to compare the recall of completed and incompleted tasks *separately across* experimental conditions; Rosenzweig (and Alper) had calculated recall differences *within* the control and experimental situations. As he pointed out, such difference scores can be obtained by a decrease in the recall of unfinished tasks under stress (the repression effect), by an increase in the recall of completed tasks under stress (*not* repression, but instead, he suggested, a more superficial process of ego defense), or by change in both. Only by an independent comparison of completed task and uncompleted task recall over the neutral and stress conditions could one know which of these three possibilities held.

The experiment involved a variety of *different* tasks which were given in test booklets to large groups of subjects. There was a relatively neutral, nonstress condition and two stressful conditions, forcefully presented as examination situations, in which incompletion clearly signified failure. In these two stress conditions, the failure-threat was very high: The subjects' intellectual abilities were being evaluated, they were told, and the task booklets were titled "Intellectual Alertness Inventory." There was a recall period in each experimental condition in which subjects were asked to remember the tasks they had worked on.

Glixman's analyses involved the comparison of the number of completed tasks recalled in each situation and of the number of incompleted tasks recalled, and these comparisons were separate and independent. There was no difference in the recall of completed tasks between either stress condition and the neutral condition—a finding Glixman had expected. With unfinished tasks, however, the neutral and stress conditions differed significantly; fewer interrupted tasks were recalled in the stress situations. These results provided straightforward support of the repression hypothesis, although Glixman advocated caution in making that interpretation of his findings: "It is probably more fruitful, at this point, to maintain the distinction between the forgetting produced in this experiment and 'repression' as defined by clinicians. Whether the same set of dynamics is involved in the two processes is an empirical question [1949, p. 294]."

The next step was to reanalyze the results of Rosenzweig's second experiment and those of Alper and to compare their findings with his own. To do this, Glixman examined the recall of completed and incompleted tasks separately, as had been done in his own experiment. By this reanalysis, the results of the three experiments looked like this:

TABLE 5.2
Glixman's Reanalysis of the Results of Rosenzweig's, Alper's,
and Glixman's Experiments[a]

| Experiment | Recall of Completed Tasks | Probability | Recall of Incompleted Tasks | Probability |
|---|---|---|---|---|
| Rosenzweig | Greater under stress | .06 (marginal significance) | Less under stress | .82 (non-significant) |
| Alper | *Less* under stress | .01 (*significant*) | Less under stress | .07 (marginal significance) |
| Glixman | Less under stress (virtually no difference) | Nonsignificant | Less under stress | .025 (*significant*) |

[a](Adapted from Glixman, 1949.)

Glixman's data were the most clearly consistent with the concept of an ego-defensive process in memory by which self-esteem is protected. It was, I believe, the strongest and most convincing experiment of the four we have considered. But there *were* four experiments, and their results were discordant. In a sharp critique of these studies, Sears (1950) pointed out discrepancies and observed that the interrupted tasks procedure was "cumbersome" and also introduced the extraneous influence of its own effect on recall—the Zeigarnik effect.

*An Exceptionally Ambitious Experiment.* There is one more interrupted tasks experiment that we need to consider—one that is distinguished by three important features. Caron and Wallach (1957) sought to examine more closely and critically the specific processes involved in selective recall under stress. They were also concerned with the role of individual differences as well as the effects of stress and failure, and last, they undertook to meet the fourth condition for demonstrating repression—providing a situation in which to observe the return of the repressed. The position that Caron and Wallach took was that ego defenses like repression are determined *both* by stressful situations *and* by the personality dispositions of individual subjects. Thus, they sought to identify subjects in the stress and neutral experimental conditions whose personality characteristics would tend to make them primarily success-recallers or failure-recallers when threatened by failure.

The subjects were selected in an unusual way. Since the personality characteristics and the measures of them associated with the tendency to repress are not well established, Caron and Wallach chose to administer a large battery of tests to all of their subjects (Harvard University freshmen) and to obtain certain biographical information from them. Thus, both personality and biographical data were obtained on all of the subjects who were given the interrupted tasks under the stress or neutral conditions. By the procedure of factor analysis, they looked for those variables with the highest relationships to success or failure recall under stress. One variable clearly stood out from the rest: whether the subject had gone to a private preparatory school or to a public high school. The preparatory school boys tended to be success-recallers under stress, in contrast to the greater failure recall of the public high school students. Other evidence suggested that the distinction between private and public high school attendance was a meaningful and appropriate one for the assessment of selective recall under stress: a higher need for achievement and greater personal security among the public high school students (McArthur, 1954, 1955), higher grades among the students with public school backgrounds despite the absence of a difference in intelligence, and personality test evidence of insecurity in the private school students. Thus, subjects were divided *post hoc* into two groups in each experimental condition on the basis of private or public high school attendance, and at this point the patterns of recall were established. The private-school boys tended to recall more successes under stress and more failures in the neutral condition; the recall pattern of the public-school students was just the reverse.

The stress situation was severe and exceptionally plausible. It was again an intelligence test, purportedly developed by the same "Stanford people" who developed the well-known Stanford–Binet intelligence test. Here are some of the other techniques that Caron and Wallach (1957) used to make the stress subjects feel that they had done very badly by failing to complete a number of tasks:

> The following means were used to make S feel that he had done badly on the test: First, E stated that most Harvard students should perform very well on this test, since they were undoubtedly at the high end of the distribution of adult intelligence. Second, Ss were tested in groups of six, and each such group included two accomplices who pretended to solve all the tasks rapidly and exuded an air of confidence throughout the session. Finally, the four naive [true] Ss received alternate forms of the test such that when any two of them failed to complete a task the other two Ss completed that same task, the result being that for any single task, four of the six testees achieved solution while two did not [p. 375].

There were actually two stress conditions, exactly alike except for their endings. In one of them, the stress continued right up to the recall period; in the other—the "Relief" condition—the experimenter revealed the hoax. "Everybody sit back and relax," he said. "From the looks on your faces I gather that this was a pretty rough test—but perhaps you didn't do as badly as you think. You'll hate me when I tell you this, but believe me, it was all in the interest of science...[p. 375]." This announcement was met with astonishment, chagrin, and great relief, and the experimenter endeavored to give the subjects an opportunity to talk about their feelings and what their failure experiences had been like—in effect, a quasitherapeutic session. The recall period then began.

If the poorer recall of failures is due to repression, the relief of anxiety and the recovery of self-esteem should make it possible to remember the painful unfinished tasks. But consider an alternative possibility: that the lesser recall of failures might be due not to repression at all but to selective learning. That is, suppose the stressed and anxious subjects simply didn't register and learn the failed tasks as well as the tasks they succeeded on. Stress and anxiety do have such effects on learning. If deficient learning were responsible for the lowered recall of failed tasks, no amount of therapeutic relief could restore recall. We considered this issue earlier, under point 2 of the conditions for the demonstration of repression.

We have already noted that Caron and Wallach found a significant drop in the recall of failures by the private-school boys in the stress condition. Did the private-school boys' recall of failures increase following relief? If so, the experiment would provide impressive evidence for repression; if not, the demonstration of repression by this experimental procedure would be left very much in doubt. The answer is that there was no suggestion of a repression effect in improved post-relief recall, even for the group that should have shown it—the private school boys.

There was one bit of evidence, however, for a repression-like effect in the reactions of the private-school subjects to the stressful test situation as a whole. One way that repression may operate to block out threatening experiences is through loss of memory for the situation as a whole. Thus, in the aftermath of the stress situation, repression would already have begun to take its toll of memory of the fact that one had done surpassingly badly on an intelligence test. It would clearly be difficult to devise a test of recall of having taken an intelligence test immediately beforehand: While repression may be effective as a defense against threat to self-esteem, it is not *that* effective. There is another avenue, however—to measure perceptual recognition of stimuli associated with the painful, repressed experience. One effect of repression should be to make it difficult to recognize stimuli which would provide cues to the threatening memory. Freud (1915) was well aware of this possibility and believed that there was no real distinction to be made between this sort of process and the afterexpulsion of repression. "The difference is not important; it amounts to much the same thing as the difference between my ordering an undesirable guest out of my drawing-room (or out of my front hall), and my refusing, after recognizing him, to let him cross my threshold at all [p. 153]."

One could measure perceptual recognition thresholds by the use of a tachistoscope for words that would revive the memory of failure (examination, reasoning, sentence, scrambled, phrases...) and for a set of control words (sunshine, cookies, agriculture, leisurely...), and this is what Caron and Wallach did. The critical comparisons are the differences in perceptual recognition thresholds for threat-related and neutral words between the stress, relief, and neutral conditions, and of course, we need to look particularly at the private-school boys. There was a very large recognition threshold difference between the threat and neutral words (the threat words had higher thresholds) in the unrelieved stress condition; the relief and neutral conditions did not differ. The public-school subjects' data did not show this pattern, and for them there were no reliable differences between the three conditions.

So there was evidence for repression, though not from the interrupted tasks procedure itself. About that procedure, Caron and Wallach concluded:

The present results impute this approach, for they suggest that repression embraces only the most general aspects of the stress situation, whereas recall of particular threatening or "nonthreatening" aspects of that situation is a function of learning. This finding seems entirely reasonable, for when a person has failed half the items on a test, what is likely to be threatening for him is not that he has failed those particular items but that he has failed the *test*. Nor can the items he passed be entirely free from threat if the total situation in which they are embedded arouses anxiety [p. 379].

The point is that the interrupted tasks technique suffers irretrievably from the problem of an intrinsic similarity of tasks, no matter how ostensibly different they might seem: All the tasks are part of a test and will share in the fate of memory of the whole experience.

Concerning the evidence for repression, we need to inquire about how convincing it was, and there are two issues to consider: (1) Was the stress situation truly stressful; and (2) did the relief condition approximate the kind of therapeutic situation in which the relief of anxiety would allow the return of the repressed? On the first issue, Caron and Wallach pointed out that:

Needless to say, the present data would have no bearing on a theory of repression if the stress situation had not induced intense ego threat. That such threat did indeed occur may be inferred from several lines of evidence— observational, introspective, and experimental. In the first place, *S*s in the stress condition showed many overt signs of emotional disturbance (little or none of which appeared among the neutral *S*s). When stumped by a problem, they would squirm nervously or shake their heads in disgust (sometimes swearing simultaneously) or would stare at the page with a very pained expression. Further, there were many attempts to conceal one's difficulty from others, either by pretending to have finished problems not actually completed, or, when able to solve a problem, by trying to make one's success very obvious to competitors (e.g., putting one's pencil down with a bang or yawning loudly while stretching). Again, depressive and hostile reactions were quite prevalent following the exam, many *S*s sitting morosely in their chairs, others openly challenging the worth of the test. Lastly, expressions of great relief—deep sighs, postural relaxation, laughter—almost always appeared when the ruse was finally explained. As to introspective evidence: First, most *S*s voluntarily reported that they had been extremely concerned prior to, and tremendously relieved following, exposure of the hoax. They attributed emotions to themselves ranging all the way from intense feelings of inadequacy ("I said to myself, 'See, you really don't belong at Harvard'") to violent hostility ("I wanted to get that supercilious bastard sitting beside me.") Secondly, continued questioning revealed that although some thought the test a poor one, no one had doubted its reality. With regard to experimental data, finally, consider the results for our indicator of anxiety: digit recall. Whereas recall of digits showed a marked pretest to posttest improvement for *S*s in the neutral condition [an effect of practice on performance on this test, the immediate recall of a series of spoken numbers], *S*s under stress showed no such improvement.... The most plausible explanation for the latter *S*s' deficiency would seem to be the disrupting effects of anxiety generated during the scrambled sentence test. These data, in sum, would seem to support the assumption that intense ego threat was aroused in the present study [p. 378].

As to the second issue, Caron and Wallach observed that the typical therapeutic strategy in real cases of neurotic repression is to change the patient's motivation (i.e., feelings and attitudes) toward the threatening experiences—to reduce his fear of them. An alternative approach was followed in the experiment: Revealing the deception had the effect of changing the motivational significance of the threat so that it no longer had any personal meaning. Caron and Wallach noted that "$E$'s revelation does not make $S$ any less of a repressor or eliminate his problem with respect to intellectual competence (nor was it intended to), but merely renders this particular event irrelevant to that problem and hence no longer something to be defended against [p. 379]."

### An Evaluation of the Interrupted Tasks Technique

We have, then, five experiments with results that do not form a consistent picture, and the one I believe to be the most exemplary of all—Caron and Wallach's—yielded persuasive evidence that the differential recall of successes and failures under stress is due to selective learning and not to repression. Their evidence of repression, as we have seen, was quite differently arrived at and involved memory of the whole failure experience. Sears, it seems, was right: The method of interrupted tasks *is* cumbersome, and it complicates the investigation of repression by introducing not one but two confounding factors. As we noted, there is the factor of the Zeigarnik effect itself, which would work against amnesia for failures, and there is the equally critical problem that Caron and Wallach's experiment revealed of the inevitable similarity of all the tasks, completed and interrupted, arising from the fact that they are all part of a test-and-failure context.

So the interrupted tasks procedure leaves the repression hypothesis largely unanswered. It was an extraordinary idea for its time, and it was responsible for some inventive and provocative experiments. That the experiments failed to answer the theoretical question is an old and oft-repeated story in the history of science; they did, however, excite great interest in the repression hypothesis and in the possibility of its experimental demonstration. They did, perhaps, help to keep the hypothesis as an *experimental* and not purely clinical question alive and thus helped to keep the way open for the other experimental approaches that we shall next consider.

## LEARNING AND MOTIVATED FORGETTING

The group of experiments that we take up now are a somewhat mixed lot. They belong together because in each of them an ego threat or the anticipation of a painful electric shock is associated with some material learned in close conjunction with the anxious event. There is a control group that is not threatened. Experimental and control subjects are tested for retention, and in the most thorough experiments there is relief of anxiety and a retention test for the return of the repressed. We shall consider three experiments of this type: Sears's (1937), Zeller's (1950), and a more recent and exceptionally clever one by Glucksberg and King (1967).

Sears trained his subjects on three lists of 10 nonsense syllables (e.g., GAX, ZEF) to a criterion of two perfect repetitions. The subjects returned on the following day and learned a new list of nonsense syllables. Then, under highly competitive and involving circumstances, half of them were made to feel that they had failed on a card-sorting task while the remaining half were given to believe they had succeeded. Sears's report of his observations of the failed subjects is convincing; they fully seemed to be distraught over their apparent inability to perform successfully. Following the card-sorting task, a new list of nonsense syllables was learned. The practice afforded by learning the first two lists should result in a decrease in the number of trials required to learn the third, and this was found in the card-sorting success group. The failed subjects, however, showed little if any practice effect: It required nearly as many trials for them to learn the post-failure list as it had for them to learn the pre-failure ones, and the difference between the success and failure groups was appreciable and reliable.

But what does this finding have to do with repression? Sears proposed that repression may be thought of in behavior theory terms as an anticipatory response to failure or other painful consequences; it results in the cessation of thinking and other actions which would bring the person closer to the threatening event. Since repression is anticipatory, Sears reasoned, there should be a "spill over" from the experience of failure at card sorting to the learning of the post-failure nonsense syllable list. That is, repression is an interfering or blocking response, and the inhibiting effects of interference would retard the processes of learning and memory.

This was an interesting approach to the problem of repression, and Sears worked it out in much more elaborate form than I have presented it here (cf. 1936). Unfortunately, it is inadequate as a theoretical account of the experiment. There is no compelling reason why an interfering or blocking response with specific effects on memory should have generalized to the learning of the post-failure list. This nonsense-syllable list was no more connected to the failure experience than the earlier ones had been, and I think the repression hypothesis would require a specific association. To the contrary, there was a strong possibility that selective learning was responsible for the poorer learning of the failure group. These subjects were anxious and upset, their thoughts revolving around their awful card-sorting performance. This was interference, all right—the sort of anxious interference that would surely have some pretty detrimental effects on learning. But these are effects on *learning*, not on memory, and the repression hypothesis demands evidence expressly concerning the impairment of memory.

Zeller carried out two elaborate experiments, the general design of which followed Sears' in looking for the generalization of a failure experience to the relearning of a list of nonsense syllables. His subjects first learned a list of nonsense syllables and returned three days later to relearn the same list. At this point, the experimental group subjects were severely failed, while the controls were given the same task under neutral conditions. The failure task involved reproducing sequences of taps on a series of blocks: The experimenter would tap the blocks in some order—say, 3-1-4-1-2-4-1-3-4— and the subject had to reproduce the pattern. Since the experimenter sat opposite the subject, it was quite easy to create and to take advantage of left-right confusions. Not only was the subject made to do badly, but the experimenter even went so far as to stop the test to ask that the subject get hold of himself and expressed his concern over the subject's bad memory and his dim prospects of success in college.

The nonsense-syllable list was then relearned, and the subject was dismissed. He returned again three days later and relearned the list. The block-tapping test was brought out at this point for both the experimental and control subjects. For the controls the procedure was repeated with the same neutrality as before; the experimental subjects were allowed to succeed in a presumably therapeutic and reassuring way. There were two more tests on the nonsense-syllable list, one immediately after block tapping and the final one three days later.

The results are shown in Fig. 5.1, and as you can see, relearning of the control and experimental subjects differed only on the two tests following failure on block tapping and before the therapeutic relief. These differences were clearly reliable. Following the block-tapping "therapy," the experimentals recalled the nonsense syllables as readily as the controls—a finding, Zeller argued, demonstrating the memorial effects of the return of the repressed.

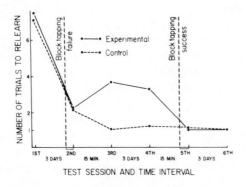

FIG. 5.1.   The number of trials to relearn the nonsense-syllable list at each test session. Block tapping failure and success were given only to experimental subjects. (Adapted from Zeller, 1950.)

Is it possible that what appears to be a strong repression effect was due, rather, to the interference of anxiety and rumination about failure? Such an alternative hypothesis could well account for the poorer post-failure relearning of the experimental group, just as we saw in Sears's experiment, and the therapeutic success at block tapping would have resulted in improved performance simply by making the subjects less anxious. Zeller considered this possibility and repeated the experiment with the addition of two new groups. Only one of these need concern us here; it was a group in which the failure experience was explicitly restricted to block tapping. In Zeller's experimental procedure, the occurrence of repression (if it could be shown to occur) depends on the generalization of feelings of failure from the block-tapping test to the nonsense syllables, and this new group was intended to determine the effect of blocking that generalization. So, while these subjects failed dreadfully on the tapping test they were told that their nonsense-syllable performance was fine.

Other than the inclusion of the two additional groups, the procedures were identical to the first experiment. The relearning of the nonsense-syllable list by the new group (failure on block tapping only) closely paralleled the performance of the control group subjects, appearing to indicate the importance of failure generalization. It is significant, however, that Zeller observed these subjects to be little if at all upset by their block-tapping deficiency, because it carried no implication of poor memory. Thus, if they were not anxious, there should have been no relearning impairment and, of course, no improvement after block-tapping success. I think the only thing we can conclude from this group is that its subjects were not threatened by failure and accordingly should have performed just as they did—that is, like the controls.

Zeller's experiment had the same flaw as Sears's: There was no reason for the *memory* of the nonsense syllables to have been affected by the previous block-tapping failure since there was no specific link between the two tests. One could be terribly worried about having a poor memory, but that would not constitute a sufficient reason for repressing the memory of the syllables. The more direct and parsimonious explanation is that the impaired relearning came about as the result of the interference of anxiety.

## An Associative Mediation Experiment

The last experiment in this group involved, like the others, a test of the repression hypothesis based on the learning and retention of verbal material. There, however, the similarity ends. Glucksberg and King (1967) used electric shock rather than ego threat, but more important, the design of the experiment has some built-in associative subtleties, and it does not depend on the vaguely defined generalization from an anxiety-inducing task to the retention test.

The experiment depends on the phenomenon of associative mediation or chaining. Think of a word—any one will do—and think of an association—another word—to the first one. Now, an association to the second word. In between writing this, mine were bacon...egg...chicken...feathers... pillow...sleep. There is probably some associative linkage between feathers and bacon; not a direct link but one mediated by the two intervening words, egg and chicken. It is known that learning can be considerably facilitated by mediational processes. An example: Russell and Storms (1955) gave subjects a paired-associates list to learn in which the stimulus member of the pair was a nonsense syllable and the response term was an English word. This is the $A-B$ list. Thus, one pair might be CEF–stem. The word stem strongly tends to elicit the association flower, and in the Russell and Storms experiment (and Glucksberg and King's) flower was an inferred mediator. A final list, $D$, was made up of associates to the inferred mediators, and subjects were trained on a list of paired associates made up of $A-D$ pairs—for example, CEF–smell. Without any explicit mention or training on the inferred mediators, the prior learning of the $A-B$ list facilitated the learning of the $A-D$ list.

What Glucksberg and King did, in effect, was to turn the whole process around, associating certain of the $D$ words with the anticipation of a painful and fearful electric shock. By the mediation of the inferred chaining words, that should make the $B$ words unpleasant to remember—given, of course, that the repression hypothesis is correct and that fear in sufficient intensity has been aroused. The lists of words used in the experiment are shown in Table 5.3. The subjects were trained on List 1, the $A-B$ pairs, the task being to learn to associate the response ($B$) words with the $A$-list nonsense syllables. Then, shock electrodes were fastened in place, and the $D$ list was shown to the subjects, one word at a time. Three $D$ words were repeatedly followed by shock. The last phase of the experiment was a single relearning (retention) trial on the $A-B$ list.

The test of repression is the comparison of forgetting of the $B$ words indirectly associated with shock with forgetting of the control words whose associates were never shocked. Note in Table 5.3 that for half the subjects, the $D$ words smell, war, and tree were shocked, and for the other half shock followed brain, good, and take. The smell–war–tree subjects were unable to remember 20.8% of the shock-associated $A-B$ pairs, but forgot only 3.6% of the control pairs. The corresponding figures for the brain–good–take subjects were 37.5% and 8.9%. These differences were significant at a probability less than .01.

Glucksberg and King repeated the experiment with the addition of a group that received money instead of shock for the three $D$ words. The purpose of this curious procedure was to test an alternative hypothesis—that learning the list of $D$ words before the retention test on the $A-B$ list might have produced interference (retroactive interference), greater for the words singled out and

TABLE 5.3
Stimulus Words Used and Inferred Associative Responses[a,b]

| List 1 | | Inferred Chained Word<br>············· | List 2 | |
|---|---|---|---|---|
| A | B | C | D | |
| CEF | stem | flower | smell | (1) |
| DAX | memory | mind | brain | (2) |
| YOV | soldier | army | navy | |
| VUX | trouble | bad | good | (2) |
| WUB | wish | want | need | |
| GEX | justice | peace | war | (1) |
| JID | thief | steal | take | (2) |
| ZIL | ocean | water | drink | |
| LAJ | command | order | disorder | |
| MYV | fruit | apple | tree | (1) |

[a](From Glucksberg & King, 1967.)
[b]The D words followed by (1) were the experimental words for half the subjects; those followed by (2) were the experimental words for the remaining subjects.

made more salient by their association with shock. If this sort of interference was responsible for the greater forgetting of the shock-associated pairs, then singling out certain D words by paying subjects money following their presentation should have the same effect. It didn't, although the shock-associated B words were again less well remembered.

## An Evaluation of the Learning–Repression Experiments

The Sears and Zeller experiments, for the reasons we have discussed, do not contribute to our understanding of repression. Glucksberg and King's experiment, however, is a different story: I cannot find a satisfactory alternative interpretation of the findings, and I think the data speak to the repression hypothesis. Among its niceties, the experimental design provides, in making use of associative mediation, an analogue of the complex associative processes involved in repression proper that Freud described and that we briefly considered earlier (pp. 122–123). The successful use of electric shock as the source of fear suggests that repression may not depend on the terrible kinds of ego threat we encounter clinically; instead, repressive amnesias can, under the right circumstances, be created by quite specific sources of fear. One bit of evidence *is* missing. How compelling it would have been had Glucksberg and King arranged for the return of the repressed— perhaps simply by removing the shock electrodes prior to the A–B retention test for one group of subjects. The removal of the source of fear should restore the memory of the critical *B* words. This is an important experiment, and it should be repeated by someone who will fill in this one crucial piece of data.[2]

## INSTIGATION TO AGGRESSION, EMOTIONAL AROUSAL, AND DEFENSIVE EMULATION

Our final experiment stands by itself, quite apart from the other groups of repression experiments. It is based on a more intricate theoretical rationale than the experiments we have been considering, and its original purpose was to test the hypothesis that persons who are dependent on the approval of others tend to repress their angry feelings. We shall take it up here, rather than in Chapter 6 which considers the approval motive, because of its bearing on the theory of repression and the design of repression experiments. The investigators were Conn and myself (1964).

### A Theory of Emotion and the Process of Repression

Let's develop the theoretical analysis of repressive defense first and, following that, the individual difference hypothesis. Pursuing a line of reasoning proposed and subjected to experimental study by Schachter and his associates (Schachter & Singer, 1962; Schachter & Wheeler, 1962), we made the assumption that anger (or any other disturbing feeling that may be subject to repression) is an emotional state that, like all emotional states, has two components: a set of verbally and symbolically mediated cues and a state of physiological arousal. Thus, for an individual to be able to define his emotional state as one of anger (or fear, depression, etc.), both a set of cognitions signifying and appropriate to a state of anger and the physiological cues contingent upon arousal must be present. As Schachter and Singer (1962) argued:

---

[2]I have a final comment to add about this experiment. It is one made in a letter from Professor Glucksberg to Professor David Rosenhan, dated January 23, 1978. I am indebted to both of them for permission to quote from it. Glucksberg wrote:

> So far as I know there have not been any follow-ups of any kind. The most likely reason is that the effect is rather a fragile one, depending critically on just the right amount of original learning... or so I believe. If the material is overlearned, then people won't forget any of it. If the material is not learned well enough, then there is too much noise in the data to detect effects of shock. We were lucky to hit just the right parameters, and the shock (coupled with a raucous loud buzzer) seemed to have tipped the forgetting just right.
>   This is not to say that I don't believe the effect, nor the analogy to repression. I do, but I've become convinced from other people's experience with the paradigm that while it is replicable, it is not robust enough to withstand any tinkering or fooling around with the conditions.

an emotional state may be considered a function of a state of physiological arousal and of a cognition appropriate to this state of arousal. The cognition, in a sense, exerts a steering function. Cognitions arising from the immediate situation as interpreted by past experience provide the framework within which one understands and labels his feelings. It is the cognition which determines whether the state of physiological arousal will be labeled as "anger," "joy," "fear," or whatever [p. 380].

The cognition by itself is not emotional. Say to yourself, "I am angry." It's not the same as anger, is it? By the same token, physiological arousal is not emotional either, as you may have experienced if you have ever had an injection of adrenalin (which arouses the autonomic nervous system) for an allergic reaction. While this sort of autonomic activation produces some noticeable physical effects, emotion is not felt or is felt in a very "cold," "as if" sort of way, as Marañon (1924) and Landis and Hunt (1932) discovered long ago by injecting subjects with adrenalin and inquiring about their feelings.

The Schachter studies attempted to assess the interaction of the cognitive and physiological arousal elements in emotional states by the artificial induction of arousal—achieved by injections of adrenalin—and manipulation of the cognitions available to their subjects to identify their emotional states. The evidence from these experiments indicates that where appropriate cognitions are lacking, subjects tend to identify their emotional states in terms of the alternative explanations suggested to them and to demonstrate behavior consistent with the alternative cognitions. Implicit in this view of emotion is the important implication that the visceral responses underlying different emotions are highly similar. Although some subtle distinctions between anger and fear are reported in the literature (Ax, 1953; J. Schachter, 1957; Wolf & Wolff, 1947), there is great overlap in the physiological manifestations of affective states. But for our present purpose the issue is not whether the discriminable patterning of physiological arousal in emotional states can be experimentally demonstrated, but whether individuals can interpret their own bodily cues as a means by which to define and label an emotional state.

Conn and I extended this line of argument to the domain of ego defenses, proposing that the effect of defenses is to block the cognitions defining a threatening emotional state. If, as Freud (1915) said, "*the essence of repression lies simply in turning something away, and keeping it at a distance, from the conscious* [p. 147]," it would not be inconsistent with the theory of repression to argue that this "something" is the cognitive labeling of anxious and disturbing emotional states. We further proposed that while defense against hostility (or any other emotional state or experience that has anxious and painful affect associated with it) affects verbal and symbolic cues, physiological arousal takes place nonetheless. Thus, in a situation in which aggression is instigated, an initial recognition of cues leading to anger occurs but is subsequently defended against by repression (or by other defenses). Recall the point made earlier in this chapter that repression has a time course; in all probablility it is not an automatic and instantaneous process. Thus, it is argued that defenses solve only part of the problem; namely, the individual's labeling and awareness of his anxiety-arousing motivational state. Dollard and Miller (1950) developed a similar analysis in proposing that repression occurs when the verbal responses labeling a drive are inhibited. It follows, then, that given the imposition of a defense—repression—that blocks labeling and thinking but fails to affect the bodily cues associated with arousal, the repressive individual will lack an explanation for a physiological state—why one feels "all stirred up." There remains, in Schachter and Singer's (1962) helpful phrase, "a bodily state 'in search of' an appropriate cognition [p. 126]."

There is one more assumption necessary to make—one also made in the Schachter studies: There is a need to explain one's feelings to oneself, and depending on the individual and the particular situational context, some attempt will be made to resolve the uncertainty created by the experience of arousal in the absence of a satisfactory explanation for that state (i.e., "I am aroused by anger"). A formal antecedent for this assumption is Festinger's (1954) concept of a drive for self-evaluation by which to explain the tendency to seek to resolve uncertainties and incongruities in one's experience by social comparison—looking to the experiences of others in a similar situation to discover how one should feel and act oneself. Have you ever covertly watched others in a dentist's office to see how they were coping with the same dreadful anticipation you were going through? That's social comparison.

## Instigation to Anger and an Alternative Cognition

The experimental design basically involved two stages. First, there was a hostility-arousing situation in which subjects were provoked to anger by an experimental accomplice who unconscionably violated an agreement just made. The second stage represented an attempt to supply the repressive subject with the opportunity to define his (hypothesized) inexpressible state of anger in terms of an alternative set of cognitions—a different emotional state. The alternative explanation selected was the emotional state of euphoria or hilarity—an emotion strikingly different and sharply at variance with the immediately preceding instigation to anger. The procedure for doing this, which was adapted from Schachter and Singer, had the same accomplice who aroused the subject to anger behave in a highly euphoric, slapstick manner, while the subject was rated by observers behind a one-way vision glass for his degree of responsiveness to the stooge's high humor and antics.

Since the "base rate" of euphoria was not known, and since the potentially repressing subject's euphoric responsiveness to the experimental accomplice might be explained on other grounds—his greater susceptibility to social influence, for example—a control group was also required. These control subjects were paired with the accomplice prior to the euphoria situation in the performance of a neutral, non-anger-arousing task.

The independent variable was a personality scale of need for approval, given to subjects some weeks previous to the experiment itself. Based on their scores, the subjects were divided into high need and low need groups. Our hypothesis was that for the approval-dependent individual, anger arousal and the harboring of hostility entails the perceived threat of alienation from others, social rejection, unfavorable evaluations, and the resulting peril of damage to self-esteem.

The major data are the ratings of euphoria of high and low need-for-approval subjects in the experimental (anger aroused) and control groups. The mean euphoria ratings of the two groups in the two experimental conditions are shown in Fig. 5.2, and you can see that the approval-dependent and low need-for-approval subjects were quite sharply divergent in the amount of euphoric behavior following instigation to anger. The two need-approval groups did not, however, respond differently in the control condition. Approval-dependent subjects instigated to anger were more euphoric than approval-dependent controls, and among low need-for-approval subjects the opposite trend was observed—less euphoria in the angered experimentals. Each subject completed some postexperimental ratings of the "other subject"—the experimenter's accomplice—which were intended to reveal how the subject would evaluate the accomplice, especially in the experimental condition. These data were consistent with the euphoria results: Approval-dependent experimentals judged the accomplice favorably, despite the fact of his dirty trick, while negative and derogatory ratings were made by the low need-approval group.

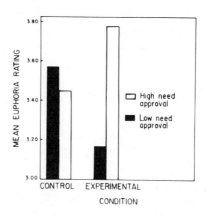

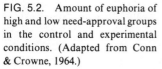

FIG. 5.2. Amount of euphoria of high and low need-approval groups in the control and experimental conditions. (Adapted from Conn & Crowne, 1964.)

An Evaluation

This experiment was predicated on a lengthy chain of assumptions about the nature of emotional states and repression—a chain, however, with empirical support from the findings of the Schachter studies. The extension of Schachter's analysis of the roles of cognitive and physiological elements in emotional states to the problem of ego defenses received some suggestive support. Given the following facts—the equivalent amount of euphoric behavior of high and low need-for-approval subjects in the control condition, the objectively equal provocation to anger of the two groups in the experimental condition, the different susceptibility to euphoria of highs and lows following hostility arousal, and the very low incidence of criticism and hostility in the postexperimental ratings of the approval-dependent experimentals—it is not easy to invoke a plausible alternative interpretation.

There is a question to raise: Were the approval-dependent experimentals really as angered as the lows? If not, the difference in euphoria between the highs and lows following instigation to anger might be more parsimoniously interpreted as due to the lower anger arousal of the high group. Note, however, that this interpretation would not handle the greater euphoria shown by the approval-dependent experimentals relative to their controls. But *were* the experimental highs and lows equally provoked, equally aroused? The data of another experiment by Fishman (1965) suggest that they were. She abused subjects in a very frustrating way, recording changes in blood pressure as one major dependent variable. Although the behavioral response of the high and low need-for-approval groups differed predictably (the highs didn't retaliate), the blood pressure changes of the two groups were equivalent. Both groups showed increases in systolic blood pressure following frustration and instigation to aggression.

The clinching demonstration of repression would have been to arrange for the return of the repressed: an angered group of approval-dependent subjects exposed to the euphoric stooge after a brief "therapy" for the repression of anger. But, since the approval-motivated individual has a presumably *habitual* problem with the awareness and expression of anger, that "therapy" would have had to be a *real* therapy going far beyond what we could hope to accomplish in the short span of a single experiment. So, there is plausible evidence for repression here, but not critical evidence.

## SOME PERSPECTIVES ON THE REPRESSION HYPOTHESIS

At the time I am writing this, Freud's concept of repression is more than 80 years old, his major statement of it 60 years old. Despite the great wealth of clinical data amassed in that long span of years and the experimental studies we have reviewed (plus others we didn't consider), there is still, I believe, a strong measure of uncertainty about the phenomenon of repression. I say that with some hesitancy, because of the extraordinary influence of Freud's hypothesis on other personality theorists, on clinical practice, on personality research, and on popular culture. But, as I believe the experimental evidence is yet incomplete and the conclusion about the hypothesis uncertain, I also feel that the clinical evidence is open to alternative interpretive possibilities. Let's consider two of them, although there are others.

1. If it cannot be shown that an experience or feeling was clearly registered, perceived, learned, then we cannot attribute its later failure to appear as the result of the memorial process of repression. Recall the second condition for the observation of repression (pp.127–128). There is some experimental evidence for selective learning rather than repression in Caron and Wallach's study, and many of the clinical observations of repression could be interpreted as reflecting the deficient registration of the original experience. Indeed, the partial, incomplete registration or perception of experiences and inadequate learning are especially likely to be the case in the kinds of emotional situations in which repression is supposed to occur.

2. The second possibility is suggested by a familiar observation: the difficulty we have all experienced in remembering the name of a person who is familiar in another context. Try as you will, the name simply doesn't come. Note that I made reference to *context*—to encountering the person in different circumstances than those you usually associate with him. Of course, if the person is highly familiar—your mother, say, or a close friend—it's doubtful that you'll have this problem. But with someone you know well enough so that in context you would have no trouble recognizing him and recalling his name, when the context of cues for retrieval is changed, you cannot supply the name. This is not a repression process but a problem of inadequate cues to enable recovery from memory.

Pribram (1971) makes this same point in connection with the ways the brain processes, stores, and retrieves: "A great deal more and much richer detail can be recalled and re-imaged when we are given the appropriate context—for instance, when visiting a neighborhood we had lived in many years earlier, shops and doorways and livingroom furniture placements come to mind which only a few hours earlier seemed forever lost [p. 162]." In the clinical treatment of a patient, the cues for retrieval of experiences differ considerably from the stimulus context at the time the experiences (ideas, feelings, etc.) were originally encountered. The therapist thinks the difficulty is a repressive one, when it may be that the retrieval situation is so different that the patient simply cannot get an associative handle to extract the memory from storage.

Neither of these alternatives is likely to be the whole story, and neither fully deals with the clinical data or the experimental evidence. Nevertheless, they cannot be dismissed, and the evidence for the repression hypothesis does not yet withstand sharp scrutiny.

There is presently a lull in research on repression. Research questions in psychology—as, I am sure, in other sciences—follow the trend of current interests and fashions. It would be too bad if what we have learned were to be consigned to some musty archive and if a great open question were abandoned without further asking. Important questions in psychology (and in science generally) have a way of reasserting themselves, however, and I think repression will be back. In fact, there is a current revival of interest in unconscious processes. The important analysis of inaccessible cognitive processes by Nisbett and Wilson (1977), that we reviewed in Chapter 2 in connection with the problems of self-description on personality tests, reflects a significant trend. Cognitive and perception psychologists (e.g., Erdelyi, 1974; Mandler, 1975; Neisser, 1967) have been emphasizing that much of our mental life as it is expressed in emotional judgments, feature analysis, language structures, and choice behavior is unconscious. We do have to distinguish between the unconscious determination of behavior and repression. Though repression is an instance of inaccessibility to awareness, it is a distinctly specific process. I think it is likely that the experimental study of repression will benefit from this recent emphasis. It is bound to capture interest and enthusiam for a concept with the most critical implications for our understanding of disturbed behavior, for psychological treatment, and indeed for the nature and dynamics of human memory.

# 6

# The Approval Motive

## ABSTRACT

*The assessment of personality by tests is troubled by the tendency of many respondents to characterize themselves in socially desirable terms. The social desirability response tendency is also a problem where personality constructs are defined by personality tests. One approach to this general problem is to treat social desirability as a source of error in tests and to take appropriate measures to eliminate it. The social desirability question also may be viewed from another perspective, as motivated and purposeful behavior. The program of research described in this chapter took the second approach. A measure of the social desirability response tendency was developed, and its relationship to other personality tests and to behavior in experimental situations was explored. Studies of compliance, conformity, and response to subtle social influence led to a miniature theory of the approval motive.*

*The concept was modified because it appeared that approval-seeking was part of a self-protective and defensive style. Studies of defensiveness confirmed this new hypothesis. They included investigation of response to psychotherapy, behavior in situations analogous to psychotherapy, defensiveness in projective tests, and the inhibition of aggression.*

*Achievement performance, intelligence, and certain cognitive processes are related to the approval motive. Studies of the development of the approval motive suggested that cold and restrictive childrearing practices lead to approval-seeking, defensiveness and inhibition, and less adequate achievement and intellectual performance.*

## INTRODUCTION

It seemed a very sour note for personality assessment when Edwards (1953, 1957) described the powerful influence of social desirability on test responses. We encountered the social desirability problem in Chapter 2, where we saw that the high correlation of a questionnaire measuring the tendency to give socially desirable responses with the Manifest Anxiety Scale made the interpretation of the MAS awkward and uncertain. Is the MAS a measure of anxiety, or does it largely reflect individual differences in social desirability? Correlations of the same magnitude were found between the social desirability scale devised by Edwards and many other personality question- naires, strongly suggesting to Edwards and other proponents that all of personality assessment was seriously infected with social desirability. The measurement of social desirability itself lent credence to the claim, since the items in the social desirability scale were selected by judges because of their clear desirability implications. The procedure thus had a high degree of plausibility about it—what is called *face validity* in the language of test construction. It was not difficult to believe that agreeing with the item, "I have diarrhea ('the runs') once a month or more" would be an undesirable thing to say about oneself, nor was it hard to accept that responses could be seriously affected by such a consideration.

There were unpleasant reverberations for a time, but out of them some important issues began to emerge. Edwards had clearly shown that personality test items differ in the degree of social desirability, and he had also forcefully established that people from divergent social classes and cultural backgrounds closely agree on the social desirability or undesirability of test items. Thus, widely shared social attitudes appeared to be the underpinning for social desirability. But was it *personality test items* that should concern us, or the behavior of *people* in test situations? Where was the proper focus to be placed—on sources of error in tests and on test construction procedures for minimizing error, or in the motives of people in being evaluated and judged? The answer to that question now seems clearer than it did at the time. If one is going to devise a personality test, procedures to eliminate such irrelevant influences on test responses as social desirability need to be followed right from the very beginning of test construction. At the same time, it is important to understand the kinds of motives that may be aroused when one is tested. In this chapter, we shall be concerned with one motive aroused by the process of being evaluated.

## THE TESTING SITUATION

Is describing oneself in socially desirable terms motivated behavior? More generally, is the behavior of taking personality tests motivated? Put that way, it almost seems a silly question deserving an impatient "of course." The answer, however, really hasn't always been so obvious, and it depends on recognizing that the testing situation is part of a large class of situations involving social evaluation. The testing situation calls forth potent motives, and they are in general the same kinds of motives that are aroused in other social situations where one is evaluated or evaluates oneself.

In the history of personality assessment, there is surprisingly little evidence that psychologists have been concerned with the testing situation as a meaningful social context that might itself influence an individual's behavior. In the effort to develop valid tests for both applied and theoretical purposes, the principal goal has been to predict an individual's behavior on some criterion measure, rather than to understand behavior in a given social setting (the test situation) and to attempt to relate this behavior and the motives determining it to behavior in other situations. The subject of testing has an important stake in self-disclosure. One does not leave one's goals in being evaluated, like a pair of rubbers, outside the tester's door; each person has a serious concern with the uses to which his or her responses will be put. That is not to suggest that the motives aroused in evaluative situations are necessarily rational and accessible to awareness. They may very well not be. Indeed, they may be part of a style of response to being judged by others and evaluating oneself that originate in childhood and are rarely, if ever, thought about. The approval motive that is the subject of this chapter apparently fits this mold. As the research on the approval motive will suggest, people dependent on the approval of others are naive, uncritical, and unreflective in their approval-seeking, and these are not the characteristics to be expected in someone whose goals are a matter of reflection and choice.

Before we take up the approval motive, we need first to consider briefly just how test responses may be motivationally determined. Test responses are influenced by two kinds of variables. These are the person's *needs*, especially those needs related to personal disclosure and to the evaluation of oneself, and *expectancies* about the consequences of responding in a particular way.

## Needs

The concept of need refers to an inferred disposition to seek certain kinds of reinforcements. There are primary or biological needs (e.g., the needs for food and water), and we also recognize in behavior the influence of many other needs that are learned in the course of personality development. Needs for affection, achievement, power, competence, nurturance and protection, and approval are examples of needs that are acquired by social learning. Among them are learned needs that may affect one's responses in evaluative situations. The basic point about the role of needs in the testing situation is simply that people's needs will dispose them to present themselves in ways that are consistent with those needs. If it is important for individuals to gain approval or acceptance, to deny inadequacies, or to obtain dependency satisfactions, we may expect that their test responses, no less than any other behavior, will be directed toward satisfying those needs. A full understanding of test responses requires that we know something about the motives behind them. The kinds of needs that could influence test responses would include at least the following: the need for recognition and status, the need for achievement, needs for approval and affection, and the need for dependence. Thus, if I (the subject) want warmly nurturant sympathy from you (the tester), the responses I give to your questions may very well reflect my need.

## Expectancies

The second principal determinant is the concept of expectancy. By expectancy we mean a subjective probability held by a person that a given behavior will result in some particular reinforcing outcome, either positive or negative. The subjective nature of the probability must be emphasized; other people might not agree on the reinforcement to be expected from the behavior or the likelihood of its occurrence. We also need to stress the point that the person himself is not necessarily aware of the expectancies he holds, nor is it probable that he thinks of his own behavior as being governed by expectancies. Expectancy is an abstraction from behavior.

The importance of taking expectancies as well as needs into account is highlighted by the frequent observation of individuals with manifestly strong needs who do not act in ways directly consistent with need satisfaction. A clear implication of the expectancy concept is that although a person may have a very strong need, test responses may not give evidence of it because of a low expectancy of need satisfaction. Alternatively, if I (the subject) want your (the tester's) approval, and I expect you to withhold it if I admit to "bad" things about myself, my test responses will be influenced by my need *and* by my expectancy.

The fact of being tested is likely to arouse needs and expectancies related to social evaluation. Thus, we have to be concerned with the ways in which past experiences dispose people to interpret evaluative situations and with the characteristic behavior that follows from those interpretations.

## SOCIAL DESIRABILITY AND
## THE NEED FOR APPROVAL

This brief discussion of the role of needs and expectancies in determining test responses suggests the process by which the social desirability characteristic of test items may be reflected in the actual responses chosen by the subject. Responses based on the desirability or undesirability of test items must reflect the individual's motives, and the question now becomes, what specific motives could impel responding in this way?

There is a serious problem in discovering the motivational significance of the test responses given by an individual. Personality test items frequently inquire about behavior reflecting *symptoms of personality disturbance* (many personality tests seek to measure aspects of disturbed behavior), or they may concern behavior (e.g., conformity) that is strongly condemned in the culture at large. The items on *clinical* personality scales are often like the following:

Criticism or scolding hurts me terribly.
I wish I were not so awkward and shy.
Sometimes I think I am losing my mind.
My greatest problem is my unhappy sex life.

When individuals deny that such characteristics are true of themselves, are they responding in a socially desirable manner, or are they genuinely free of those problems? The answer is that we really don't know. Rejection of items like these *may* imply a tendency to respond in a socially desirable manner, but it is also quite possible that persons responding *false* are simply not overwhelmed by criticism, awkward and shy, troubled by worries of going crazy, and sexually maladjusted. Notice that when an investigator devises a social desirability scale from items with strong desirability implications (like these) that are also characterized by pathological implications, it becomes impossible to discriminate between the true absence of symptoms and the disposition of persons to present themselves in a favorable light. Such a social desirability scale cannot indicate the motivated willingness or unwillingness of individuals to acknowledge maladjustive symptoms, but simply indicates whether they do admit to symptoms or not.

There is another possible approach to the problem. Consider a set of personality test items that have two defining attributes: (1) they may be characterized as "good" or "bad" (a social desirability dimension); and (2) they are very likely to be true of most people or untrue of most people. The diagram below shows the four possibilities. What we want are items that fall in the two quadrants with Xs. Endorsement of the "good" items means

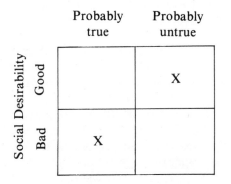

TABLE 6.1
Some Illustrative Social Desirability Scale Items[a]

---

I sometimes feel resentful when I don't get my way.

On a few occasions, I have given up doing something because I thought too little of my ability.

I'm always willing to admit it when I make a mistake.

I don't find it particularly difficult to get along with loud mouthed, obnoxious people.

I would never think of letting someone else be punished for my wrongdoings.

There have been times when I was quite jealous of the good fortune of others.

---

[a]From Crowne & Marlowe, 1960.

claiming some very improbable things about oneself, and rejection of the "bad" items entails denial of some very common human frailties. Table 6.1 gives some illustrative items. To the extent that a person responds this way, we may say that he or she is displaying a social desirability response set.

This was the approach that David Marlowe and I took in trying to make sense of the social desirability problem. Our initial investigation (Crowne & Marlowe, 1960) involved the development of the desirability scale characterized above and an analysis of its relationships with the Minnesota Multiphasic Personality Inventory (MMPI). The MMPI consists of a number of clinical scales with names like Hypochondriasis, Depression, Hysteria, Psychopathic Deviate, and Schizophrenia. Although the interpretation of these scales is far more complex than their individual names would suggest (the pattern or configuration of scores on all of the scales is the basis of test interpretation), each scale does contain items of clinical significance. There are also three "validity" scales designed to detect defensiveness (the K scale), flagrant "faking good" (the Lie scale), and confusion and/or carelessness (the F scale). In addition, since the MMPI contains a very large number of items (more than 500), they have been recombined in other research scales such as the MAS, an Ego Strength scale, and Anxiety and Repression scales. The correlations of our social desirability scale with these MMPI scales are shown in Table 6.2 along with the correlations that Edwards (1957) had originally reported for the social desirability scale he developed.

Let's consider the clinical scales first—those set apart in the center section of Table 6.2. There is a general tendency for the two social desirability (SD) scales to show negative correlations with most of the clinical scales, and these correlations are consistently higher for the Edwards scale. These correlations suggest two conclusions. First, the greater the tendency to respond in a socially desirable way as measured by the two SD scales, the lower (i.e., more in the normal direction) the MMPI clinical scale scores are likely to be. Second, the more closely the SD scale items resemble the clinical scale items, the higher will be the correlations. The Edwards scale was constructed from MMPI items with strong desirability implications, and it is not surprising that it should show such sizeable correlations. This fact, of course, makes interpretation of the correlations difficult: Are those large correlations due to consistent individual differences in the tendency to respond in a socially desirable way, or do they mainly indicate that when a person rejects a clinical item it is likely that he does so because he simply doesn't have the symptom?

There is one other fact to note about Table 6.2—the difference made by the subtle and obvious items on several of the clinical scales. On some of the clinical scales, the items can be divided into a group with obvious pathological (and desirability) implications ("I frequently think of killing myself") and a group of subtle items with no clear implications of disturbance (or desirability) ("I like to read detective and mystery stories"). The two SD scales correlate higher with the obvious than with the subtle items. This is a finding we should expect, and it rather suggests that persons who respond in a socially

TABLE 6.2
Correlations Between the Social Desirability Scales and the MMPI[a]

| MMPI Scale | Marlowe–Crowne SD Scale | | | Edwards SD Scale | | |
|---|---|---|---|---|---|---|
| | Correlation | Subtle Items | Obvious Items | Correlation | Subtle Items | Obvious Items |
| K (defensiveness) | .40 | | | .65 | | |
| Lie | .54 | | | .22 | | |
| F (confusion/ carelessness) | -.36 | | | -.61 | | |
| Hypochondriasis | -.30 | | | -.62 | | |
| Depression | -.27 | .14 | -.37 | -.72 | .33 | -.78 |
| Hysteria | .15 | .32 | -.23 | .09 | .54 | -.71 |
| Psychopathic Deviate | -.41 | -.21 | -.46 | -.73 | .27 | -.85 |
| Paranoia | .21 | .37 | -.18 | -.02 | .06 | -.72 |
| Psychasthenia | -.30 | | | -.80 | | |
| Schizophrenia | -.40 | | | -.77 | | |
| Hypomania | -.24 | .04 | -.32 | -.42 | .40 | -.53 |
| Ego Strength | .17 | | | .46 | | |
| MAS | -.25 | | | -.75 | | |
| Anxiety | -.23 | | | -.61 | | |
| Repression | .28 | | | .07 | | |

[a]From Crowne & Marlowe, 1964.

desirable way are concerned to avoid acknowledgment of statements that would imply that they are different or deviant.

## The Motivation of Socially Desirable Responding

The correlations we have just considered show that an SD scale made up of items that themselves do not imply psychopathology enables us to account for *some* of the variation in personality test responses, but by no means all. Could the magnitude of these correlations be taken to reflect the influence of a *need* to give socially desirable responses? That seemed a plausible hypothesis.

What might the motive be? Our initial interpretation was that high scorers on the SD scale were conforming to social stereotypes of what is acceptable to acknowledge about oneself as a means of obtaining approval. Thus, the new SD scale we had devised was an indirect measure of a *need for approval*. Our concept of an approval motive could be set forth in two propositions.

1. People differ in the need to be thought well of by others.
2. Those with a high need generally tend to hold the expectancy that approval is gained by engaging in behavior that is culturally acceptable and by avoiding behavior that others would not approve of.

Thus, the person with a high need for approval is sensitive to the evaluations of others and concerned to achieve favorable ones. The approval motive construct seemed to account pretty well for test-taking behavior, and it also implied that dependence on the approval of others would be reflected in a wide range of social behavior. One specific implication was that approval motivation should be associated with compliance and conformity.

## SOME COMPLIANCE AND CONFORMITY EXPERIMENTS

The first of a series of experiments attempting to test this hypothesis (Marlowe & Crowne, 1961) was based on the common-sense notion that if you want someone to approve of you, one of the things you can do is to say what you think he wants to hear. The essential requirement for such an experiment is to create an *implied* demand for conformity to the views or wishes of someone important to the subject—the experimenter—and to make that implied conformity demand strongly contrary to the subject's own views and wishes.

That was done in two steps. The first step involved giving each subject a long, drawn-out task to perform that he would find unutterably boring. The task was packing empty thread spools in a box one by one, unpacking them one by one, refilling it and emptying it over and over for 25 minutes. The subject was told nothing more than that the experiment concerned "measures of performance," and he was not told of the long duration. All the while, the experimenter appeared to be busy taking notes on and timing the subject's performance. At the end of the spool-packing period, a questionnaire was handed to the subject asking him to give ratings on four 10-point scales:

1. Was the task interesting and enjoyable?
2. Did the experiment give you an opportunity to learn about your abilities and skills?
3. From what you know about the experiment and the task involved in it, would you say the experiment was measuring anything important?
4. Would you have any desire to participate in another similar experiment?

This was step two. The hypothesis was tested by comparing the mean ratings of high and low need-for-approval subjects. The SD scale had been given to each subject just before the spool-packing task was introduced with a questionnaire measuring conforming tendencies. The need-approval groups were formed by dividing the distribution of scores on the SD scale at the mean into a high (above the mean) group and a low (below the mean) group. Table 6.3 gives the results. On each of the four rating scales the mean responses of the high-scoring subjects were more favorable than the neutral midpoint on the rating scale and appreciably more so than the low SD group. Scores on the SD scale correlated significantly with the conformity questionnaire (the higher the need-for-approval score, the higher the conformity score), although the conformity questionnaire did not as successfully predict the favorability of attitudes toward spool packing.

Thus, the first experiment appeared to lend support to the interpretation of the SD scale as an indirect measure of approval motivation. It seemed

TABLE 6.3
Attitudes of the High and Low Need-for-Approval Groups on the Four Questions[a, b]

| | Expressed Attitude Scores | |
| --- | --- | --- |
| Questions | High Need-for-Approval Group | Low Need-for-Approval Group |
| How enjoyable the task was | 7.17 | 5.70 |
| How much they learned | 5.37 | 3.22 |
| Scientific importance | 7.37 | 5.67 |
| Participate in similar experiment | 8.63 | 6.67 |

[a] Adapted from Crowne & Marlowe, 1964.
[b] All differences between the high and low need-for-approval groups are significant. The attitude scores shown are means on scales ranging from 0 (negative end) to 10 (positive).

plausible that subjects, especially those concerned about approval, would view the experimenter as a person of prestige and authority, identify him with a professorial role, and anticipate approval satisfactons from pleasing him. The rating scales left little doubt about how to do that. Those subjects less dependent on approval would, of course, be freer to express what they really felt about the spool-packing task.

But no single experiment, particularly of an R–R type such as this one, can establish the validity of a theoretical concept. We need a series of experimental tests covering the range of the behavioral predictions implied by the concept. The next set of experiments examined the role of need for approval in a very different kind of influence situation.

## Subtle Social Influence

The attempt to influence attitudes  in the implied demand experiment was deliberately blatant, and approval-motivated subjects responded to the obvious cues given them. Would they be similarly responsive to the subtle and non-obvious—to social influence that only hints at the desired behavior and that rewards small and imperceptible steps toward it? There are really two questions here: would persons with a high need for approval *detect* subtle cues, and would the slight and intermittent rewards provide sufficient approval-relevant satisfaction?

Subtle social influence is an ever-present fact in interpersonal relationships, and there are several ways to accomplish it in the laboratory. One of them is verbal conditioning, a procedure devised long ago by Greenspoon (1955). It is eminently simple. The subject is instructed to say words—just words. Without telling the subject, the experimenter has selected some response class; in Greenspoon's experiments, and in the first of our subtle influence studies (Crowne & Strickland, 1961), it was plural nouns. In the course of saying words, some are going to be plurals, and the experimenter's response to any plural noun is to lean forward slightly, indicating interest, and to say "Mmm-hmm." We compared the proportion of plurals in such a reinforced group with a nonreinforced control group, and the subjects in each group were divided into high and low need-for-approval subgroups. We added one more group to the experiment to further test the sensitivity and responsiveness of approval-motivated subjects—a negative reinforcement group in which the experimenter's response to plural nouns is a slight shake of the head and an "Uh-uh."

We see the results in Fig. 6.1 and 6.2. Plural nouns increase in the high need-for-approval group when positive reinforcement is given, and there is an immediate reduction in plurals in the negative reinforcement condition for the approval-dependent subjects. The low need-for-approval subjects are indistinguishable from the nonreinforced control group. As Fig. 6.1 and 6.2 suggest, there was a stronger effect for positive reinforcement than for the

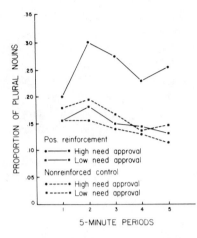

FIG. 6.1. Proportions of plural nouns given by high and low need-for-approval groups in the positive reinforcement and nonreinforced control conditions. (From Crowne & Strickland, 1961.)

negative "Uh-uh." Apparently, an approving reinforcer is more effective in increasing responses than is mild disapproval in inhibiting them for persons sensitive to and motivated for approval.

Verbal conditioning experiments have raised an interesting and provocative issue: How much of the "conditioning" effect is under the subject's direct, voluntary control? Early experimenters like Greenspoon claimed on the basis of postexperimental interviews that nearly all of their subjects were unaware of the reinforced response class and the increase in their plural responses. If this were true, it would make the verbal conditioning phenomenon a striking instance of instrumental learning without awareness. We conducted such interviews with our subjects and at that time concluded that they—or a large majority of them—were unaware. Subsequent verbal conditioning research has rather convincingly demonstrated that the sort of postexperimental interview that we used (it was patterned after Greenspoon's) is notably insensitive to what the subject knows or thinks about the experiment—his

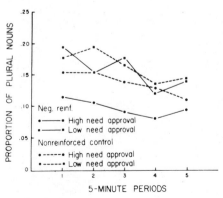

FIG. 6.2. Proportions of plural nouns given by high and low need-for-approval groups in the negative reinforcement and nonreinforced control conditions. (From Crowne & Strickland, 1961.)

hypotheses. Thus, it seems probable that subjects *were* aware of the response class and the response–reinforcer contingency. Those who showed "conditioning" were more sensitive to the experimenter's approval or disapproval and sought to behave in the one way that would attain approval or avert disapproval. It should be noted, though, that Strickland (1970) found verbal conditioning among approval-motivated subjects classified as unaware on the basis of careful postexperimental interviews. Perhaps aware–unaware is too crude a dichotomy, and what is needed is the *scaling* of degree of awareness.

Two other verbal conditioning studies followed, and these experiments examined the effect of subtle social reinforcement on high and low need-for-approval subjects in more lifelike and realistic situations, similar to those in which subtle influence is naturally exerted. One of these studies (Marlowe, 1962) was an attempt to alter the way people high or low in need approval talk about themselves by the same "Mm-hmm" technique. The situation was a personal interview conducted with each individual subject, and the response class was positive self-references. Thus, in talking about himself, anything favorable that the subject mentioned ("I get pretty good grades," and "I have a lot of friends.") was rewarded by "Mm-hmm." There were nonreinforced control groups of high and low need-for-approval subjects who simply talked about themselves for the duration of the interview without any response from the experimenter. No negative reinforcement was used in this study because of its potentially upsetting effects.

There was a conditioning effect for the reinforced high need-for-approval group only. These subjects increased their positive self-references, as Fig. 6.3 shows. Their decline in positive self-references in the last period of the interview is curious. It is perhaps best explained in the words of one subject: "It's awfully hard to sit here and toot your own horn."

In the two experiments we have just reviewed, subtle social influence was applied *directly* to the subject. But not all social influence is direct; we

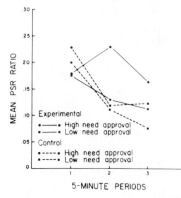

FIG. 6.3. Positive self-reference (PSR) ratios of the high and low need-for-approval groups in the experimental (reinforced) and control (nonreinforced) conditions. The PSR ratio is the number of positive self-references divided by the total number of statements made. (From Marlowe, 1962.)

sometimes observe influence attempts on other people and may modify our own behavior in the implied direction. This is *vicarious* influence, and the more we are concerned to create a favorable impression, to be positively evaluated, to gain approval, the more we are likely to be sensitive to cues signaling behavior that will achieve these things.

A vicarious influence experiment needs three conditions. First is a condition in which subjects *observe* another person (in this case a pre-instructed confederate of the experimenter) being reinforced for responses in the chosen class—a *vicarious reinforcement* condition. Second, a condition is required in which subjects observe another person responding but no reward is given. Here, the subject gains an idea of the nature of the situation but is given no cues about what specific responses may be desired. This is called the *information* condition. Finally, we need a control condition. These subjects never see the influence situation at all.

Now, subjects respond in the influence situation but are not themselves reinforced, and what we want to see is whether the vicarious influence of the first condition takes. This experiment was done by Marlowe, Beecher, Cook, and Doob (1964). The task was a simple one—making up two-word sentences from verbs and pronouns. The choice of I–we pronouns was the dependent variable, and what subjects had observed in the vicarious reinforcement condition was a high rate of increase in these words by the confederate.

Approval-motivated subjects in the vicarious reinforcement condition increased their use of I–we pronouns, but low need-for-approval subjects exposed to the same vicarious influence did not. No change in the critical response class occurred in the information or control conditions for either approval motive group, nor should it have since no cues were provided in these conditions.

These subtle social influence experiments established that people motivated for approval are alert to minimal social reinforcement and responsive to it, while those less approval-motivated are not. Could *any* response be shaped by the verbal conditioning technique in an approval-dependent person? Some studies to be discussed later suggest that there may be limits—for example, acknowledging very undesirable things about oneself. Dixon (1970), however, was able to show the verbal conditioning of negative self-referring statements in approval-motivated females. The statements, however, were not the subjects' own spontaneous self-descriptions but were presented to them on cards. Self-references were made by choosing the personal pronoun. To form a sentence from elements given you does not entail the same degree of individual accountability as to utter the sentence spontaneously.

There have been failures to replicate these subtle social influence studies (Bryan & Lichtenstein, 1966; Spielberger, Berger, & Howard, 1963). In both of these experiments, however, the experimenters were undergraduate students who could not have represented a source of approval as important to the subject as the professors and advanced graduate students who conducted the studies we have just reviewed. Replication of experimental findings demands that the conditions under which the phenomenon is observed are reproduced. The condition for successfully influencing someone else by subtle reinforcement appears to include both a degree of approval dependence in the person to be influenced and a measure of importance—a significant source of approval—in the influencer.

## Conformity

A number of years ago, Asch (1951) devised a beautifully simple means for exerting group pressures to conform on an individual subject. The influence exerted is not subtle; it is quite evident, and it arises in the form of a conflict between some obvious fact and the unanimous judgments of the members of a social group. The subject in this situation must set himself apart from the others if he chooses the objective fact, and if he aligns himself with the group he must deny what he knows to be true. There is a price to conformity, thus, as there often is in real social situations: One must violate a personal conviction to achieve concensus with the others. It is a powerful and painful procedure.

There are several techniques for creating conformity pressure. Asch's original experiments used accomplices who were pre-instructed by the experimenter to argue on an incorrect judgment. It is so arranged that all accomplices respond before the single subject. Most commonly, the judgments are perceptual—length of lines or the number of dots in a cluster. This procedure is an expensive and demanding one; several people have to carry out complex roles for each individual subject. Modifications of the Asch situation have been developed to make the creation of conformity pressure more economical. One such modification simulates the oppositional majority; the subject is led to believe that the others are in adjoining rooms or that they have responded previously. He is exposed to their judgments and must decide whether to agree or to remain independent.

The implied demand and subtle influence studies found approval-motivated persons to be more responsive to the influence attempts. In those experiments, however, there was no "price" for giving the implied or rewarded response; they were not conformity procedures. Would motivation for approval lead to the surrender of personal beliefs under pressure to conform? This question led to the following experiments.

Strickland and Crowne (1962) used the simulated group procedure. Female subjects were required to judge the number of "knocks" presented on a tape recorder. Each series of knocks was followed by the responses of three "previous subjects," and the real subject was to announce her judgment immediately after. The judgments of the "previous subjects" differed from the actual number of knocks on a majority of the trials. High need-for-approval subjects were responsive to the conformity pressure, giving the same response as the simulated majority on a significantly greater number of trials than the low need-for-approval group.

The next experiment (Crowne & Marlowe, 1964, pp. 79–82) followed Asch's original procedure, creating social pressure by a physically present group. Pre-instructed accomplices of the experimenter unanimously gave the incorrect response on a majority of trials in a "perceptual discrimination" task, and again approval-motivated subjects conformed more often than those low in need for approval.

A rather different conformity pressure was involved in a study by Miller, Doob, Butler, and Marlowe (1965). They gave subjects a large number of personality test items mainly drawn from the MMPI. Beside each item was a "prediction" of the subject's own response ostensibly made by one of four judges. The judges varied in expertise and in the importance of agreeing with them. When the judge was perceived as expert and agreeing with him as important, approval-motivated subjects tended to conform more than the low group, accepting a greater number of predictions as true of themselves.

Skolnick and Heslin (1971) also studied the tendency to agree among subjects varying in approval motivation. These investigators manipulated the validity of persuasive arguments and the credibility of the source. Logical and well-reasoned or poor and weakly-reasoned arguments were attributed to highly credible or less credible sources. Subjects with strong approval motivation were more easily persuaded overall, and they did not discriminate as did the low approval-motivation subjects between good and bad arguments or believable versus less believable sources.

A similar susceptibility to undiscriminating agreement was shown in another persuasion experiment by Buckhout (1965). Subjects with positive attitudes toward television were reinforced for choosing anti-television statements. Those high in approval motivation more often selected the anti-television statements, and this effect lasted beyond the reinforcement period.

## Attitude Change

Persons dependent on approval are more vulnerable to the persuasive efforts of others, responding uncritically to arguments or to reinforcing comments by modifying their attitudes. Attitude change, however, may come about in other ways than by the direct influence attempts of others. One important way is through the arousal of inconsistency, or dissonance as Festinger (1957) has called it—for example, by publicly committing oneself to a position one doesn't privately hold. That inconsistency ("I said something I really don't believe") is uncomfortable, and there is a great deal of evidence to show that once aroused, efforts will be made to reduce it. There are a number of potential avenues by which such a state of dissonance may be reduced—disparaging the situation, the importance of one's hearers, or the significance

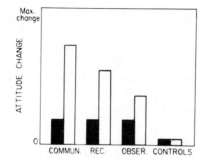

FIG. 6.4. Predicted attitude change of the high and low need-for-approval groups in the various role assignments: Commun.—Communicators, Rec.—Receivers, Obser.—Observers. (Adapted from Salman, 1962, in Crowne & Marlowe, 1964.)

of the issue. One may also change one's private belief to conform to the public position one has avowed, and if one feels constrained not to dismiss or disparage this may be the alternative. The approval-motivated person is especially likely to feel constrained not to devalue (if you care strongly about what others think of you, you are unlikely to belittle as a means of rationalizing your public commitment). Thus, private attitude change should be the means of inconsistency reduction when the approval-dependent person has committed himself to a personally discrepant position.

To test this hypothesis we need to induce subjects to avow in public an attitude to which they are opposed. Salman (1962; see Crowne & Marlowe, 1964, Chap. 8) designed an experiment to do this. High and low need-for-approval subjects were assigned to one of four conditions. In the critical condition, subjects were given the task of preparing and delivering a persuasive argument on an issue about which their attitudes had already been assessed. Subjects in the second condition were "receivers"—the ones to be persuaded. The two other groups were observers, who merely watched the persuasion attempt, and a control group not exposed to the persuasion. Figure 6.4 shows the predicted attitude change for the high and low need-for-approval groups in each condition of the experiment.

Salman found that approval-motivated communicators initially opposed to the position they had to advocate showed significant attitude change in the direction they had argued. Weaker attitude change was shown by approval-motivated receivers and observers, and the low need-for-approval group did not change at all. Approval-dependent subjects in the communicator role, especially those privately opposed to the issue, were faced with an uncomfortable degree of dissonance. Because of their concern to be thought well of, they were less able than the low need-for-approval subjects to treat the persuasive task, the role they were required to play, and the position they had to advocate as personally inconsequential. The remaining avenue to achieving consonance between personal belief and public commitment was private attitude change.

Conformity and compliance to both direct and subtle influence attempts seem to be distinguishing features of the behavior of people who characterize themselves on a personality test as nearly perfect persons. The test behavior enabled prediction of social behavior by means of concept of need for approval. The concept implies both behavioral outcomes. As the discussion of R–R research strategy in Chapter 2 revealed, we measure one set of responses as the principal index of the concept and use it to predict other responses. The clarity and explicitness of the concept are critical: If the theoretical concept is vague and not well defined, the extensiveness and the specificity of the implications that may be derived from it will be limited.

In an important way, that was a problem with the concept of need for approval at this stage in its development. It could account for the findings we have just considered and some related ones—conventional or even stereotyped social behavior (Barthel, 1963; Horton, Marlowe, & Crowne, 1963), and greater effort on laboratory tasks, especially under conditions of approving feedback (Strickland, 1965b; Willingham & Strickland, 1965) among approval-motivated subjects. It was not clear that need for approval implied more than this relatively limited range of self-descriptive and social behavior. There was also an even more basic question: Why would people engage in such blatant, uncritical, naive, approval seeking? This sort of behavior is often not rewarded and in fact is the target of contempt. A simple concept of *need* to be approved of seemed inadequate to account for the behavior we observed, particularly when we reasoned that in many real life situations the approval-dependent person must encounter disapproval or rejection for his compliant and yielding behavior.

Thus, it seemed likely that the construct we had developed represented only part of a more complex motive. What we had missed in the initial emphasis on the need for approval was the defensiveness and self-protectiveness implicit in the very test behavior from which we inferred the approval motive. To describe oneself in such a way as to deny the slightest wrongdoings and to claim the most implausibly favorable attributes may be characterized as approval-currying. It is also recognizably *defensive*: The person is unwilling to acknowledge, or unable to recognize in himself, certain unfavorable characteristics. These implications to socially desirable test behavior suggested that the need for approval might involve avoidant and self-protective defenses—defenses to avert threat to self-esteem from anticipated social rejection and from severe uncertainties about self-worth. One might then think of a defensive style based on repression, denial, and reaction formation (the turning of disturbing feelings into their acceptable opposites) —a defensive style patterned on stereotyped and conventionally acceptable social behavior. Both approval-seeking and socially desirable self-description could then be understood as efforts to maintain self-esteem and to secure in relationships with others the reassurance of approval. Cohen (1959) clearly described this defensive style:

> the use of avoidance defenses permits the individual to organize a cohesive and encapsulated self-picture. After they have been developed as a means of handling inner impulses, avoidance defenses become behavioral modes

themselves and determine the social reality to which the person exposes himself. Consequently, persons with avoidance defenses can turn away from experiences which reflect unfavorably on their self-picture. . . . Persons whose defenses are more expressive may not be able to deal so selectively with external stimuli [p. 117].

## DEFENSIVENESS

Some very different implications follow from this defensiveness hypothesis. It entails all the approval-related findings, but it suggests in addition that we should see distortions of those thoughts and feelings that arouse fears of rejection or of disruptive self-recognition, and the avoidance of threatening situations.

### A Conflict in Psychotherapy

There are many possible ways in which we can observe avoidant and self-protective defenses. One of them is to create a requirement for frank self-disclosure. In this case, the desire to please, to gain approval for complying with the demand, conflicts with the fear aroused by having to reveal intimate personal feelings, thoughts, and impulses. Psychotherapy should involve just this kind of conflict: Please the therapist by talking freely about oneself versus the anxiety aroused by the threat entailed to one's defensive self-image. This sort of conflict should be especially acute in the beginning stages, before the patient has come to trust and to feel secure with the therapist.

How would an approval-dependent patient cope, faced with these conflicting motives? Defy the therapist and risk disapproval? (Even though he might not actively disapprove, the approval-dependent person is likely to *expect* him to do so.) Attempt to talk openly and speak the unutterable? This is an avoidance–avoidance conflict, and what we frequently observe when people are caught between two painful alternatives is behavior characterized as "leaving the field." In psychotherapy, leaving the field would amount to premature termination. If the patient finds the conflict insoluble, he may convince himself that he has already accomplished what he came for—he feels much better, is no longer bothered by his problems, etc.—or that psychotherapy is not worthwhile.

These considerations led Strickland and Crowne (1963) to obtain scores on the need-for-approval scale from a large number of patients in an outpatient psychiatric clinic, together with several other measures. These included the number of hours of psychotherapy before termination, therapists' ratings of each of their patients on a case-rating scale, and each patient's rating of his own improvement. There is a design flaw in this study that could be overcome only in part. Most patients could not be given the need-for-approval scale at the clinic while they were actually in treatment and so the questionnaire was mailed to them within three months of termination. There was, however, a smaller group of patients who did take the scale while at the clinic and in treatment. Thus, the personality scale that is the major predictive variable was not administered at the beginning of therapy, and it was not taken by most patients under controlled conditions. Did patients respond differently on the need-for-approval scale as a result of having taken it at home after therapy was over? Further, what might have been the effect, if any, of the experience of psychotherapy on the personality scale?

There are some partial answers to these questions. The mean need-for-approval scores of the patients who mailed the questionnaire and those taking the scale at the clinic were compared, and no difference was found. As a check on the potential influence of psychotherapy on need-for-approval scores, the scale was readministered to a small number of patients after five months in therapy. A fairly sizeable test–retest correlation of .68 was found, and in addition there was no systematic shift in the mean. Were these checks on the comparability and stability of scores adequate to compensate for the basic procedural flaw of the study? That is, can conclusions be drawn about any possible relation between the approval motive and length of stay in psychotherapy? You may judge for yourself whether the problem was adequately answered.

The threatened and defensive patient should leave the field of psychotherapy by premature termination and should thus have fewer hours of psychotherapy than the less threatened patient. The relation between need-for-approval scores and the number of hours of psychotherapy is shown in Table 6.4. You can see that there are few approval-motivated patients who remained in psychotherapy for a long period; instead they tended to stop by 30–40 hours of treatment. Quite the opposite picture is seen for the low need-for-approval group. These patients were much more likely to stick it out.

Was the earlier termination of the approval-motivated patients a *defensive* response? The therapists' ratings suggest that it was. One of the items on the

TABLE 6.4
The Number of Hours of Psychotherapy for High and Low Need-for-Approval
Patients[a]

| Number of Hours of Psychotherapy | Number of High Need-for-Approval Patients | Number of Low Need-for-Approval Patients |
|---|---|---|
| 71+ (to 284) | 5 | 11 |
| 61–70 | 1 | 1 |
| 51–60 | 1 | 5 |
| 41–50 | 0 | 5 |
| 31–40 | 7 | 2 |
| 21–30 | 10 | 9 |
| 11–20 | 11 | 5 |
| 1–10 | 8 | 4 |

[a]From Crowne & Marlowe, 1964.

case-rating scale concerned the therapist's judgment of the defensiveness of the patient, and the correlation between these ratings and need-approval scores was -.67 (the lower the score on the rating scale, the higher the defensiveness). Approval-dependent patients were not considered by their therapists to be more improved than the long-remaining lows: Indeed, the correlation between therapist-rated improvement and need for approval was negative, though not significant.

This study suggests—if one believes that its flaw is not fatal—that approval-motivated patients were threatened by psychotherapy and quit prematurely. Although there is no direct evidence, their early termination and higher ratings of defensiveness imply that these patients could not cope with the conflict between complying with the therapist and open self-disclosure. The findings thus fit with a view of approval motivation as entailing a defensive self-image maintained to avert threat to self-esteem.

## Approval Seeking versus Defensiveness

Mosher (1965) pitted approval-seeking against defensiveness in a study designed to assess the acceptance of undesirable personality characteristics attributed to subjects. We earlier saw that approval-dependent persons are especially responsive to subtle social influence, modifying their choices of words, self-descriptive statements, and attitudes in the direction indicated by the reinforcing nods and "Mm-hmms" of experimenters. Would they also agree with personality interpretations, some of them highly unfavorable, made by an expert? In this study subjects were presented with interpretive statements by a clinical psychologist, presumably based on a previously taken test. Some of the statements, which were actually MMPI items, were highly favorable, some were slightly unfavorable, and some were highly unfavorable (e.g., "You sometimes feel as if you must injure yourself or someone else."). Approval-dependent subjects were more likely to accept the favorable and mildly unfavorable interpretations than low need-for-approval subjects, but they accepted significantly fewer of the very unfavorable interpretations. Acceptance of these statements, Mosher suggested, would have entailed a threat to self-esteem—a threat these subjects coped with by denial. The situation appears to resemble that of the patient in psychotherapy who has to cope with the esteem-jeopardizing problem of self-disclosure. Although most of Mosher's statements would not have been true of any individual subject, there must have been a great grey area of uncertainty, surely fed by an authoritative expert confidently making personality predictions.

## Two Psychotherapy Analogues

Two other studies, both modeled on psychotherapeutic processes, bear out the implications of these initial studies of the vulnerable self-esteem hypothesis. Efran and Boylin (1967) gave subjects a choice of participating in a group discussion of the social interactions of its members or simply observing. Approval-motivated subjects more often chose to be observers, suggesting avoidance of the potential threat to self-esteem of critical evaluations from the other members of the group. In an experimental analogue of psychotherapy, Kanfer and Marston (1964) gave subjects a series of topics to discuss with interviewers who made reflective or interpretive comments on the subjects' responses. The subjects could choose which interviewer—reflective or interpretive—they wanted to hear. Those who chose the less threatening reflective interviewer had significantly higher scores on the need-for-approval scale.

These defensiveness studies we have reviewed suggest that approval-dependent persons not only *present* themselves as adjusted, self-controlled, responsible, and self-content, but *think* of themselves that way. When this image is threatened, they recoil in an avoidant retreat to protect it. The most salient dimension by which they judge themselves is an evaluative, good–bad one (Pervin & Lilly, 1967). That may be largely true of all of us—the other two dimensions of semantic "space," activity and potency, less compellingly reflect our self-concerns—but it appears to be especially true of those high in the need for approval. That finding helps to make sense of the defensiveness studies: if one is sensitized to goodness–badness and must think of oneself as good, threat is going to abound.

## Defensiveness on Projective Personality Tests

It will not be surprising that threat is perceived and defensiveness evoked when approval-dependent subjects are given projective personality tests, whose very rationale is to undermine—or indeed, not even to engage at all—defensive responding. There are two principal studies. Tutko (1962) gave three widely used projective tests to a group of 60 hospitalized psychiatric patients. The tests were given to half the patients with "stress" instructions: "the results of these tests can find out a great deal about people and they are often used to find out if people are mentally sick." The other half received "supportive" instructions emphasizing anonymity and the interest of the investigator in the tests themselves. The patients' test responses were given to a large number of experienced clinical psychologists to rate, blind, on three dimensions—the degree of revealingness in the test responses, defensiveness, and the amount of pathology. High need-for-approval patients were generally rated as less revealing and more defensive, and their projective responses were also briefer and less productive. The stress instructions tended to make approval-dependent patients much more guarded and defensive, but the supportive test procedure did not reduce their defensive responding to the level of low need-for-approval patients. Defensiveness also had its effect on ratings of pathology: The projective responses of approval-dependent patients in the stress instructions condition were given low pathology ratings, especially on the least disguised test. This seems to reflect the success of defensive and constricted responding and not lesser disturbance in these patients. Card rejection (refusal to give any responses) on projective tests is considered to be highly defensive; a small number of responses, most of which are banal and innocuous, also suggest defensiveness. Tutko's high need-for-approval patients showed these characteristics also.

A later study by Lefcourt (1969) investigated defensive responding on projective tests among college students. He administered one of the inkblot-type tests to two groups of subjects under two conditions—threat (the test is a mental illness detector), and a "creative" instruction condition. The dependent variable was the number of human movement responses, which are presumed to reflect imaginativeness, expressiveness, and intellectual effort. Compared to low need-for-approval subjects, the high group gave fewer movement responses, especially when threatened, and those they gave were produced later in the test session. Lefcourt also assessed subjects on another test, a measure of repression versus sensitization. Approval-dependent subjects who were also repressors gave the fewest movement responses. The usual interpretation given to a low number of movement responses includes constriction and defensiveness, and so Lefcourt's findings nicely bear out Tutko's.

## The Inhibition of Aggression

There is one more set of studies to review under the general heading of defensiveness. These are some experiments showing the inhibition of aggression in subjects provoked to anger. These studies suggest that approval dependence involves not only a defensive self-image but a very specific difficulty in expressing anger, even when it is called for. The first of these studies in particular suggests the kind of defense raised against anger, and perhaps also against other disruptive incursions that would undermine approval and esteem from others or that would undermine self-esteem. That defense is repression, and we considered this study by Conn and Crowne (1964) earlier at the end of Chapter 5 under the heading, "Instigation to Aggression, Emotional Arousal, and Defensive Emulation." In that experiment, subjects in an arousal condition were instigated to anger and then exposed to a euphoric model. The hypothesized tendency of approval-dependent subjects to repress awareness of anger was expected to interfere with angry cognitions, leaving them with an unexplained state of arousal. A process of social comparison would lead to adoption of the model's euphoria as their own emotional state. Control subjects and those low in need for approval would show much less euphoria. These predictions were confirmed, and the data of this study rather strongly suggest that repressive defense is a principal means by which approval-dependent persons cope with thoughts and feelings they cannot accept in themselves.

A follow-up to the Conn and Crowne experiment, a study by Fishman (1965), was also mentioned in Chapter 5. She severely frustrated subjects as they performed an experimental task. The subjects were then asked, ostensibly by a higher authority, to evaluate the experimenter—that is, they were afforded the possibility of counter-aggression. Fishman also took readings of systolic blood pressure at several points in the experiment to measure degree of arousal. We earlier noted Fishman's finding that high and low need-for-approval groups were equally aroused by her abusive frustration tactics. The high need-for-approval group showed less counter-aggression. One additional result in this experiment helps to understand the reason for the high need-for-approval person's difficulties in the expression of aggression. Not all the highs failed to counter-aggress against the unfairly critical experimenter. Fishman compared the systolic blood pressure readings taken at the time of frustration and immediately following the opportunity to counter-aggress. Low need-for-approval subjects showed a significant decrease, rather suggestive of a "catharsis" effect—their critical evaluations of the experimenter relieved their anger. There was no such drop for the high need-for-approval group, and the maintenance of an aroused state in these subjects suggest what has been termed "aggression anxiety"—the person is made fearful by his own angry arousal. The Conn and Crowne experiment implies that anxiety over aggression may be so severe that repressive defense must intervene to dispel it. Note that in the Fishman study, aggression toward the ill-tempered experimenter would have taken the form of a critical evaluation of her performance and was appropriate and justified. Though some approval-dependent subjects could aggress in this mild and sanctioned way, they experienced no relief of frustration-induced emotional arousal, and most approval-motivated subjects couldn't so aggress.

Various other aspects of the problem of aggression in approval motivation have been studied: retaliation for unfairly administered electric shocks (Taylor, 1970), preference for aggressive cartoons (Heatherington & Wray, 1964), and the imputation of hostile motives (Palmer & Altrocci, 1967). High need-for-approval subjects tend not to retaliate when unfairly shocked by an experimental partner, see less humor in aggressive cartoons except when given alcohol, and make intuitive "gut" judgments that impute less hostility to others.

There are two ways in which these aggression-inhibition findings might be interpreted. One possibility is that aggression is withheld so as not to jeopardize approval from others. The second possibility is repressive defense against anxiety. Approval-dependent persons are unaware of, unable to recognize, anger arousal in themselves. Although there is no direct evidence on which to base a choice between these alternatives, I believe the weight of the data we have reviewed is strongly on the side of repressive defense.

## ACHIEVEMENT, INTELLIGENCE, AND
## COGNITIVE PROCESSES

There is no obvious reason to expect that dependence on the approval of others, vulnerable self-esteem, and reliance on avoidance defenses would be related to intellectual and cognitive abilities. If one were to make a prediction, I would hazard the guess that one would predict higher performance from the approval-motivated—a guess based on the assumption that one would expect the high need-for-approval person to try harder in the effort to please. The problem with this prediction is that in the intellectual and cognitive realm, trying hard to please in order to gain approval doesn't necessarily enhance one's performance. If concern for approval is accompanied by the expectancy—perhaps dread would be a better term—of failure, we might then see less adequate accomplishment. Anxious anticipation tends to disrupt thinking and problem solving and to motivate a variety of attempts at avoidance (e.g., to quit as quickly as possible, or to get it over with in any way possible).

The findings here are mainly from studies of children, using a scaled-down-for-age version of the measure of need for approval (Crandall, Crandall, & Katkovsky, 1965). In the first study, Crandall, Crandall, and Katkovsky found a small but significant negative correlation between need for approval and intelligence in older children. This finding was pursued further by Allaman, Joyce, and Crandall (1972), who investigated the relation between need for approval in adulthood and intelligence test scores obtained on several occasions between early childhood and adolescence. Although they found some inconsistencies, the general trend was for approval dependence to be associated with lower intelligence test scores.

Crandall (1966) examined the relations of IQ, achievement test scores, and need approval in elementary and high school age children. At each grade level, the children were divided into high and low need-for-approval and high and low intelligence groups; achievement test performance was the dependent variable. Crandall's results are shown in Fig. 6.5. Among children below the mean in IQ, the lowest rank order of achievement belongs to those high in need for approval. The results are more complicated for the high IQ group. In younger bright children, approval dependence is associated with lower achievement test performance (rank 2 versus rank 1), but in the older children the high need-for-approval group shows the highest achievement test rank. Perhaps as bright approval-dependent children have successful experiences in school, they overcome their fear of failure and begin to develop achievement expectancies consistent with their abilities. They learn that accomplishment yields approval and expend greater effort.

The subjects in this study included a group of children who were members of the subject population of a human development research institute. The

| | | High IQ | Low IQ |
|---|---|---|---|
| High need approval | Younger | 2 | 4 |
| | Older | 1 | 4 |
| Low need approval | Younger | 1 | 3 |
| | Older | 2 | 3 |

FIG. 6.5. Rank order of the mean achievement test scores of younger and older children grouped according to intelligence and need for approval. (Adapted from Crandall, 1966.)

data collected on each child included annual behavior observations of free play during a summer day camp, observations that were then rated on a number of social interaction and achievement scales. Each child was also given various achievement tasks to perform, and expectancies of success were determined. This was accomplished by having the child indicate the level of each task, graded from easy to hard, that the child would be able to complete. Correlations were computed between the need-for-approval scale and the free play behavior ratings and expectancy measures. They are shown in Table 6.5. There are no relationships among girls between achievement play or

TABLE 6.5
Correlations of the Children's Need-for-Approval Scale
with Achievement and Expectancy Measures[a]

| | Correlation for | |
|---|---|---|
| Measure | Girls | Boys |
| Free play achievement behavior | | |
| Gross motor mastery attempts | –.15 | –.09 |
| Fine motor mastery attempts | –.02 | –.46* |
| Time spent alone involved in achievement tasks | .08 | –.48* |
| Achievement effort | .10 | –.53* |
| Task persistence | .24 | –.35* |
| Achievement expectancies | | |
| Intellectual | .11 | –.66* |
| Physical skills | .13 | –.64* |
| Artistic | –.12 | –.52* |
| Manual–mechanical | –.20 | –.50* |

[a]Adapted from Crandall, 1966.
*Significant correlations.

achievement expectancies and need for approval (though there were significant correlations for girls in the achievement test data described above). The boys, however, show consistent and substantial relationships—less achievement and persistence and lower expectancies of success in each achievement task area among the approval-dependent boys.

It begins to appear that high need-for-approval boys anticipate failure in a variety of achievement situations; their anxious anticipation leads to minimal involvement or outright avoidance. Girls who are approval-motivated don't show the fear of failure and avoidance of the boys. Why is the relationship not there for them? We don't know; perhaps it has to do with the fact that achievement problems are far more common and salient for boys than for girls, and perhaps the high need-for-approval boys become especially sensitized to failure and loss of esteem.

The effects of anxious anticipation on learning are shown in two experimental studies, one by Crowne, Holland, and Conn (1968), and one by Harter (1975). The Crowne, Holland, and Conn experiment investigated discrimination learning in high and low need-for-approval children. Approval-dependent children, especially boys, showed poorer discrimination learning, tended to respond impulsively, and had higher heart rate. We interpreted these findings as evidence of the interfering effects of anxiety on attentional processes in discrimination learning:

> if one supposes that achievement and test situations represent a persistent source of anxious arousal for approval-dependent children, especially boys, one of the consequents of such apprehension could well be a kind of failure in learning how to learn in the attentional domain. If apprehension is associated with autonomic arousal and if arousal impairs stimulus input and processing, it is not difficult to see how a child might fail to acquire the repertoire of strategies or hypotheses which facilitate...[the] discrimination of cues. That is, it is ordinarily not profitable to persist in attending to only certain and selected aspects of the stimulus situation...to the exclusion of other stimuli [pp. 428–429].

Harter found less persistence in high need-for-approval children on a difficult discrimination task; these approval-dependent children also required more trials to learn an easier discrimination.

## THE DEVELOPMENT OF APPROVAL DEPENDENCE

If we know that a person has a high need for approval, we can make some rather specific predictions about his or her behavior in a variety of situations and interpersonal interactions. Although it is unlikely that a given individual will show all of the behavioral characteristics that have been identified by the studies we have reviewed, he or she should display a consistent and coherent tendency to act in an approval-dependent way. That means, as we have seen, greater susceptibility to social influence attempts ranging from frank pressure to conform to subtle reinforcement of verbal behavior; uncritical persuasibility; reliance on self-protective defenses, which is seen in over-favorable self-description, avoidance of self-disclosure and other potential sources of threat in psychotherapy, and inhibited or even repressed anger; and somewhat lower intelligence, less adequate problem-solving, and poorer school achievement. There is some evidence to suggest that low self-esteem and expectancies of failure lie behind the defensive façade.

How does one get that way? What kinds of experiences in childhood would produce such personal vulnerability, the protective defenses masking it, and the persisting need for approval from others? That is not an easy question to answer. The experiences of childhood are generally not readily accessible to psychological inquiry. The most widely used procedures for investigating child behavior and childrearing—interviews or questionnaires in which subjects themselves are asked about childhood experiences or informants (mothers) are asked about childrearing—have major problems both of reliability and validity. The rearing of children is a day-to-day business of little details, difficult to remember, and complex feelings about sometimes very emotional events that are hard to sort out. Also, children are extensions of their parents' egos, and many parents distort the truth of childrearing in the interest of self-protection. Moreover, investigation of the childhood antecedents of personality variables is likely to stumble over the sheer lack of clear hypotheses about the relevant experiences. It is not impossible to extract meaningful antecedent data by these methods, but it is very difficult. Because of the uncertainties in integrating the data, we can have only limited confidence in the findings.

A far more adequate approach would be to have *observational* data on child and parent behavior over a period of several years—ideally the critical years for the development of the personality characteristic. Those observations, transformed into ratings on important dimensions of childrearing and child behavior, would be correlated with scores on the personality variable during childhood and in adulthood. There are only a few research centers where the opportunity exists to collect such longitudinal data on children who remain as research subjects throughout their development. At one of them, the Fels Research Institute, Allaman, Joyce, and Crandall (1972) investigated the childhood antecedents of need-for-approval.

A measure of need for approval, the Children's Social Desirability Scale, was given to two groups of children who were subjects in the longitudinal research program—a younger (ages 6-9) and an older (ages 9-12) group. A sample of young adults, also members of the subject population studied by the institute, was also included; they took the standard, adult need-for-approval scale. The antecedent measures were ratings of maternal and child behavior based on direct observations made semiannually by trained staff

TABLE 6.6
Correlations of Parent Behavior Ratings with Children's Need for
Approval[a]

| Parent Behavior Ratings at Infancy | Need for Approval at Early Elementary Age (6–9) | | Need for Approval at Late Elementary Age (9–12) | |
|---|---|---|---|---|
| | Boys | Girls | Boys | Girls |
| Warmth | | | | |
| Affectionateness | −.62* | .20 | −.51* | .01 |
| Use of praise | −.41 | .07 | −.53* | .00 |
| Control | | | | |
| Restrictiveness | .40 | .01 | .04 | .03 |
| Severity of penalties | .43 | −.10 | .22 | −.05 |
| Coerciveness | .34 | −.01 | .05 | .05 |
| Encouragement of skill development | −.20 | −.07 | −.19 | −.08 |

| Parent Behavior Ratings at Preschool | | | | |
|---|---|---|---|---|
| Warmth | | | | |
| Affectionateness | −.07 | −.22 | −.15 | −.22 |
| Use of praise | .04 | −.03 | −.30 | .07 |
| Control | | | | |
| Restrictiveness | .40 | −.05 | .34* | −.05 |
| Severity of penalties | .32 | −.08 | .39* | −.22 |
| Coerciveness | .35* | −.13 | .36* | −.13 |
| Encouragement of skill development | −.03 | −.17 | −.39* | −.18 |

[a]Adapted from Allaman, Joyce, and Crandall, 1972.
*Significant correlations.

members. In this study, ratings made during the age-periods of infancy (up to 40 months) and preschool (41–80 months) were examined. The parent behavior ratings were clustered into three broad variables—maternal warmth, maternal control, and maternal encouragement of skill development; each variable was made up of more specific rating scales (e.g., affectionateness, restrictiveness).

Correlations were computed between the parent behavior ratings and need-for-approval scores of the children. As you see in Table 6.6, there are some significant relationships with a rather surprising pattern to them.

The results are quite different for boys and girls: While a number of significant correlations are found for the boys, there are *none* for girls. Rather than make the obvious interpretation—whatever the antecedents of approval dependence in females, they are not to be found among maternal warmth, control, or encouragement in the early years—let's hold off until we examine one more set of findings.

For the boys, the findings seem pretty clear: Less affection and praise during the very early years—less maternal warmth—show up in a higher need for approval when the child reaches elementary school. The pattern seems to be pretty well set by the age of six years or so. During this early period, the severity of control practices doesn't have much of an effect in producing approval dependence. When boys are a little older, however—after about age 4, roughly—strict discipline does show a relationship: the stricter and more coercive the mother at preschool age, the more likely her child is to be approval-dependent when he reaches elementary school age. One other relationship seems to belong in the package, and that is the tendency of mothers of children later to become approval-dependent to fail to encourage the developing skills of their sons.

It is the sample of young adults given the need-for-approval scale, whose mothers were also observed and rated, that suggests an answer for the question of the origins of feminine need approval. The data, again in correlations between parent behavior ratings and need-for-approval scores, are in Table 6.7. What mothers do to their daughters *does* affect the development of need for approval, but it is a kind of "sleeper" effect, not

TABLE 6.7
Correlations of Parent Behavior Ratings and
Young Adults' Need for Approval[a]

| | Correlation Between Young Adult Need Approval and | | | | | |
| --- | --- | --- | --- | --- | --- | --- |
| | PBR at Infancy (0–3 Years) | | PBR at Preschool (3–6 Years) | | PBR at Elementary (6–10 Years) | |
| Parent Behavior Rating | Males | Females | Males | Females | Males | Females |
| Warmth | | | | | | |
| Affectionateness | .05 | –.38* | –.04 | –.39* | –.25 | –.25 |
| Direction of criticism | –.04 | –.48* | –.01 | –.62* | –.31* | –.45* |
| Intensity of contact | .10 | –.34* | –.12 | –.42* | .22 | –.08 |
| Control | | | | | | |
| Restrictiveness | .13 | .24 | .06 | .53* | –.06 | .65* |
| Severity of penalties | –.05 | .41* | –.04 | .56* | .26 | .50* |
| Coerciveness | .11 | .14 | –.12 | .53* | .13 | .57* |
| Encouragement of skill development | .22 | –.14 | .12 | –.04 | .06 | .12 |

[a]Adapted from Allaman, Joyce, and Crandall, 1972.
*Significant correlations.

appearing until long afterwards—some time between age 12 and early adulthood. Almost the same pattern of relationships appears as with the boys: Maternal coldness and severe control appear to be the antecedents of need for approval in young women.

There is a surprise in Table 6.7: The relationships for boys have dropped out. Though early maternal ratings may predict sons' need for approval from 6–12, they do not do so in young adulthood. What other antecedents are there for approval dependence in males? What about the role of fathers? Allaman, Joyce, and Crandall did not have parent behavior ratings on fathers—the observations weren't available—and so they gave to their adult subjects a parent behavior questionnaire asking for retrospective ratings of their fathers. There were significant correlations among the males on two scales, rejection and hostile detachment. The approval-dependent males tended to recall their fathers as having been rejecting and hostile. Perhaps, then, a boy may be given an early push toward approval dependence by his mother's relative coldness and strictness, but other mitigating experiences may intervene by early adolescence. For example, Allaman, Joyce, and Crandall think that high intelligence may be a sort of "antidote" to a persistent need for approval. If the boy has a father who conveys rejection and hostility, however, it is more likely that he will be approval dependent in young adulthood.

Much of this developmental sequence is speculative, going well beyond the specific correlations of parent behavior ratings or recalled father's behavior and need-for-approval scores of offspring. A developmental interpretation needs longitudinal data—both parent behavior ratings during significant childhood periods *and* measures of need for approval and approval-related behavior on the children. Data such as these could tell us *when* the effects of parental behavior begin to emerge, what specific child behavior is affected, and what kinds of compensations or antidotes there may be. This longitudinal study will have to wait for a new generation of subjects. In the meantime, Allaman, Joyce, and Crandall believe that there is persuasive evidence for a hypothesis relating cold and restrictive childrearing practices by either or both parents to the development of the need for approval. That hypothesis goes as follows:

> It appears that parental child-rearing practices which communicate overt disapproval, threat, and rejection sensitize the child to the tenuousness of parental positive regard. In fact, even sharp reduction of previous maternal interest, attention, and responsiveness may contribute to this end. As a history of parental rejection and negative evaluation accrues, the child may develop both a generalized concern with others' evaluations of him and a low expectancy that those evaluations will be approving (or conversely, a high expectancy that they will be disapproving). We suggest that such a combination of high value for approval (or avoidance of disapproval), but a low expectancy of attaining it, results in apprehension in evaluative situations [p. 1156].

## A CONCLUDING VIEW

This brings us to the end of the study of need for approval. There are some other experiments—variations on the ones I have discussed and others on cheating (the approval-dependent person tends to cheat if detection is unlikely and if approval can be gained by the results of cheating) and on expenditure of effort (approval-dependent subjects work harder). But we have covered the main studies that outline the patterns of R–R relationships on which the concept of need for approval is based.

Although we have reviewed other R–R studies in earlier chapters, this is the first time that we have encountered a concept wholly defined by correlations between response measures. Since I am so intimately involved in this research program, it is awkward for me to judge it dispassionately. I do think I can say, however, that it seems to me to exemplify both the strength of this research strategy in the study of personality and its weakness. The design of the response measure (the SD scale) and the selection of behavioral situations to relate to it can yield a rich and complex concept. We could not hope to achieve an experimental manipulation in the laboratory that would create approval dependence in subjects, overriding their own lifelong dispositions, and enduring just long enough for the experiment to take place. Though it is possible to imagine some experimental ways in which we might arouse an approval motive, they are pallid beside the results of the "experiments of nature" assessed by the need-for-approval scale.

The great potential weakness of R–R research, as we saw in Chapter 2, lies in failing to make the network of correlational relationships sufficiently tight so that alternative interpretations become highly improbable. How secure is the concept of the approval motive? Is there a viable competing alternative? Perhaps. The difference may be one principally of emphasis, but there is a competitor to the need for approval. Allaman, Joyce, and Crandall believe their childrearing evidence affirms an avoidance-of-disapproval concept. Thus, the motive is entirely fear-based, and such apparently positive, approval-seeking behavior as verbal conditioning is really engaged in to avoid expected censure. Which interpretation is correct? I am not inclined to dismiss the approval seeking (with which we first started), but Allaman, Joyce, and Crandall are equally insistent about the preeminence of fear and avoidance. We clearly need more studies. Allaman, Joyce, and Crandall suggest that we need to assess the anticipation or expectancy of approval or disapproval as well as the need. I agree that that would help to decide.

# 7 Internal Versus External Control of Reinforcement

## ABSTRACT

*The concept of internal versus external control of reinforcement refers to generalized beliefs or expectancies about the control of reinforcement. Internal control is the expectancy that one's own behavior determines rewards and punishments; external control that rewards and punishments are meted out by powerful and capricious others or by fate or luck. The study of internal versus external control began with experiments on learning in skill and chance situations. These learning studies were followed by the development of a personality scale to measure individual differences in expectancies of internal and external control. Thus, the concept became a dimension of personality, and its implications were extended to a broad band of social behavior and social learning in important life situations. We review and evaluate studies of internal versus external control in five major areas: (1) coping or avoiding; (2) being influenced and exerting influence; (3) achievement; (4) a belief system; and (5) the development of expectancies about the locus of control.*

## INTRODUCTION

It is sometimes helpful in designing an experiment to outline the procedures to some subjects and ask them how they would react. The purpose is to detect flaws in the experiment that only a subject's-eye view may reveal. To begin this chapter I would like to outline an experiment (Rotter, Liverant, & Crowne, 1961) to you, but for a different purpose. This is an experiment long

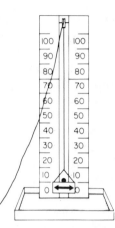

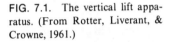
FIG. 7.1.  The vertical lift appa-
ratus. (From Rotter, Liverant, &
Crowne, 1961.)

since conducted; I shall try to give you a subject's perspective of it to see if the
core idea of the experiment comes across to you. You are going to see two
principal conditions of an experiment as subjects saw them—"see," that is,
through the medium of a verbal description.

You are escorted to a small cubicle where you see the apparatus shown in
Fig. 7.1. A small platform with the double-ended arrow on it rides in the
groove between the two upright panels. Connected to the platform is a pull
string that passes over a pulley at the top. A little steel ball rests in the center of
the platform. The experimenter gives you these instructions:

This experiment is to see how well you can succeed in raising this ball without its
falling off and also to see how accurate you are in estimating your success.

The object of this task is for you to try by pulling this string to raise the ball on
the platform as high as possible before the ball drops off. You will be given a
number of trials. The apparatus is built with a very slight tilt forward so that the
ball is more likely to fall off the platform the higher it is raised. Of course if you
raise the platform very quickly the ball can't drop off because of the momentum,
therefore the platform must be raised slowly. Now, in order to be clearly
successful you must score 80 or better on a given trial.

Before each trial I would also like you to estimate how certain you are that
you can succeed, that is, get 80 or better. You are to estimate your degree of
certainty of success on a scale going from 0 to 10. For example, if you feel fairly
sure that you will succeed, that is, that you will get 80 or higher, you may rate
yourself with a nine or ten. If you feel moderately sure that you will succeed you
may rate yourself with a 4, 5, or 6. If you feel pretty sure you will *not* be
successful, that is, not get 80, you may rate yourself with a 0 or 1. Use any
numbers on the scale (0, 1, 2, 3, 4, 5, 6, 7, 8, 9, 10) to indicate how successful or
unsuccessful you think you will be. It is important that you select your estimates
carefully on the 0 to 10 scale and that they correspond closely with how certain
you *really* are. They should be an accurate description of the degree to which
you really feel that you will or will not succeed.

Suppose that your scores for the first 14 trials run like this: 80, 60, 70, 80, 90, 60, 50, 90, 60, 40, 70, 60, 30, 70. . . . After trial 8, you no longer achieve success. What are your estimates of success on each trial after the 14th one? Write a series of trial numbers on a sheet of paper (15, 16, 17. . .), and for each trial put down your estimate of success. Continue until you have given two successive estimates of 0 or 1. Stop at this point, and note the number of the trial on which the second of the two successive estimates occurs.

Now, let's go to the other condition. This would not actually have happened if you had been a real subject in the experiment; each subject served in only one condition. For you to see the experiment, however, you will have to do double duty and risk a little contamination in your performance in the second condition from exposure to the first.

Again, you are taken to a small experimental room. This time, you are seated before a large screen or shield in the center of which is an opening covered by a small door. Your instructions are as follows:

> This experiment is to see how well you can do at telling me beforehand which of the two kinds of cards will be exposed in this opening [the experimenter points to the opening] and also to see how accurate you are in estimating your success.
>
> In this box [here, the experimenter shows you a box of cards] we have a large number of cards marked with either an X or an O.
>
> These cards are divided into sets of five. Each set has been *shuffled* and there are not necessarily the same number of X's and O's in each set. Each time I will select *at random* one of these sets of five cards and place it behind this closed shutter [the experimenter points to the opening; he then removes the box of cards]. You are to tell me whether the top card is an X or an O. After you tell me, this shutter will open and you will know whether you were right or wrong. I will remove that card and the next card in the set will be in front of the closed shutter and again you will tell me whether it is an X or an O. In this way we will go through a number of these sets of 5 cards. I will also be keeping score and will let you know how well you did at the end of each trial, that is, at the end of a set of five cards.
>
> Now in order to be successful on a trial you must get at least four or more cards right out of five. Four or five cards correct will mean that you have succeeded. Any number of cards correct below four will mean that you have *not* succeeded.

These are your scores: 5, 3, 2, 4, 5, 3, 1, 4, 2, 1, 3, 3, 0, 3. . . .

You are not successful on any trial after the eighth one. Give your estimates of success trial by trial, writing them down on a different sheet of paper, and of course don't look at your previous estimates. Continue until you have made two successive estimates of 0 or 1, and write down the number of the final trial.

There were in fact other conditions in the experiment, but the ones in which you have just "served" will give us the critical data we need. What was the experiment all about? It concerned the perception of skill or chance and the effects of believing one's performance to be due to one's own ability and effort or to external forces—luck or fate in the card-guessing task. We predicted that (1) persistence in the face of failure (called resistance to extinction), (2) the amount of increase or decrease in estimates of success (expectancies) following success or failure, and (3) "gambler's fallacy" expectancies (a failure increases the probability that a success will follow) would differ in the skill and chance conditions. We predicted also that these three expectancy measures would be affected by subjects' experiences of reinforcement on the skill or chance tasks.

We now need the other conditions of the experiment—the conditions you didn't "participate" in. The design of the experiment is represented in Table 7.1. On each task, there were four training conditions in which subjects got a prearranged reinforcement schedule—25%, 50%, etc. Scores on the first eight trials, and, indeed on every trial thereafter, were entirely controlled by the experimenter. This was necessary if we were to compare the effects of reinforcement history in skill and chance situations. How was this done? On the skill task, the platform made electrical contact via the metal grooves through which it moved. Concealed within the platform was an electromagnet, and fastened under the table was a battery. With the circuit on, the ball remained on the platform; interrupting the circuit immediately caused the little steel ball to fall. Beneath the table on which the apparatus rested was a lever-actuated switch that could be operated (silently) by a slight movement of the experimenter's leg. The deception had to be extraordinary if subjects were to believe that their scores were the result of their own skills. On the

TABLE 7.1
The Design of the Skill–Chance Experiment[a]

| Group | Training Trials | | | | | | | | |
|---|---|---|---|---|---|---|---|---|---|
| | 1 | 2 | 3 | 4 | 5 | 6 | 7 | 8 | |
| Skill | | | | | | | | | |
| Success in training | | | | | | | | | |
|   25% | + | − | − | − | − | − | − | + | |
|   50% | + | − | − | + | + | − | − | + | |
|   75% | + | + | − | + | + | − | + | + | Extinction |
|   100% | + | + | + | + | + | + | + | + | |
| Chance | | | | | | | | | for |
| Success in training | | | | | | | | | all |
|   25% | + | − | − | − | − | − | − | + | |
|   50% | + | − | − | + | + | − | − | + | Groups |
|   75% | + | + | − | + | + | − | + | + | |
|   100% | + | + | + | + | + | + | + | + | |

[a]Adapted from Rotter, Liverant, and Crowne (1961).

chance task, control of correct and incorrect guesses was achieved by the use of the single card with an X on one end and an O on the other. It slid in a groove just behind the small door. If the subject was supposed to be correct and had guessed X, the experimenter simply moved the card to the X end and opened the door for the subject to see.

## LEARNING AND THE CONTROL
## OF REINFORCEMENT

The experimental hypotheses were based on the idea that learning in skill and chance situations is quite different. If you believe that the occurrence of a reward (or, indeed, a punishment) is specifically related to your own behavior, the response–reward association will be stronger than if you believe the reinforcement is a matter of luck, fate, or the unpredictable behavior of others. Your expectancies about the connection between behavior and reinforcement reflect your beliefs about the task. In a skill situation, your expectancies are likely to follow the occurrence of success or failure pretty closely—increases after success and decreases when you have failed. Highly successful performance would strengthen your expectancy about the efficacy of your behavior; if there were now to be a series of failures, it would take some time for you to come to believe that your skill was lost or temporarily diminished. It would take a long time, that is, for you to extinguish. What about the case when you have been only partially successful—as an example, the 50% training schedule? The most likely belief to develop is that you are not very good at this particular skill, and if you now experience a succession of failures your expectancies will decline rapidly, and extinction of any expectancy of success will occur.

Chance tasks—let's call them *externally controlled* tasks—produce very different effects. After a series of successes you begin consistently to fail. You have not learned very much about the relation between your response and the reinforcement, and there is then little or nothing you can do in the way of changing your behavior to affect the outcome. You will soon arrive at the conclusion that your luck has changed or that somehow the situation has changed. You then extinguish. With partial reinforcement (e.g., 50% success) in externally controlled situations, it takes longer to detect the change when failures begin to occur since you have had experiences of failure. Thus, the effects of 100% and partial reinforcement on extinction in externallly controlled tasks should be the reverse of skill learning. Actually, the prediction for the externally controlled situation is based on a classic finding. It is called the partial reinforcement effect (see Lewis, 1960), and the general rule by which it operates is that training under partial or intermittent reinforcement produces greater resistance to extinction than continuous reinforcement.

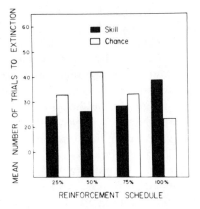

FIG. 7.2. The mean number of trials to extinction of the skill and chance groups under the four reinforcement schedules. (Adapted from Rotter, Liverant, & Crowne, 1961.)

The extinction findings are the most important part of the experiment; they are shown in Fig. 7.2. The data plotted are the mean number of trials to extinction of each group, and you can see that the schedules of reinforcement produced very different effects in the skill and chance situations. The chance task gave a typical partial reinforcement effect, most clearly seen in the comparison of the 50% and 100% groups. Skill-trained subjects produced a set of data points directly opposite to the partial reinforcement effect; the 100% group showed the greatest resistance to extinction.

Skill-trained subjects changed their expectancies in the direction of previous reinforcement (success or failure) to a greater extent than did chance-trained subjects. They were more responsive to the first success, and at each reinforcement schedule had higher expectancies on the last training trial than chance-trained subjects. The gambler's fallacy prediction was not borne out. We had no ready explanation for that at the time, and I have none now. A previous experiment by Phares (1957) had found more unusual shifts (up after success and down after failure) among subjects who were told the task was a matter of luck, and so this hypothesis probably requires another experiment.

Skill learning and learning under conditions of external control produce large differences in the expectancies people state. Are only verbal expectancies affected? The answer is no. Holden and Rotter (1962) investigated the resistance to extinction of skill and chance groups trained on a 50% reinforcement schedule by providing them with money to bet on each trial. Extinction occurred when the subject was no longer willing to bet, and the skill subjects quit first. There have been several other experiments in which the effects of skill and chance on extinction were studied. The findings are uniformly consistent with the Rotter, Liverant, and Crowne study.

What one learns about the consequences of his behavior and the functional value of learning are different in skill and chance situations. Phares (1962) designed a clever experiment that shows this clearly. He used a tachistoscope to expose nonsense syllables for very brief intervals. Subjects were told that some of the nonsense syllables would be followed by shock. There was a skill condition in which subjects were informed that the shock could be avoided by learning which of several buttons to press following the exposure of each nonsense syllable. In an externally controlled condition, the instructions were that any of the buttons might be pushed; whether or not shock occurred was a matter of chance. The two groups were equated for shock by running the skill group first and administering shocks to the chance group on the same trials and for the same nonsense syllables as the skill subjects received them. At the end of training the recognition thresholds of skill subjects had significantly decreased, while those of chance subjects had not. Phares interpreted this finding to mean that the skill subjects developed an expectancy that they could learn to avoid the shocks—an expectancy that led to more vigilant and effective perceptual responses. Subjects exposed to uncontrollable and unpredictable shock did not acquire such coping responses. In mild form, perhaps, they might be said to have been more helpless; although I wish to be properly cautious, there is the suggestive hint of a parallel between their behavior and the unadaptive helplessness of the dogs in Seligman's experiments that we reviewed in Chapter 4.

Learning situations in the laboratory and in daily life may be arrayed along a continuum that ranges from skill at one end to complete determination by external forces at the other—e.g., luck, fate, the exercise of control by powerful others, the unpredictable. This is a continuum of *perceived control*, for we are concerned with what people believe about the relation between their behavior and the occurrence of reinforcement. One's belief may represent the control of reinforcement accurately, but it is also possible to develop mistaken beliefs. Our "skill" task subjects did that, being fooled by its apparent requirement of motor steadiness. One could also inappropriately believe that a true skill is mostly a matter of luck; common expressions such as "a lucky break" and "I got lucky" suggest that people do sometimes think of skills as "a chancy business." What we have, then, is a continuum of belief in the *locus of control of reinforcement*. At one end, as we have noted, is the expectancy of *external control*: Reinforcement is not in one's own hands. At the other end is the expectancy that reinforcement occurs as a result of one's actions, abilities, or personal characteristics, and so this is a belief in *internal control*. Most learning situations are perceived to contain elements of both skill and chance; they occupy intermediate positions on the locus of control continuum. Thus, it is the relative expectancy of internal or external control that we need to consider.

## INTERNAL VERSUS EXTERNAL CONTROL AS A DIMENSION OF PERSONALITY

Generalized expectancies about causal relations between behavior and reinforcement are acquired in the course of cultural learning in a great variety of learning situations. We do not all acquire the same expectancies about the locus of control of reinforcement, however, even though we all go to school, learn about social relationships, develop motor skills, and have experiences with the accidental and unpredictable. There are important individual differences: Some people learn strong generalized expectancies in internal control, while others develop beliefs about a greater degree of external control in the same kinds of situations. This is to say that generalized expectancies about the locus of control of reinforcement constitute a dimension along which people vary, a personality dimension.

If a way of measuring expectancies about internal and external control could be devised, we might then study social learning and behavior to see the ways in which the attribution of control make a difference. We need a personality scale consisting of items about beliefs in internal or external control in a variety of situations. Some items will ask for endorsement of beliefs in the caprices of luck, fate, or the basic unpredictability of people; pitted against these will be items stressing the importance of care, effort, and skill in determining life events. There were some early efforts to construct such a personality scale, first by Phares (1957) and by James (1957), and to use it to predict expectancy changes in skill and chance tasks. The results of these studies were weak but encouraging: Endorsement of externally controlled test items was associated with less responsiveness to success and failure and with more unusual shifts. Thus, subjects identified by the personality scale as believing in external control tended to show the kinds of expectancy changes that are characteristic of learning in chance situations.

More careful test development followed, undertaken principally by Liverant. It appeared to Liverant that expectancies of internal or external control might be more successfully measured by a forced-choice method than by separate internal and external items. Forced choice pits alternatives against each other, and the respondent must select one or the other. This appeared to be an ideal way assess expectancies of internal or external control. Each item would consist of an internal and an external statement involving the same context and situation. If these statements were about equally socially desirable, the choice of one or the other would reflect belief about the locus of control. The test construction procedures were exhaustive; they included a careful assessment of the relation of each test item to a measure of social desirability and elimination of items with high correlations. The result was a personality measure called the I–E Scale, and some representative items from it are shown in Table 7.2.

As research on internal versus external control has proliferated, new I–E scales have been developed, especially scales for children. There are presently five I–E measures for use with children. We shall eventually have to consider the problem raised by these many devices for measuring the same variable: To what degree are they measuring the same thing?

TABLE 7.2
Some Representative Items from the I–E Scale[a]

I more strongly believe that:

2.a. Many of the unhappy things in people's lives are partly due to bad luck.
b. People's misfortunes result from the mistakes they make.

4.a. In the long run people get the respect they deserve in this world.
b. Unfortunately, an individual's worth often passes unrecognized no matter how hard he tries.

7.a. No matter how hard you try some people just don't like you.
b. People who can't get others to like them don't understand how to get along with others.

9.a. I have often found that what is going to happen will happen.
b. Trusting to fate has never turned out as well for me as making a decision to take a definite course of action.

12.a. The average citizen can have an influence in government decisions.
b. This world is run by the few people in power, and there is not much the little guy can do about it.

[a]From Rotter, 1966.

## COPING OR AVOIDING

The locus of control studies we have so far reviewed have been concerned with how behavior is acquired and changed in learning situations. The development of personality measures of internal versus external control was based on the belief that the learning studies could represent a major facet of the social learning that is responsible for the development of personality. The idea for those studies did not come originally from the psychology of learning but from clinical observations made in psychotherapy of patients who seem to make little behavioral progress. For these patients, there are always new difficulties that emerge, bad breaks, unpredictable happenings, or the uncontrollable actions of others to block important achievements. The patient doesn't seem to learn from experience or to be able to generalize from psychotherapeutically acquired insight. Behavior such as this is frequently seen, puzzling, and difficult to treat.

The concept of generalized expectancies about the locus of control of reinforcement helped to make sense of repetitive and self-defeating helplessness, and it also suggested that such behavior might be modified by a therapeutic focus on changing the patient's expectancies of external control. Because of the great complexity of psychotherapy, the learning studies were designed to test the expectancy hypotheses in controlled experimental situations. The powerful outcomes of these studies suggested that it would be worthwhile to extend the investigation of expectancies of internal and external control to realistic and ego-involving life situations and experiments.

Some of the first studies to be undertaken were based on the general hypothesis that expectancies of external control would lead to less effective coping—to passivity and inaction when faced with difficulties or barriers. On the other side, if one has learned that his own efforts can make a difference, he is more likely to attempt to change his situation when it doesn't meet his needs. What is needed to study the influence or internal versus external control expectancies on coping behavior are situations of manifest importance to the individual—ideally, situations that challenge his coping skills but also provide an avenue of least resistance.

## Coping with Hospital Confinement

One situation like this is to be in the hospital, especially in a hospital for such long-term, chronic diseases as tuberculosis. A tuberculosis patient is deprived of much of the control one is accustomed to exercise over one's life. Subject to the rules of an authoritative and bureaucratic staff, one is wholly dependent on experts whose opinions about one's case may or may not be fully divulged to the patient. There are things one can do to cope in this situation, or one can make little effort at all in the alienated belief that there is nothing that can be done to change things. This was the setting for a study by Seeman and Evans (1962) of internal versus external control and learning. From a large number of tuberculosis patients in several hospitals, a smaller sample of internals and externals (based on a division of I–E scores at the overall mean) was selected. These patients were carefully matched for education, occupation, and for specific experience in the hospital by pairing internals and externals from the same ward.

The measures were an abbreviated version of the I–E scale described earlier, and three "knowledge" scores. These were a test of information about tuberculosis, ratings by the staff of each patient's understanding of the illness, and an attitude scale assessing what Seeman and Evans called "subjective knowledge"—the patient's satisfaction with the amount and quality of information provided. On each measure, the internals and externals differed. The internals knew more about tuberculosis, had reputations among the staff for greater knowledge, and were *less* content with what they were told about their own illnesses.

These findings suggest more active coping with the fear, the restrictions, and the loss of personal control accompanying long confinement in a tuberculosis hospital: The internals learned more about the disease, about their own cases, and they demanded more information. As Seeman (1972) pointed out about this study, however, there is a problem. Strictly speaking, the causal link between internal versus external control and learning is a weak inference. Patients' failures to learn about their serious illnesses might have resulted in feelings of powerlessness, of external control; patients who were able to acquire satisfactory amounts of information felt more in command. Though the original interpretation may be more plausible, it is important to be able to rule out its competitor.

## A Coping Study with Reformatory Inmates

Therefore, a second study of institutional inmates followed, this time with prisoners in a reformatory. Seeman (1963) again examined internal versus external control and learning, but this time the measure of learning was a test of retention of new material presented to the subjects. Three kinds of information were presented to the prisoner-subjects: immediate, prison-relevant facts ("A survey at Chillicothe showed that 65% of the men had no disciplinary actions on their record."); parole-relevant facts ("In 60% of the cases where parole is delayed beyond the date set by the parole board, difficulty in arranging employment is the main reason for the delay."); and facts about future opportunities ("It's been estimated that the demand for unskilled workers will continue to decline in the 1960's, with the loss of about 2,500 such jobs per year."). A number of these information items, all randomly arranged, was given to the inmates "to get your reactions to some statements that are listed below. First, we'd like to get your judgment about how interesting these statements are. . . ." The subjects weren't told about the test of retention of the information that was to come immediately after the interest ratings—a multiple choice test based on the items. Springing the test like this controlled for the potential effect of such motives as pleasing the investigators that might have obscured the relation between internal versus external control and learning.

The inclusion of the three kinds of information had a clever purpose. The specific hypothesis was that internal and external inmates would differ only on the parole-related items; the internals would learn more of this information because of their general expectancies that they could plan for their futures. Neither the immediate nor the remote information involved possibilities of affecting one's life, and thus these items served as a control for intelligence, school achievement, criminal record, and whatever other variables might influence learning. Since only one set of information was relevant to the expectancy hypothesis, each patient would serve as his own control in the learning of the other two.

There was a correlation, small but significant, between the I–E scale and learning of the parole-related information and no relation to the other kinds of items. We should expect the I–E–parole-learning correlation to be small because expectancies of future control are only part of the behavior equation. One also has to *value* the goal itself (rehabilitation and parole) for the information to be personally relevant and worth learning. That is likely to be the case for men who are, as the prisoners say, "Square Johns," but not for the "Real Cons" who reject the whole intent of the reformatory. A division of the inmates into Square Johns and Real Cons was made from prison records, and the I–E–learning correlations were computed separately for the two groups. Again, the reformatory and remote information correlations were not significant, but there was a striking difference in the parole information correlation between the inmate groups. The Real Cons showed no relation between the I–E scale and learning, while a sizeable increase was seen for Square Johns.

## Prejudice and Social Action

In these two studies, coping behavior in situations entailing severe limits on the exercise of personal freedom and choice was related to expectancies of control. The studies revealed avenues through which a measure of control over important life events could be achieved. The next two studies we consider also entail these features. The situation, however, was a far more general one: the deprivations of freedom of choice and action and the degraded living conditions imposed by prejudice. The subjects were blacks in southern United States. These studies were undertaken at a time when the old, established order of discrimination and segregation was being challenged by concerted social protest. Protesters were often jailed, threatened with violence, and sometimes physically attacked. The question asked in these studies was whether involvement in social action against racial discrimination is influenced by expectancies of internal or external control.

In the first study, Gore and Rotter (1963) administered some personality measures, including the I–E scale, to students in a southern black college. Several weeks later, a confederate of the experimenters entered the classes in which the personality measures had been taken and solicited volunteers for civil rights action. He ended his appeal by passing out the forms seen in Fig. 7.3. One could express no interest at all or commit oneself to one or more degrees of social protest. The seriousness of any commitment to action is underscored by a footnote in Gore and Rotter's article: "Shortly before the time of testing, a large number of Negroes were arrested and placed in jail for a similar march on the state house of a nearby state [p. 62]."

The various categories of commitment do not lend themselves to the usual method of dividing scores on the personality measure into "highs" and "lows" and finding the mean value for each group on the behavioral measure; the categories are discrete, and combinations of them need to be considered to represent strong or weak commitment. So, Gore and Rotter used the categories to classify subjects and looked at the mean I–E scores of each one and of the combinations. Strong commitment is represented by categories B, C, and D, little or no commitment by A and E. The mean I–E score of those checking any of the strong categories was significantly more internal than that of the weak categories alone or combined. The single categories of A and C differed significantly as did E and C; in both cases, commitment was associated with more internal scores.

These differences are impressive: persons signing up to make some active protest against segregation are more internal. The commitments, however, consisted of check marks and signatures on slips of paper. Despite the

---

### Students for Freedom Rally

Please check any or all of our program in which you
would be willing to participate.
I would be interested in:                                          Check here:

(A)   Attending a rally for civil rights.                          _____

(B)   Signing a petition to go to local government
and/or news media calling for full and immediate
integration of all facilities throughout Florida.             _____

(C)   Joining a silent march to the capitol to demonstrate our plea for full and immediate integration
of all facilities throughout Florida.                         _____

(D)   Joining a Freedom Riders Group for a trip during
the break.                                                    _____

(E)   I would not be interested in participating in any of
the foregoing.                                                _____

Signature: _____

Address: _____

Tel. No.: _____

---

FIG. 7.3.   The form for eliciting commitment to social action. (From Gore &
Rotter, 1963.)

subject's intent and probable belief at that time that to sign anything of this
sort could be dangerous, no social *action* was yet involved. Strickland (1965a)
tested the coping–social-action hypothesis by comparing the I–E scores of
civil rights activists with the scores of uninvolved blacks. The activists were
members of the Student Nonviolent Coordinating Committee (SNCC) or
other similar civil rights groups. The degree of their commitment is suggested
by Strickland's observation that:

> Every active subject stated on the civil-rights questionnaire that he had
> participated in some phase of civil rights protest, such as voter registration, sit-
> ins, and demonstrations. The mean number of arrests per person in conjunction
> with civil rights activities was about five, with a range of zero to 62. Nineteen of
> the subjects answered that because of their involvement they had received
> threats of violence directed either at themselves or their families [p. 355].

The uninvolved group was made up of black students in three southern
colleges who were, according to professors in the classes in which they were
tested, largely inactive in the civil rights movement. Strickland found a

sizeable and significant difference in I–E scale scores between the two groups. The activists were more internal, and it is interesting to note that their mean I–E score is almost identical to the I–E means of the signers of the two most committed categories in Gore and Rotter's study.

## Socioeconomic Opportunity, Coping, and Internal–External Control

What can be said of the uncommitted subjects in Strickland's and Gore and Rotter's studies? Did belief in the external control of important life events contribute to their passive roles? That is certainly suggested by these findings, and in fact other studies show that people whose lives are marked by deprivation of opportunity believe more strongly in external control. There are several studies showing blacks to be generally more external than whites when other variables of potential influence were controlled. Among reformatory inmates (Lefcourt & Ladwig, 1965) and children matched on social class (Battle & Rotter, 1963), as examples, blacks hold more external beliefs. In the latter study, the most external scores were obtained by lower class black children—the group with the greatest disadvantages.

That social disadvantage and denial of opportunity are associated with external control is strongly demonstrated by two further studies. One of them (Jessor, Graves, Hanson, & Jessor, 1968) was a major research project examining the relations among sociocultural variables, personality, and deviant behavior. The subjects were members of the ethnic groups making up the population of a small southwestern Colorado town—"Anglos" (whites of English, German, or Italian extraction), Spanish, and Indians. The groups differ greatly in their access to the "opportunity structure." As Jessor et al. described it:

> There is a definite hierarchy in the community, with the Anglos occupying the dominant position and maintaining control over most of the community institutions and resources. The Spanish and Indians occupy minority positions, the Spanish being more accepted by the Anglos and less the object of prejudice and even hostility than the Indians. Economically, however, due to the tribe's substantial assets, the Indians are . . . significantly more advantaged than the Spanish [p. 14].

In stratified samples of adult members of these groups, I–E scale scores reflect access to opportunity. The Spanish had the most external mean I–E score of the three groups, and although the mean I–E score of the Indians did not differ much from the Anglos', the Anglos' were more internal. An index of objective access to opportunity correlated substantially (.50) with the I–E scale, greater opportunity going with internal scores. There was a tendency for parental beliefs to influence the expectancies of their children: A measure of mothers' teaching of internal versus external control to their children correlated significantly with the I-E scores of their high school children. Thus, the socioeconomic opportunity or disadvantage experienced by adults is seen in beliefs about the locus of control that are communicated in the socialization process to children.

Stephens and Delys (1973) reported that preschool children from disadvantaged homes are more external than middle class chidren, suggesting that some critical socializing experiences contributing to beliefs in internal or external control occur early in development. A previous study by these investigators found that children from families below a poverty income level tended to have more external beliefs than children whose families were just above it. In this group of studies, then, social and economic deprivation affect expectancies about the locus of control of reinforcement beginning in childhood. In adults, those expectancies are related to coping with personal or social adversity. That is not to suggest that socioeconomic conditions are the principal source of beliefs in internal or external control. They constitute one contributor, but we shall see in a later section that childrearing attitudes and practices in the family shape the child's expectancies.

## Smoking

We can round out the theme of coping behavior with some data on the relation of internal versus external control to smoking. The U. S. Surgeon General's report on the effects of smoking made very clear the adverse physical effects of tobacco. How would one cope with knowledge that smoking could pose a long term threat to health? The determinants of coping with awareness of the dangers are surely many (the degree of dependence on tobacco, belief in the evidence, reliance on the defense of denial, as examples); one of them should be internal versus external control. Internal expectancies ought to lead to avoidance of smoking in the first place or planful effort to quit. For the person with external beliefs, there is an obvious out: Whatever happens will be a matter of luck or fate. Since there are a lot of people around who smoke and haven't gotten ill . . .: the argument is a natural. Straits and Sechrest (1963) compared smokers and nonsmokers, finding the smokers to be more external. James, Woodruff, and Werner (1965) not only replicated this result but found that male smokers who quit and kept for a time their resolve to stay off were more internal than subjects, equally believing in the cigarette-smoking–cancer link, who continued to smoke.

## BEING INFLUENCED AND EXERTING INFLUENCE

One of the very earliest studies of internal versus external control investigated the hypothesis that externals should more readily conform to social influence (Odell, 1959). The tendency to passivity of external persons and their dispositions to believe that important events in their lives are controlled by forces outside themselves should make them more susceptible to manipulation. Odell found a significant relation between the I–E scale and an Independence of Judgment scale that Barron (1953) had shown to be related to social conformity.

## Conformity

The conformity hypothesis can be specified more exactly. External persons should find it especially difficult to resist pressures to conform even when they have a stake in the issue, when a price is exacted for conformity. This situation should challenge the confidence of externals in their own judgments, making them vulnerable to the influence of others. Internals, however, should strongly resist when it matters, and their trust in their own judgments should be little diminshed by conformity pressures. A test of this hypothesis could be accomplished by making independence more valuable and at the same time punishing conformity. We did that in an experiment (Crowne & Liverant, 1963) in which subjects bet money on the correctness of their judgments. The conformity situation was an adaptation of Asch's procedure: Subjects had to make perceptual judgments in the presence of others who announced their judgments first. The special feature of our experiment was the betting condition: Each participant was given a sizeable amount of money to bet with, and he could keep a proportion of his winnings. In the group were one true subject and four accomplices of the experimenter who made their judgments first, were unanimous in their incorrect judgments, and bet on them.

In this condition, external subjects conformed significantly more than internals, although in two other non-betting experimental conditions this difference was not found. There were differences in the amount bet by internal and external subjects. On those trials when externals successfully resisted the influence of the group, their bets were significantly smaller than on trials on which they yielded. Internals bet about the same, whether they remained independent or conformed. These betting results, then, suggest that the externals had little confidence in their judgments when they departed from the majority view. We should expect that from persons who tend to believe that they do not have much personal control over their lives.

## Subtle Social Influence

Social influence does not always involve the heavy, overt demands to step into line that conformity situations do, as we saw in the last chapter. Sometimes it is subtle in form, exacting small measures of compliance. Verbal conditioning experiments revealed the responsiveness of approval-dependent persons to subtle social influence, and they have also been used to test the hypothesis that internal control should entail resistance to perceived manipulation. Getter (1966) reinforced subjects for using words ending in -*ion* during the conditioning period of his experiment. This was followed by extinction, the experimenter now no longer making the reinforcing response. He divided his subjects into groups on the basis of their performance in the conditioning and extinction periods: conditioners, who showed an increase in the reinforced response class; nonconditioners, who failed to produce an increase; and *latent* conditioners, who increased their use of -*ion* words only in extinction. Conditioners were the most external and latent conditioners the most internal of the three groups. Getter proposed that:

> [The internally controlled latent conditioners] have negative feelings toward being manipulated. They are apparently attuned to the reinforcement contingency, since increment eventually occurs, but they do not allow themselves to show it. It is only during the subsequent extinction trial when they feel "on their own" that the conditioning is exhibited [p. 404].

Strickland (1970) divided the subjects in her verbal conditioning experiment into three major groups on the basis of a postexperimental interview: subjects who were unaware of the experimenter's subtle reinforcement; subjects who were aware and who acknowledged being influenced; and aware subjects who denied influence. In the aware–denied-influence group, those who did give evidence of conditioning had more external scores on the I–E scale than nonconditioners. As a whole, this group had the lowest (most internal) mean I–E score of the three. Though some of these subjects were in fact affected, they described themselves as immune to the influence.

A verbal conditioning experiment by Doctor (1971) investigated the responsiveness of internal and external subjects to subtle verbal reinforcements made by internal or external experimenters. He found no effect of the experimenter's locus of control, but external subjects who were aware of the reinforcement and response class did respond to the influence. Although these three subtle influence experiments used different procedures and varied somewhat in their findings, there is a consistent conclusion to be drawn from them. It strongly appears to be an internal characteristic to find subtle influence unpleasant and to resist it.

## Resistance to Influence

The internal's resistance doesn't seem to be simply a negativistic response to any influence attempt, as a study by Gore (1962) makes clear. She gave portions of the TAT to subjects, telling them that the research was to learn which cards yielded the longest stories. There were three experimental conditions, two involving influence and a control condition. One influence condition was obvious and direct: The experimenter openly indicated the card to which she thought longer stories would be told. The other was a subtle condition in which the experimenter presented the same card, smiled, and said, "Now, let's see what you can do with *this* one. " Internals and externals did not differ in the length of their TAT stories in the control and obvious conditions; they did in the subtle condition, the internals telling significantly shorter stories. Given what they perceive as a choice, internals may accept the influence attempt; when the influence is subtle, it seems to appear to them as manipulative, and if detected it is likely to be resisted. The findings of the James, Woodruff, and Werner study on smoking that concluded the section on coping are relevant here. The internals in that study responded favorably to the persuasion of the U. S. Surgeon General's report.

Are external persons generally and indiscriminately more open to influence, subtle or overt? An attitude change experiment by Ritchie and Phares (1969) suggests that they are not. Internal and external subjects were exposed to persuasive communications attributed to high or low prestige sources (the U. S. Secretary of the Treasury or a college student). The externals changed their attitudes, measured earlier in the experiment, more to the high than to the low prestige source. Internal subjects did modify their attitudes in comparison to a control group, but about equally to the two communications. It rather appears that they responded more to the content of the argument, while the externals were affected by the persuader's authority.

## Influencing Others

Turn the influence situation around and we have the question of effectiveness in influencing others. The hypothesis is clear enough: the internal person should be more persuasive than the external because of the general belief that people's behavior can be changed by thoughtful effort (the importance of thought, plans, effort is a theme that appears in many of the internal alternatives on the I–E scale). The best of several experiments is one by Phares (1965). Subjects with internal or external scores on the I–E scale were given the task of changing the attitudes of college students like themselves on such campus issues as requiring class attendance, the place of fraternities and sororities, and parking for student cars. Though the persuading subjects had to adhere to a script provided to them, which very likely minimized the possibilities for exerting influence, the internals were more successful in shifting the attitudes of their subjects than the externals. Indeed, the externals' subjects did not show reliable attitude change. What made the internals effective? Unfortunately, the strict control over the persuasive arguments, though important in keeping out unwanted variability in the influencers' attempts, masked what the internals did—and what the externals didn't or did less of. There is a hint about the differences between internals and externals from Doctor's verbal conditioning study (1971) mentioned earlier. Doctor didn't find his internal experimenters to be better conditioners

("There is a considerable difference," says Phares, 1976, "between saying 'Good' to a subject's verbal production and trying to influence a person by reading from a long prepared script [p. 67]"); he did, however, find them to be perceived differently by their subjects. On a device for measuring the semantic structure of language, the Semantic Differential, internal experimenters were judged by their own subjects to be more potent than external experimenters by their subjects. "Strong," "powerful," and "effective" are examples of attributes that might define potency. So, although the limiting conditions of the experiment did not permit the internals to elicit greater conditioning, their individual approaches to their subjects were apparently more forceful.

This set of influence experiments, together with the coping studies, forms a cornerstone of the locus of control data. The hypotheses about being influenced and exerting influence derive very explicitly from the concept, and they relate closely to the hypothesis of personal effectiveness that guided the coping studies. It was the encouraging results of the initial studies in these areas that led to seeking other correlates of beliefs in internal or external control.

## ACHIEVEMENT

If you believe in the instrumentality of your actions in attaining rewards and avoiding failures and punishments, you are likely to be concerned about mastery and accomplishment in situations that are important to you. If your belief is that luck or the uncontrollable behavior of others are often responsible, you may trust them rather than your own efforts. Further, because of the belief in external control, specific expectancies about the effect of your behavior on the occurrence of important reinforcements will not be strengthened. Thus, we readily derive the prediction that belief in an internal locus of control should be associated with higher school achievement. Let me express a caution, however. There are many determinants of achievement in school—intelligence and *need* to achieve and situational ones as well—so we ought not to expect the locus of control to contribute a large effect. We also need to recognize that the age of the subjects being studied will likely make a difference. In children, whose learning habits are less securely formed, internal or external expectancies should be more influential in shaping achievement behavior. Among college students, we shall mainly find those who successfully acquired a repertoire of achievement behavior; many externally controlled individuals who did not learn how to study and learn will no longer be represented. The external students in college have learned enough about the effort-achievement relation to survive or even to do well, and as a result we shall see a minimal internal–external control relation to achievement at this age level.

There is a large number of studies on the achievement hypothesis. One by Chance (1972) is a good example. She administered a locus-of-control scale

TABLE 7.3
Correlations Among Internal–External Control, Need for Achievement, IQ,
and Achievement Test Scores[a]

| | Internal–External Control | | Need for Achievement | |
|---|---|---|---|---|
| | Boys | Girls | Boys | Girls |
| IQ | .34* | .33* | .26* | −.13 |
| Achievement tests | | | | |
|   Reading | .50* | .45* | .01 | −.22 |
|   Arithmetic | .46* | .51* | .27* | −.27 |
|   Spelling | .56* | .38* | .22 | −.25 |
|   Need achievement | −.28* | −.44* | | |

[a]Adapted from Chance, 1972.
*Significant correlations.

specifically developed to measure achievement-related internal–external control beliefs (Crandall, Katkovsky, & Crandall, 1965) to a sizeable sample of school children in grades three through seven. The children were also given a projective measure of need achievement, and Chance had standardized achievement test scores for each child.

Her results, shown in Table 7.3, show quite powerful and generally consistent relations between the locus-of-control measure and IQ, specific areas of the achievement test, and need achievement. This internal–external control scale is scored in the internal direction, so that internal scores are associated with higher IQ and achievement. They are, curiously, related to *lower* need for achievement. The more typical finding with need for achievement is either to obtain no relationship or small but significant correlations in which internality and high need for achievement are associated (Odell, 1959; Wolk & DuCette, 1973). Chance thinks that her reversed finding has to do with the way independence training was carried out with the children in her study, who came from well-educated middle- and upper-middle-class families. The problem that interferes with the relation of internal–external control to need for achievement is, as Rotter (1966) proposes, that:

> People who are high on the need for achievement, in all probability, have some belief in their own ability or skill to determine the outcome of their efforts. The relationship is probably not linear, however, since a person high on motivation for achievement might not be equally high on a belief in internal control of reinforcement, and there may be many with a low need for achievement who still believe that their own behavior determines the kinds of reinforcements they obtain [p. 3].

Other achievement research has produced findings similar to Chance's, although some complications have emerged. The results are not uniform over the grade levels of the children studied. Crandall, Katkovsky, and Crandall

(1965) found belief in internal responsibility for (control of) achievement *success* to be a better predictor of standardized achievement test performance in third and fourth grade *girls,* while achievement test scores for fifth grade *boys* were better predicted by belief in internal responsibility for *failures.* Among older children, there were only occasionally significant correlations of internal–external control and scholastic achievement test scores. There is nothing in the expectancy construct itself to help us to explain these curious irregularities. The other major complication is that relations to achievement tests are generally higher and more consistent for boys than for girls (Crandall, Katkovsky, & Preston, 1962; Strickland, 1972). The results of the Chance study are discrepant. This difference is probably related to the commonly-obtained finding (cf. McClelland, Clark, Roby, & Atkinson, 1958) that feminine achievement is motivationally different and more complex than achievement in males.

A study by Nowicki (1973) suggests a resolution of this problem for internal versus external control. He reasoned that the typical socialization of girls entails a conflict between the conventional feminine role and achievement—a conflict that results in the minimization of achievement motivation and the control of achievement behavior by other, more affiliative motives. That conflict is likely to be especially acute for girls who are high in approval dependence, while those less concerned with approval may be freer to depart from the conventional mold and pursue achievement for its own intrinsic satisfaction. Only in the latter group, he argued, would there be a relation between expectancies of internal or external control and achievement. Among both third-grade children and college students given measures of internal–external control and need approval, Nowicki got strong confirmation of his hypothesis. Low need-for-approval internals had reliably higher achievement than approval-dependent externals; no difference appeared among high need-for-approval girls.

We need to note one other aspect of these school achievement findings. Internal–external control is consistently more highly related to school grades than to standardized achievement test scores (Crandall, Katkovsky, & Crandall, 1965; Phares, 1976). That makes sense if, as is surely the case, the grades given by teachers reflect the teachers' perceptions of attitudes and effort expended. Remember Doctor's finding of the differential judgments of internal and external experimenters by their subjects. It is plausible indeed that internal children may impress teachers with characteristics that influence their evaluation of achievement.

## Some Supporting Findings

There is a nice generality to the achievement data, as the following bits of evidence attest. Crandall, Katkovsky, and Preston (1962) found that the choice of intellectual activities in free play and persistence in them (the same sort of free-play situation as that in which need for approval was studied) is substantially associated with internal control in young boys. As Crandall, Katkovsky, and Crandall (1965) later said about these data, "The child who feels responsible for his successes and failures should show greater initiative in seeking rewards and greater persistence in the face of difficulty [p. 108]."

The internally-controlled person should reveal not only greater initiative and persistence: We should see other evidences of involvement in accomplishment as well. One of those evidences should be the time taken to decide when choices are important and depend on one's ability. Rotter and Mulry (1965) covertly timed subjects during the performance of a difficult perceptual judgment task. Half the subjects got instructions that despite the difficulty of the task, skill was an important factor in performance; half were told it was so hard as to make success a matter of luck. Internals took longer to decide than externals in the skill condition and were quicker than the externals in the chance condition. This finding rather suggests that the importance or value of skill-determined reinforcement is greater for the internally-controlled person than the value of lucky outcomes. The nearly equal decision times of external subjects in the two conditions suggests an indifference to this source of reinforcement.

Persistence and the ability to delay gratification were shown by Mischel, Zeiss, and Zeiss (1974) to be specifically and distinctively related to expectancies about the control of positive and negative reinforcements. Among young children, persistence in one experimental condition in which instrumental acts yielded a rewarding outcome was related to belief in the internal control of positive events. In another condition in which an aversive outcome could be prevented, persistence was related to belief in the internal control of negative events. I find such highly specific relationships as these compelling. It is not necessarily the case that one should hold consistent expectancies about the internal or external control of successes and failures. One could believe in personal responsibility for achievements but see the cause of failures as lying outside oneself. A general point is worth noting: The more specific predictions we are able to make, the more detailed the theoretical concept must be and the more thorough must be our understanding of the predictive situation.

## ASPECTS OF THE BELIEF SYSTEM

Ordinarily, if you want to know what someone believes you ask him. Formal psychological methods for investigating belief systems include attitude scales and interview techniques. To know about the more extended beliefs of internally or externally controlled persons, the usual procedure would be to administer attitude measures or an interview designed to assess the belief dimensions of interest. Collins (1974) did a thoughtful and creative study of the I–E scale; although intended as an analysis of the belief structure that is directly assessed by the scale, I think it is far more revealing. The import of some classical theory and research on the attribution of causality (Heider, 1944; 1958) suggested to Collins that the beliefs about the locus of control of reinforcement that define internal versus external control are more than two-dimensional. We do not see this in I–E scale scores as the test is usually given; we only obtain the respondent's relative position on internal versus external control. The concept of causality that is embodied in beliefs about internal or external control can be divided into two components: *Predictability* and *lawfulness versus chance* (there is regularity, order, and controllability in our own dispositions and in the events that confront us versus a more chaotic, unpredictable view in which uncertainty, fate, and luck reign); and *personal versus situational control* (important reinforcements are determined by personal attributes or by the nature of situations). One might believe, "I'm a lucky person," or one might believe in fateful control by outside forces. Then again, as Collins proposes:

> The world is equally predictable to a student who believes, "There is a direct connection between how hard I study and the grades I get [the internal alternative for (I–E) Item 23]," and the student who believes, "Professors always give good grades to people who complain about their test scores [a situational, hence external, attribution]." An observer endorsing either of these internal or external attributions should disagree with the statement, "Sometimes I can't understand how teachers arrive at the grades they give [...the external alternative for Item 23]." But one observer attributes the cause of grade assignment to some attribute within the student (trying hard, being smart, etc.), and the other observer finds the cause in some reliable attribute of the environment (professors' gullibility). [B]oth observers...[are internally controlled] in the sense that they can predict and control the grade they receive (by studying hard or by complaining about a grade) [p. 382].

The forced-choice pairing of internal and external alternatives in the I–E scale masks the complexity of the belief systems. Because internal (personal efficacy) and external (events out there) alternatives are pitted against each other as if they were logical opposites, the respondents can't show the dimensions along which their expectancies fall. Collins broke up the I–E scale into unpaired, individual items and added some new ones. The response options for each item on this new measure ranged from strongly agree (+3) to strongly disagree (–3), a procedure we call the Likert scale. Collins gave his revised I–E scale to a large number of subjects and then applied the technique of factor analysis to the responses to each item. Factor analysis reveals the pattern or clustering of the correlations among many measures. The output of the factor analysis of a test is a set of factors, each consisting of items that *inter*correlate more highly than they correlate with other items. The items defining a factor "load" on it; these factor loadings tell us that an item elicits responses that are consistent with the other items making up the factor. The number of factors varies according to the characteristics of the particular test.

Collins found a substantial general factor with loadings by each internal and external item save one. This factor describes internal versus external control as Liverant and Rotter intended to measure it. But he found four other factors defined by distinctive groupings of items.

1. *Belief in a difficult versus an easy world.* This factor is entirely made up of external alternatives, eleven of them, that reflect a view of life as hard, perplexing, and inscrutable. That is what you acknowledge if you agree with these items. As one item puts it, "Many times I feel that I have little influence over the things that happen to me." Rejection of these items implies that you believe there are things you can do to bring reinforcements under your own control. It is important to recognize, Collins points out, that "this factor is not to be equated with a belief in an unlawful world ruled by Lady Luck [p. 385]." Rather, "Misfortunes are caused by an attribute of the environment (task complexity), and this state of affairs prevents the respondent from controlling or manipulating his environment to seek reinforcement and avoid punishment [p. 390]."

2. *Belief in a just versus an unjust world.* Agreement with the eleven items defining this factor, most of them internal alternatives, expresses a belief in fairness and just recognition of effort (especially in the academic sphere) and dismissal of the idea that the cards are stacked against one. Collins suggests that from endorsement of this factor's items we may infer:

A belief in a just world [that] results from a combination of (a) internal attribution to effort and ability, (b) an external attribution of justice and equity in the environment, and (c) and admission of the importance of discriminative stimuli in the environment that specify the specific strategy appropriate for that specific environmental situation [p. 390].

3. *Belief in a predictable world versus one ruled by luck.* Six of the seven items of this factor feature the word "luck." Two items give the flavor of the contrasting views of the world that the extremes of this factor represent: "Many of the unhappy things in people's lives are partly due to bad luck;" "Getting people to do the right things depends upon ability; luck has little or nothing to do with it."

4. *Belief in political responsiveness versus the political steamroller.* This factor comes from the I–E scale items concerning the relation of citizens to politics and government. Internal alternatives show positive loadings, and external alternatives load negatively. We see a belief in the responsiveness of the political system or an opposing belief in its capriciousness and indifference ("This world is run by a few people in power, and there is not much the little guy can do about it").

It seems to me that Collins' analytic procedures have uncovered some quite differentiated beliefs that internals and externals may hold about causality, themselves, and their environments as they perceive them. To be internally controlled is to hold a set of beliefs that could not have been inferred simply from knowledge of a score on the I–E scale, and that is also the case for the external. The expectancies of internal and external control involve cognitions about self and about life situations that require the label "belief system" to characterize adequately.

There is little research on the belief systems of internals and externals. Collins' study suggests that there ought to be more. The factors that Collins discovered are robust and have been replicated in other analyses (Zuckerman & Gerbasi, 1977a; Zuckerman, Gerbasi, & Marion, 1977). Zuckerman and Gerbasi (1977b) believe, however, that the belief system is not as inclusive as the research of Collins and others implies. They argue that the dimensions of the belief system have been extended inappropriately to political and social attitudes and involvement, trust in others, the belief that people tend to get what they deserve, and firmness and forthrightness of beliefs and values. These things, according to Zuckerman and Gerbasi, are more legitmately considered to be correlates of belief in a just world than of internal–external control. Though it is proper to question unwarranted extensions of concepts (I shall raise that issue at the end of the chapter), expectancies about the locus of control could plausibly entail a belief system one of whose features concerns the justness of the world.

One bit of evidence we have fits neatly into the scheme discovered by Collins. Hamsher, Geller, and Rotter (1968) investigated the attitudes of internals and externals toward the Warren Commission Report on the assassination of President Kennedy. They administered an attitude questionnaire on the Report to introductory psychology classes that had some time previously completed the I–E scale. Among males, there was a strong tendency for internals to believe the conclusions of the Report and for externals to select the options implying a conspiratorial suppression of evidence. Hamsher, Geller, and Rotter also found a substantial correlation between the I–E scale and a measure of interpersonal trust (Rotter, 1967)— again, for males only—with the externals obtaining less trusting scores. It is not entirely clear to me why a relation between internal–external control and belief in the Report was not found for females (trust did predict for them). Among the males, however, the externals' belief in high malevolence could be aptly derived from unjust and politically unresponsive world beliefs. This is not Hamsher, Geller, and Rotter's view. They argue that it was a special and distinct group of "defensive" externals who disbelieved the Report— externals who blame "the system" in a projection of responsibility for their own feelings. I think a more consistent and parsimonious interpretation is afforded by Collins' belief-system analysis, but the question really needs to be answered by further data.

# THE DEVELOPMENT OF EXPECTANCIES
## ABOUT THE LOCUS OF CONTROL

The childhood origins of internal versus external control have been investigated by three procedures: interviews with mothers; retrospective reports of young adults of their parents' childrearing practices; and observations of maternal and child behavior like those used to study the development of need for approval. The results obtained with two of these methods, as we shall see, are reasonably consistent, but they differ in some important respects from the findings yielded by the third. Let's examine the studies in the order just given; then we can see if there is a possible way to reconcile the differences.

Chance's (1972) study of internal–external control and achievement that we reviewed earlier was also concerned with the childrearing antecedents of control expectancies. She conducted interviews with the mothers of each of her child subjects. These interviews were carefully structured procedures that yielded scores on maternal control, hostility–rejection, democratic attitudes, and independence training. Chance found that boys' expectancies of internal control were associated with earlier independence training and with less concern by their mothers about the need to control their children's behavior. The mothers of the internal boys also tended to be more highly educated. No significant relation between internal–external control and maternal attitudes was found among the girls.

Davis and Phares (1969) obtained retrospective reports of their parents' childrearing from college students; they also contacted their subjects' parents to get both I–E scores and a measure of childrearing attitudes from them. Internal and external subjects characterized their parents differently on two major dimensions—warmth and acceptance–rejection. The internals remembered their parents as having shown positive involvement to a greater degree than the externals, and less rejection, hostile control, and withdrawal. These findings were true of both males and females. When Davis and Phares examined the childrearing attitudes of the parents themselves, no relation could be found with their children's I–E scores. Neither was there a direct relation between the I–E scores of the parents and that of the child. That must have been surprising to Davis and Phares, and they next undertook a more complex analysis of their data. Perhaps children only come to resemble their parents in beliefs about the locus of control when childrearing attitudes and practices tend to foster identification. The subjects—parents and their children—were divided into groups differing in the similarity of parent–child I–E scores. Thus, for example, one group contained families with closely matched I–E scores, and another was made up of families in which the parents and children greatly diverged. The childrearing attitudes of the parents in the similar-score families were more indulgent and less strictly disciplinarian than the attitudes in different-score families. There needs to be a small reminder about this result: It applies equally to internal and external family resemblances and thus does not tell us anything about the distinctive things that parents do to create internal or external expectancies in their children.

Two studies of childrearing antecedents clearly stand out from the others because of their use of observations of mother–child interactions at home. These studies followed a plan nearly identical to the need-for-approval antecedents research that we considered in the last chapter, and in fact they were undertaken by the same research group. In the first of them, Katkovsky, Crandall, and Good (1967) obtained I–E scores on a group of elementary-school-age children who were members of the research sample of the Fels Institute. Home visit observations were rated on a large number of scales, and correlations with the children's I–E scores were determined. The mothers of internal children were judged to be more protective, nurturant, affectionate, and approving-rather-than-criticizing than the mothers of children holding external expectancies. The correlations were quite substantial for data of this sort and generally consistent for boys and girls. For boys and girls combined, the correlations were: protectiveness, .64; nurturance, .64; affection, .38; and approval, .57. Katkovsky, Crandall, and Good also interviewed mothers and rated these interviews on variables similar to those derived from the home observations. Only nurturance correlated with both boys' and girls' I–E scores; the only other relationship to be found was between parental rejection and daughter's I–E score. Rejection and criticism were associated with external beliefs. No ratings resembling Chance's assessment of independence training were made from either the home observations or the interviews. A rating of acceleration attempts was made from the observational data, but it failed to relate to internal–external control.

The other study was an even more ambitious effort to establish the relations of internal–external control to observed parent behavior. This research, by Crandall (1973), studied young adults whose parents had been observed in home visits years earlier when they were children. The observational data came from three periods in each child's life: birth to age 3, age 3 to 6, and age 6 to 10. The analysis consisted of correlations between the ratings on each maternal variable and the young adulthood scores of the offspring on two I–E scales. One was the standard I–E scale used in all the research with adults that we have reviewed (the Rotter scale, it is often called), and the other was a specially-devised scale of internal versus external expectancies concerning achievement and the mastery of skills. Tables 7.4 and 7.5 present samples of these correlations for each of the I–E scales. There is a somewhat different pattern of relationships for males and females, and it is quite evident that there are some important differences that distinguish these findings from other studies. Most of the significant correlations between maternal behavior and internal or external beliefs among the males involve the achievement I–E scale; for the girls, the general I–E scale yeilds the significant correlations.

Why should the relationships cluster in this way? First, we need the fact that the two I-E scales are not highly correlated, suggesting some degree of specificity in expectancies of control. Second, Crandall suggests the plausible hunch that the maternal antecedents of internal-external control in males might involve achievement because of the greater salience of achievement and skill development for them. For females, expectancies about the locus of control will range more generally over social relationships and beliefs about the regulation of human affairs. In what follows, it is important to note that Crandall treats the two I-E scales as measures of the same conceptual variable, ignoring the specificity found among the males. It would be reassuring to have some data to support the legitimacy of doing that, but there

TABLE 7.4

Correlations Between the I-E Scale[b] and Ratings of
Observed Parent Behavior in Childhood[a]

| | | Correlation for | | |
|---|---|---|---|---|
| Age | Variable Name | Males | Females | Combined |
| 0–3 years | | | | |
| Maternal reward of dependency | | –.16[b] | –.43* | –.20 |
| Maternal intentional independence training | | .14 | .50* | .25 |
| Maternal affection | | –.08 | –.46* | –.22 |
| Severity of penalties | | .07 | .39* | .15 |
| 3–6 years | | | | |
| Maternal participation with child in achievement activities | | not rated | .82* | — |
| Intensity of contact | | –.29* | –.16 | –.24* |
| Maternal affection | | –.28 | –.36 | –.32* |
| Maternal criticism of child | | .24 | .53* | .36* |
| Direction of criticism (high rating = approval) | | –.32* | –.37* | –.34* |
| Maternal intentional independence training | | .26 | .45 | .32* |
| 6–10 years | | | | |
| Maternal value for child's motor ability | | –.03 | –.79* | –.14 |
| Affection | | .08 | –.46* | –.13 |
| Direction of criticism (high rating = approval) | | .11 | –.46* | –.13 |
| Intensity of contact | | –.01 | –.56* | –.20 |
| Adjustment of home | | .04 | –.44* | –.12 |

[a]Adapted from Crandall, 1973.
[b]High scores on the I-E scale indicate internal control.
*Significant correlations.

TABLE 7.5

Correlations Between the Achievement Responsibility Scale[b] and
Ratings of Observed Parent Behavior in Childhood[a]

| Age | Variable Name | Correlation for | | |
|-----|---------------|-------|---------|----------|
| | | Males | Females | Combined |
| 0–3 years | | | | |
| | Maternal value for child's motor ability | −.18[b] | −.52* | −.31* |
| | Adjustment of home | −.13 | −.46* | −.24 |
| | Direction of criticism (high rating = approval) | −.42* | .11 | −.23 |
| | Intensity of contact | −.38* | −.08 | −.22 |
| 3–6 years | | | | |
| | Adjustment of home | .06 | −.52* | −.14 |
| | Intensity of contact | −.36* | −.09 | −.28* |
| | Direction of criticism (high rating = approval) | −.48* | −.05 | −.34* |
| | Maternal affection | −.44* | .11 | −.20 |
| | Maternal criticism of child | .49* | .26 | .39* |
| | Maternal intentional independence training | .35 | .32 | .36* |
| | Maternal reward of dependency | −.26 | −.38 | −.31* |
| 6–10 years | | | | |
| | Clarity of policy | −.30* | .39* | −.04 |
| | Justification of policy | −.27 | −.47* | −.34* |
| | Intensity of contact | −.27 | −.50* | −.34* |
| | Maternal participation with child in achievement activities | −.15 | .77* | .24 |

[a]Adapted from Crandall, 1973.
[b]High scores on the Achievement Responsibility Scale indicate internal control.
*Significant correlations.

aren't any that clarify the male–female differences. We shall have to accept provisionally that both scales are equivalent measures of internal–external control.

Crandall's interpretation of her results begins with an expression of surprise. Her interpretation, however, is a credible one, and it helps to reconcile some of the divergences in the earlier data.

Like the findings of others' investigations, our own previous study of I–E in childhood (Katkovsky, et al., 1967) had shown *positive* maternal antecedents. Since that study had been conducted with a Fels [Research Institute] sample very similar to the present one and had used the same sort of observed maternal data, we began to conclude that the explanation for the antecedent reversal must lie in the difference in the ages of the subjects when internal–external perceptions were assessed. It may be that warm, protective, supportive maternal behaviors are necessary for the assumption of personal responsibility during childhood, but in the long run, militate against internality at maturity. Perhaps internality at later developmental stages is best facilitated by some degree of maternal "coolness", criticality, and stress, so that offspring were not allowed to rely on overly indulgent affective relationships with their mothers, but were forced to learn objective cause–effect contingencies, adjust to them, and recognize their own instrumentality in causing those outcomes [p. 11].

The hypothesis that Crandall offers proposes that nurturance and warmth and the security they foster are necessary for the development of internal expectancies only *in young children.* For internal beliefs to become a stable and lasting feature of adult personality, however, a critical requirement is relatively early and consistent independence training. In effect, the internals' mothers may need to say, quite coolly: "Get out of my hair and go do something, kid!" This kind of mother may generally tend to insist that her child encounter the reasonable consequences of his or her actions, good and bad, leading to the development of expectancies about the instrumental effects of his or her behavior.

If independence training and some degree of withholding of nurturance, warmth, and approval are necessary for the enduring acquisition of internal control, why is it that internals as young adults remember their parents as having been warm and accepting? Crandall does not have a hypothesis, and I can only suggest that perhaps the coolness and criticality and the intentional push toward independence that she found were relative and that the internal young adult is able to detect the generous and loving *intent* of his or her parents. I suspect that we are stuck with some measure of uncertainty here for a considerable period of time to come. There is going to be great difficulty in replicating these findings because of the rarity of longitudinal observational data.

Although there are some imporant consistencies in the findings of these childrearing antecedent studies, it would be well to conclude this section with two cautions mentioned in the last chapter. I hope that in ending this way the reader will not feel I am being unduly severe or carping over minor issues. It needs to be said that the childrearing attitude/practice interview with parents is not a powerful technique. The problem is that we cannot be sure that parents characterize their actual behavior toward their children accurately. The same must be said for retrospective acounts of parental childrearing by their offspring. Though we may find consistency between personality test scores and characterizations of parent attitudes and behavior, it is difficult to know whether the reported attitudes and practices were actual or reflect some consistent disposition in the subject in the characterization of himself and others. For example, is the tendency of externals to view their parents as having been rather cold, disapproving, and unnurturant a conceivable expression of a general belief that others in authority tend to be unjust, or is it perhaps an attribution of blame for their own perceived failures? It is critical to our understanding to be able to distinguish between what parents really did, the feelings and attitudes they reflected, and such beliefs of the recallers.

## SOME SUMMARY COMMENTS

In a critical analysis of research on internal versus external control, Rotter (1975) reported finding over 600 published studies, and there are no signs of diminishing interest. The concept, the instruments to measure it, and the initial studies clearly struck a responsive chord in personality psychology. The early research on internal–external control is a model of the best we can do in the study of personality dispositions, and that may account in part for the great appeal. It must be said, however, that a burgeoning literature has produced some misconceptions and raised some issues.

On the positive side, I believe the research strategy was a creative and effective one. It has some of the distinguishing features of the study of conflict that we reviewed in Chapter 3. Like the experimental analysis of conflict, research on internal versus external control began with clinical observations about the behavior of patients. These observations were interpreted and expressed by a theoretical concept—the concept of expectancy. The very first studies were experiments on learning and extinction, because of the important implications for behavior change that grew out of the theoretical analysis. As Rotter (1975) says:

> Our interest in this variable developed because of the persistent observation that increments and decrements in expectancies following reinforcement appeared to vary systematically, depending on the nature of the situation and also as a consistent characteristic of the particular person who was being reinforced. We were interested, in other words, in a variable that might correct or help us to refine our prediction of how reinforcements change expectancies [p. 56].

The powerful and consistent results of those experiments encouraged the development of personality measures to assess generalized expectancies about the control of reinforcement. From the very beginning, internal–external control was conceived of both as a personality disposition and as an attribute of situations leading to beliefs about the locus of control of reinforcement. The concept and a good bit of the research well reflect the point about situation–person interactions made in Chapter 1.

Many of the individual difference studies are models of the use of significant life situations in which to explore the role of personality variables. The tuberculosis hospital and reformatory studies and the civil-rights–social-action research are elegant examples of the use of field study methods in the investigation of personality. They made full use of the sophisticated analysis of personality disposition–situation interaction afforded by the expectancy concept.

These noteworthy accomplishments have been paralleled by the emergence of some problems. They have to do with the measurement of internal–external control, with the kinds of predictions that may be made and the level of predictability, and with the ways in which the concept is interpreted.

## Measurement

Some time ago, I was the discussant at a symposium on recent developments in research on the locus of control. One of the things that impressed me in reviewing the research was the proliferation of measures of internal–external control and an unfortunate consequence of that. What I said then I should like to repeat here as a critique of the assessment of locus of control expectancies.

Three of the papers presented alluded to the problem of obtaining results with one measure of I–E but not with another, or finding substantial differences between the results with one I–E scale and another. In one paper, this is interpreted as evidence of the multidimensionality of locus of control expectancies, and its author is hopeful about it. In another, divergent results from two adult I–E scales are thought to stem from the generality of one measure and the specific assessment of achievement-related expectancies by the other. The author of a third paper is distressed by these discrepancies, and so am I. Whatever the several things are that are being measured by the several I–E scales, we still lump them all together under the same rubric, and only after the fact do we make any gesture toward the acknowledgment of discrepant findings and what they might mean. Our history suggests that what we then do is to revert to our summary trait label, as if the disquieting contradiciton had never appeared.

Fiske (1973) has recently pointed to exactly this problem, and the seriousness with which he regards it is evident in his title: "Can a personality construct be validated empirically?" Fiske delineates the problem very sharply and clearly.

> The investigation of construct validity must study a construct–operation unit, not a construct and some casually selected procedure for its measurement. The specific measuring procedure must be involved integrally in the total conceptual formulation being subjected to the empirical test. If an investigator seeks to validate a construct and its abstract conceptualized relationships to other constructs, he may find that he obtains positive support when he uses one measuring procedure but no support when using another. Hence the delineation of the construct must itself identify at least one (and preferably more than one) specific measuring operation congruent with the conceptualization [p. 89].

In an earlier paper, Fiske (1971) had argued for an "extrinsic convergent validation": "that concept," he said, "refers to estimating the degree to which two measuring operations can be said to be interchangeable, as determined by comparing their profiles of correlations with other variables [p. 245]." Some of the data presented here, and other studies as well, indicate that we may be nudging uncomfortably close to diverging profiles . . . and thus to diverging concepts. One paper has taken a promising step in pointing to the possible sources of variation among the various measures of I–E. But it does not seem reasonable to me to continue to identify competence and mastery expectancies, self-attribution of responsibility, and an active–instrumental versus passive–wishful cognitive style by the same singular label. As Fiske (1973) goes on to say, "The empirical investigation of construct validity assesses the validity of the integration of the method with the construct, that is, the validity of that form of the construct which is measured by the test [p. 92]." The articulation of the various possible meanings of I–E has not been worked out theoretically, and the operational differences and disparities of profiles might, strictly speaking, be taken to suggest that we have several concepts.

In the four years that have elapsed since I made those remarks nothing has happened to change my view; I believe that the investigation of internal–external control would greatly profit by careful articulation of its measuring instruments. What was said in Chapter 2 about the derivation of response measures of personality variables applies no less to internal–external control than to anxiety.

## Predictions and Predictability

The enthusiasm that greets a popular concept often results in unwise and overgeneralized extensions of its implications. The genuine limits on the predictions entailed by the theoretical concept are not recognized, and greater generality and a higher level of predictability than are truly warranted come to be expected. In the flush of high zeal, no one wants to be reminded of limits and cautions, of the necessity of carefully parsing the concept to make sure that its response elements are well understood. But the alternatives are a literature padded with weak, probably unreplicable, and theoretically unrepresentative findings, and a growing discouragement from the accretion of negative results that must follow from ill-conceived studies. Some of the large body of research on internal–external control is faulted by inattention to the concept of generalized expectancy. It would be difficult to find clear theoretical support for a prediction relating expectancies of internal or external control to hypnotic suggestibility, although I recently encountered a study attempting that. The results were weak and to my eye inconclusive, and I am not surprised. Response to hypnotic suggestions does not seem to entail *expectancies about the control of reinforcement,* and I suspect that the investigators in this particular piece of research were guilty of taking the name of the variable—external control—far too literally.

The other problem that needs to concern us is the inappropriate expectation of highly accurate prediction. Internal versus external control is a *generalized* expectancy, and its level of predictability in any specific situation must necessarily be limited. Conformity, social action, and achievement are examples of complex behavior with many determinants. Internal–external control is but one variable among many that may play a role. In addition, as Rotter (1975) points out:

> Some measure of a very broad generalized expectancy allows prediction in a large number of different situations, but at a low level. A narrower or more specific generalized expectancy should allow greater prediction for a situation of the same subclass but poorer prediction for other kinds of situations that are nevertheless to some degree similar [p. 59].

There is an inescapable trade-off between specificity and generality, and one's purposes must determine which will be pursued. If the goal is to develop a network of relationships to establish the validity of a theoretical construct, predictive accuracy must give way to predictive generality, because in this case we seek *lawful relationships* rather than specific prediction of the behavior of individual subjects.

## "Good Guys" and "Bad Guys"

We personality psychologists seem to have a tendency that at times borders on the uncontrollable to lapse into a good-guys–bad-guys sort of thinking about our variables. In most individual differences research, there are clear value implications about which end of the dimension is healthier, more adaptive, perhaps personally more appealing. These value-laden judgments are difficult to avoid, but they may seriously interfere with objectivity. Many of the behavioral consequences of a belief in external control pretty clearly imply that it would be far preferable to be an "internal." Such thinking, however, reveals that we have fallen into a trap, confusing a *dimension of expectancies* with a personality typology. There really *is* no such thing as an "internal" or an "external," and we must be scrupulously careful to keep that recognition distinct. What we are after is an objective analysis of a set of beliefs about how reinforcing events are controlled, the antecedents of those beliefs, and the consequences of them. Though we many hold personal preferences about desirable and undesirable beliefs, a disciplined regard for a science of personality rather mandates that preferences not intrude on research and the interpretation of findings. There is a robustness to the concept of internal versus external control of reinforcement. It doesn't need any boost or body English from sources that should remain outside of science.

# 8 Personality Research in Perspective

## ABSTRACT

*The six areas of research covered in the preceding chapters do not represent all the numerous and varied concerns of experimental research in personality. There are several senses, however, in which they can be taken as representative. We can find in them some important characteristics of contemporary research in personality, some of the most commendable features of personality research, and we can also see certain problems of method and conceptualization that have been persistent sources of bedevilment.*

*This chapter is about the specific ways in which the six areas do represent the larger whole of experimental research in personality. We shall begin with some substantive characteristics of personality research, turn to questions of method and research strategy, and conclude by examining our research areas for hints about where personality research may be going.*

## SOME SUBSTANTIVE CHARACTERISTICS

### Origins

French and Viennese psychiatry gave personality theory its beginning toward the end of the 19th century, as we saw in Chapter 1, and it was in a clinical context that personality research originated. Clinical concerns are still powerfully influential; they are seen in theoretical concepts and the problems we choose to investigate, and in the application of personality theory and research the clinical area is paramount.

218

The clinical origins of research in personality are represented by chapters on anxiety, conflict, stress, and repression. These are among the classical problems in the understanding and treatment of disturbed behavior, and the extent of research devoted to them reveals the intimate liaison of personality theory and research with abnormal psychology. Though research on some specific areas has abated (for example, repression and conflict), clinical involvement is still very evident. Research on anxiety and stress is ongoing and vigorous, and there is strong interest in current research on such clinically relevant problems as self-esteem, aggression, depression and hopelessness, and fear of success in women.

The significant interest of personality psychology in *individual differences* is seen in the chapters on need-for-approval and internal versus external control. A major portion of the research on anxiety and some of the repression studies as well, have assessed differences between persons in these variables, relating them to theoretically prescribed consequences—conditioning and learning, or memory failure. These individual difference studies are correlational, employing R–R research designs. This individual differences emphasis would not exist without the R–R strategy. Despite the problems that correlational analysis raises for solid theoretical inference—problems that we discussed in Chapter 2 and will encounter again later in this chapter—R–R research design is a strong tradition in the experimental study of personality. R–R research is on firmer ground now in both conceptualization and application, for reasons to be discussed below, and thus the place of individual differences in personality study is secure.

## Two Contemporary Emphases

The experimental study of personality is a huge enterprise, its diversity only hinted at by the research we have reviewed. There are many conceptual emphases; two especially prominent ones appear in the chapters on stress and internal versus external control. The first of these is a contemporary concern for *cognitive processes* and a cognitive emphasis in the study of coping or avoiding.

In the past, investigators tended to explore the debilitating effects of personality dispositions, usually clinically conceived ones. Much of the research on repression and anxiety, for example, was of this type. In a variant of this theme, the facilitating qualities of such dimensions as need for achievement were the focus of investigation. These were really studies of the behavioral *outcomes* of personality dispositions, often conceived along an abnormal–normal dimension. There was thus a prevailing concern to demonstrate the consequences of being anxious, repressive, etc., with quite nakedly evaluative interpretations of the data. Little attention was devoted to the *processes* involved, to the ways in which cognitive activity is modified and contributes to behavioral outcomes. This was a severely limiting approach to personality study, and the current emphasis is a considerable advance.

The complex cognitive processes that stress research has shown to be involved in the appraisal of stress and the great range of stress response— coping/avoiding behavior, affective responses, and somatic responses—that are mediated by those cogntive processes clearly show the current emphasis and the accomplishments in understanding that it makes possible. The cognitive components of internally and externally controlled belief systems also well exemplify cognitive personality psychology. The concept of expectancy itself as an anticipation or subjective probability about the consequences of one's behavior is a cognitive process concept. It leads naturally to a concern for the mediating role of expectancies in the way people categorize situations and in the choice of behavior, and it discourages the crude caricature of behavioral outcomes (except, perhaps, for some poorly informed investigators who simply haven't grasped these implications). A distinctive characteristic of the research on internal versus external control is its stress on the ways in which the process concept of expectancy mediates learning, belief, and action in a variety of situations. This cognitive emphasis is a pervasive one. A major behavioral analysis of personality that appeared a short while ago was titled, "Toward a cognitive social learning recon- ceptualization of personality" (Mischel, 1973); it gives a decisive role to expectancy concepts in determining behavior and in accounting for the importance of situational influences. Table 8.1 shows the cognitive variables that Mischel regards as critical to an understanding of individual behavior. Bowers (1973), one of several critics of Mischel's analysis, has based his own argument on a cognitive approach emphasizing "cognition as an organizing structure that determines our perception and knowledge of reality [p. 333]." Beyond the polemics, the interest in cognitive processes is encouraging. We simply could not have remained at the level of behavioral correlate or outcome analysis.

TABLE 8.1
Cognitive Social Learning Variables Important to the Prediction of Individual Behavior[a]

1. *Construction competencies:* Ability to construct (generate) particular cognitions and behaviors. Related to measures of IQ, social and cognitive (mental) maturity and competence, ego development, social–intellectual achievements and skills. Refers to what the subject knows and *can* do.
2. *Encoding strategies and personal constructs:* units for categorizing events and for self- descriptions.
3. *Behavior-outcome and stimulus-outcome expectancies:* specific expectancies about the consequences of different behavioral possibilities in [specific situations]; stimuli ("signs") [that] essentiallly "predict" for the person other events that are likely to occur.
4. *Subjective stimulus values:* motivating and arousing stimuli, incentives, and aversions.
5. *Self-regulatory systems and plans:* rules and self-reactions for performance and for the organization of complex behavior sequences.

[a]From Mischel, 1973.

The second emphasis is the concern for the developmental origins of personality concepts, as seen in the childrearing antecedent studies of need for approval and internal–external control. This emphasis is not reflected in a large number of studies, for there are special difficulties to the investigation of the developmental antecedents of personality variables, as we saw in the discussion of the need for approval and internal–external control research. There are the problems of reliability and validity that plague retrospective reports of childrearing. Neither those who rear nor those who are reared may—or may be able to—tell us in accurate detail what actually happened. There are unusual problems of access to behavioral observation of parent–child interaction. There is the difficulty of conceptualizing the antecedents—formulating hypotheses to guide investigation and to subject to specific test; personality theory and miniature theoretical concepts are not very explicit about antecedent events. There is the long time span to face when longitudinal studies are contemplated, and there is the problem of replication, often simply not feasible to attempt. These difficulties are in addition to those that center on the establishment of a network of correlations that will yield unambiguous interpretation—the difficulties that challenge R–R research generally. Despite these formidable obstacles, there are psychologists and research institutes willing to endure them for the impressive advances in our understanding of personality concepts that these studies can bring.

The developmental emphasis is also seen in investigations of personality variables in children. The construction of scales to measure need for approval and internal versus external control in children and the extensive body of experimental research that has followed exemplify this aspect of the concern for personality development. Experimental studies of personality routinely appear in the pages of the major developmental journals, and one may often find personality studies of children in the *Journal of Personality* and the *Journal of Personality and Social Psychology*. The experiments are mainly cross-sectional, studying samples of children of different ages. Only rarely is there a longitudinal investigation permitting study of stability or change in the personality disposition. In this emphasis we see a healthy departure from our longstanding reliance on accessible populations of college sophomores and the static view of personality implied by the study of a single age group in a common cultural context.

## METHODS AND RESEARCH STRATEGIES

### The Use of Naturalistic and Clinical Settings

We noted above that clinical contexts have been an important source of concepts and research problems in personality. Hypotheses and research questions have also come from naturalistic settings—patients facing surgery, the awesomely stressful experience of the concentration camp (Bettelheim, 1943), indeed even the society at large that suggested parallels between the alienation produced by mass society and the expectancy of extenal control. Among the research areas that we have reviewed, conflict, stress, and internal–external control stand out in their creative use of complex life situations and of psychotherapy to develop important theoretical analyses.

Naturalistic and clinical settings have been ingeniously used to test hypotheses. The analysis of conflict and displacement in psychotherapy, the study of conflict in sport parachutists, the surgery stress research of Janis (1958), and the hospital, reformatory, and community studies of internal–external control are fine examples. These investigations have several distinguishing features. Clinical studies such as Murray's (1954) analysis of conflict and displacement in psychotherapy show well-conceived categories of patient responses, accurately translating conflict and displacement theory into operational terms, and clear predictions from conflict/displacement theory. The same care in theoretical derivation and the analysis of interview responses is evident in Janis' (1958) study of the work of worrying. Conflict-based displacement is not easy to recognize, nor are the cognitive processes of coping with anticipatory fear and their delayed postoperative effects.

The selection of compelling life situations clearly marks the parachuting conflict research and the learning–information-seeking and social action studies of internal–external control. We also see in these investigations the effective use of control procedures to isolate the effects of the variables studied—the assessment of parachute jumpers at a remote interval and on the day of the jump, and the learning of material of varying relevance, as examples. Indeed, the adequacy of the controls in these studies suggests that in naturalistic or field research—or, for that matter, clinical research—weak and ineffective control procedures are not inevitable.

Finally, these studies are distinguished by the careful choice of dependent measures—the measurement of drive arousal to parachute-jumping–related stimuli and the assessment of fantasy responses to reveal the ways in which fear is handled, or the use of incidental learning as a means of assessing one of the consequences of expectancies about personal control. What we see in these life setting and clinical studies, then, is the highly inventive application in challenging circumstances of those procedures that make for a powerful and informative experiment.

## S-R Research Design

We dealt with the logic and strategy of S–R research design in Chapter 2 and have seen many examples in the subsequent chapters. Though it should not be necessary to defend S–R design, it has come under sharp attack from some person-oriented psychologists sympathetic to the pursuit of individual differences (Bowers, 1973; Carlson, 1971). To Bowers, "the experimental method as generally employed is differentially sensitive to the impact of situations, and correspondingly insensitive to organismic variables [p. 309]." Carlson takes to task our current methods for the limitations they impose on the questions we may set for inquiry:

> We cannot study the organization of personality because we know at most one or two "facts" about any subject. We cannot study the stability of personality, nor its development over epochs of life, because we see our subjects for an hour. We cannot study the problems or capacities of the mature individual, because we study late adolescents. We cannot study psychosexuality, because we avoid looking at distinctive qualities of masculinity and femininity as a focal problem. We cannot study how persons strive for their important goals, because we elect to induce motivational sets. We cannot study constitutional, temperamental variables because (apart from a few glances at increments in galvanic skin response under stress) we do not consider biological bases of personality. We cannot study the development and power of friendship—nor the course of true love—because we choose to manipulate interpersonal attraction. . . . Personality psychology would seem to be paying an exorbitant price in potential knowledge for the security afforded by preserving norms of convenience and methodological orthodoxy [p. 207].

Though persuasive, I belive the criticisms are unfair to the intelligently conceived, designed, and executed experiment in the true Galilean tradition for two reasons. One, set forth by Postman (1955), defends the experiment thus:

> Even if we were to agree, then, that the purpose of psychology is to systematize our knowledge of behavior as it occurs in the organism's habitat, it does not follow that the analysis and explanation of such behavior can be pursued only under "natural" conditions. In behavior analysis, as in problem solving, the *detour principle* may provide the optimal road to solution. By turning our backs on the complexities of behavior in the organism's natural habitat we may arrive more speedily at useful tools of analysis than if we allow ourselves to be guided by the apparent lack of uniformity in daily behavior [p. 218].

In the same vein, there is the point Miller made to explain the use of simplified experimental analogues in testing the propositions of conflict theory: It is often more advantageous to work out the laws governing a phenomenon in well-controlled experimental situations before trying to observe their operation in complex, difficult-to-control life situations. Note that I, like Miller, did not say that it is *always* more advantageous; there is no conflict with the discussion above about naturalistic and clinical research.

   The other reason has to do with the genuine interplay of naturalistic or clinical observation and the experimental study of personality, or the interplay of S–R and R–R approaches. Where this occurs, the criticisms lose force and are not well founded. There are experimental studies of conflict, of stress, and of internal versus external control, for example, that have tested hypotheses drawn from complex life situations or have established principles to be verified in those situations.

It is true that many aspects of human personality cannot be investigated by S–R designs as we now understand and implement them. Critics like Carlson are correct in this respect. But the study of personality is not narrowly contricted by dependence on a single research method. There is a great deal of R–R research, there are clinical studies, and we find the occasional field study. I believe it is important to reiterate the point mentioned earlier about the theoretically relevant experiment that truly manages to represent the behavior under investigation. The effective differences between successful and unsuccessful experiments are to be found in how well the investigators conceptualized the problem, abstracted its essential features, and represented them operationally in the experimental design. In the research that we have reviewed there are examples of both unsuccessful experimental designs (the repression studies of Sears and Zeller) and some highly adept and very successful ones (the basic conflict studies, many of the experimental studies of stress, the initial experimental investigations of internal–external control). It is not the maladroit experiment nor some hypothetical average experiment that should serve as an example of what S–R research can and cannot accomplish but the well-designed and carried out experiment. We have all too much of woefully designed research, and it is less informative about the limits of particular research strategies than it is of bad research whatever its method. I agree that Carlson and another contemporary critic, Wachtel (1973), are correct in deploring the unimaginativeness and inflexibility that characterize all too much of current research design in personality. Wachtel has a biting sobriquet for this kind of personality psychologist: It is "the implacable experimenter." I must again come back to a point stressed in Chapter 1: We do not need to reproduce in experiments the great complexity of events in their life settings. Indeed, when we attempt that, we have lost an elemental part of the meaning of the experiment. Implacable experimenters are going to produce tedious and unimportant findings that fail to capture any aspect of what personality psychology is all about—persons and the magnificent intricacy of their cognitive life and behavior. But it is not that the experiment breeds implacable experimenters; *they* breed bad experiments.

## R–R Research Design

The research of several chapters illustrates R–R design. The investigation of need for approval made exclusive use of R–R designs, and this has also been the principal research strategy in the study of anxiety and of internal–external control. We also encountered R–R studies of stress and of repression.

The power of R–R design and its important weaknesses were reviewed in Chapter 2. Both of these features are revealed in the R–R studies we have discussed. R–R and S–R research seek the same goal, a point emphasized in Chapter 2. They are not in principle different, as Dulaney (1968) makes clear: "R–R relations and S–R relations have the same logical status and equal weight in supporting *theoretical* statements about the *causal influences* of *unobservables* [p. 369]." Some experimental psychologists have been harshly critical of correlational, R–R designs. One eminent psychologist (Hilgard, 1955) branded correlation "an instrument of the devil" in the belief that it lent itself perniciously to *any* interpretation the investigator was committed to. Correlation is probably not such a hellish device; instead, it is better regarded as a useful and adaptable technique for the investigation of individual differences that could not be studied, by and large, by manipulative S–R designs. It is a useful and adaptable technique, that is, when employed with careful regard for the limitations and frailties that we have discussed.

It is worthy of comment that one of the significant dangers of R–R design is that it lends itself to the *passive experimenter*. I have so named him because he does so little. The passive experimenter collects correlations between personality measures, or between personality measures and simply obtained behavioral measures. There is no variation of the situation, no use of control procedures. There also appears to be no limit to fearless interpretation by this type of experimenter. It is all to easy to obtain such correlational data, and the literature is too heavily burdened by them. There is a place for R–R designs that simplify a problem to its essentials, ridding it of unnecessary and confusing complexity; there is not a place for the passive experimenter whose simple studies betray paucity of idea and poverty of design.

There are great strengths to be discerned in the contemporary study of R–R relations. One of them is the sophisticated study of situation–person interactions. "Traditionally," Mischel (1973) writes, "trait [R–R] research has studied individual differences in response to the 'same' situation [p. 277]." That was the bad flaw in the older study of personality variables—failure to recognize the mutual interplay of person *and* situation in behavior. Traditional personality psychologists were preoccupied with the personality disposition itself to an extent that did not let them see the influence of situations. They were thus theoretically naive in their insistence that individual differences—traits—were dominant and methodologically limited in their failure to study the *interaction* of person and situation. There have been some manful struggles with this problem, and competent investigators now show both a keen theoretical understanding of situation–person interactions and the astute use of experimental designs to reveal them. The anxiety–drive conditioning and learning studies and some of the need for approval and internal–external control research manifest this new found achievement. It is now understood—except by a hopefully diminishing number of passive experimenters—that a correlation between a personality measure and some behavioral index is simply not enough to make a secure theoretical inference. The behavioral context must be varied as well, so that the situational discriminativeness of the variable can be shown. We need to know the *conditions* responsible for eliciting the behavior associated with the disposition.

This discussion might appear to raise a question: are situations or persons more important? The question, as Mischel (1973) points out, is a meaningless one. The expression of personality variables is shaped by situations, and situations themselves exist differently for different persons as a function of their distinctive personality characteristics. Mischel says it clearly:

> Some of the most striking differences between persons may be found not by studying their responses to the same situation but by analyzing their selection and construction of stimulus conditions. In the conditions of life outside the laboratory, the psychological "stimuli" that people encounter are neither questionnaire items, nor experimental instructions, nor inanimate events, but they involve people and reciprocal relationships (e.g., with spouse, with boss, and with children). The person continuously influences the "situations" of his life as well as being affected by them in a mutual, organic two-way interaction. These interactions reflect not only the person's reactions to conditions but also his active selection and modification of conditions through his own cognitions and actions [pp. 277-278].

I believe that here lies an answer that should quiet a furious debate between "situationists" and trait psychologists (cf. Alker, 1972; Bowers, 1973; Mischel, 1968; Wachtel, 1973, for some of the principal arguments). The debate was probably necessary to clarify the issues, though the participants took more extreme positions in the interest of argument than they were really committed to. But it has become clear as the debate has subsided that it is *interactions* that are of theoretical importance, although on occasion we may choose to emphasize person or situation for specific purposes (e.g., in the therapeutic manipulation of situations to treat certain neurotic symptoms behaviorally, or the study of personal beliefs that are resistant to situational variation).

An explicit understanding of the situation–person interaction helps to formulate an answer to the question raised by critics of R–R research: Why are the correlations of personality variables with behavior so low? The critic has in mind compelling an admission that individual differences are weak and trivial contributors to the variance in observed behavior. The answer, however, is a more complex one. There are at least four possible alternatives that we can see when we view behavior from a situation–person perspective.

1. The interaction of personality disposition and situation has not been conceptualized adequately and represented well in the experiment. If experimental situations are not carefully chosen as clearly defined points along a dimension salient to the personality variable, and if the personality

variable is not adequately conceptualized, we are unlikely to see strong effects. Why, for example, did Folkins (1970) not find a relation between the coping or avoiding appraisals of individual subjects and their autonomic responses to stress (see pp. 111–112)? Was it because a complex interaction of the nature of the threat, threat anticipation time, individual cognitive appraisal, and stress response was not fully worked out? Thus, the first possibility we have to consider in accounting for marginal or incomplete findings is an ill-understood interaction.

2. The cognitive processes of the personality variable have not been taken into account. In retrospect, it is implausible that subjects disposed to repress would banish quite specific and detailed recollection of the experimental tasks under conditions of close experimental scrutiny. This is, I think, a major reason why the otherwise ingenious Caron and Wallach (1957) experiment (see pp. 136–140) failed.

3. Complex behavioral events such as conformity, stress response, and social action have many determinants, of which a single personality variable is but one. We have to be clear about the purpose of prediction. If our purpose is to explain conformity or social action, then the amount of variance accounted for is important, and we shall be properly disappointed in small relationships even though they are reliable. If our interest is in the laws relating a personality disposition to many behavioral consequences, however, the amount of variance accounted for is a less critical concern. We want to show reliable differences. Of course, it will eventually be a mark of our theoretical sophistication to be able to specify the contribution of a given variable in a given situation under given conditions.

4. Having a clear regard for these possibilities, we are better prepared to recognize and to take some adaptive steps when there are problems in the measurement of the personality variable leading to weak relationships. The embarrassments suffered in the anxiety–drive research through the weaknesses of the MAS might have been anticipated and averted had there been a clearer conceptualization of the anxiety–arousal situation relation.

## The Interplay of Research Methods

One of the distinctive attributes of research in personality is its methodological eclecticism. Personality psychologists have unabashedly borrowed experimental procedures and designs, as well as research problems and hypotheses, from many other areas of psychology. Sometimes, eclecticism means indiscriminant borrowing, without sensitivity to the issues involved, but I do not believe that fairly applies to experimental personality research. We see a variety of methods being used, often very systematically, to answer particular questions in the most informative way, to seek the generality of a phenomenon, or to apply experimental results clinically.

At its best, personality research starts with clinical or naturalistic observation, operationalizes the critical features of those observations in carefully controlled experimental designs, and tests the generality or ecological validity of the experimental findings in clinical or field studies. Of all the research we have considered in this book, I believe the conflict studies best exemplify this intelligent and disciplined use of a variety of methods and research settings—and, indeed, species of subject. Some of the internal-external control and stress research, as I have said earlier also deserve to be acknowledged for moving with thought and skill between complex life situations and the laboratory. There is a point of considerable importance to be made from this. As a distinguished psycholinguist, Brown, has said about his own area of inquiry (Brown and Hanlon, 1970):

> The history of psychology generally and of psycholinguistics in particular shows that careful experimental work provides no sure path to the truth. Neither does naturalism. There are rich opportunities for error in either method. But on the whole, the opportunities arise at different points, and when the methods are used in combination, the truth has a chance to appear [p. 52].

## DIRECTIONS FOR THE FUTURE

It is a risky enterprise to predict the future course of a scientific discipline. Sometimes in science there emerge periods of great development not clearly foreshadowed by immediate history—developmental leaps that stem from the creative talents of one great mind or a few of them. New problems also emerge to capture the imaginations of investigators, and within a short time there is an impressive literature. Anxiety–drive theory and the MAS had such an effect, and so too did the concept of internal versus external control. Then there is the fact that personality psychology is a young and exceedingly diverse discipline, and this is likely to encourage new research trends not distinctly anchored in the problems currently being investigated.

But if specific directions—problems to investigate, theoretical models, and experimental approaches—are uncertain for these reasons, it is also true that rarely do new developments wholly overthrow the conceptual models and experimental methods they may eventually come to supplant. Scientific revolutions, as Kuhn (1970) points out, do have a basis in the traditions of "normal science." Perhaps, then, some modest trends can be foreseen. I believe that for some time to come the course of scientific research in personality will show the influence of four major trends.

1. I alluded above to the situation versus trait debate that was sharply though indecisively argued for a considerable period. That debate was part of a larger conflict between an old tradition, profoundly influenced by Freud,

emphasizing intrapsychic dynamic concepts, and a radical behaviorism that utterly rejected this sort of conceptualization in favor of an objective analysis of the relation of responses to their antecedent stimuli. The behaviorist found the distasteful taint of a nonoperational mentalism in inferences to motivational states and cognitive processes. The trait psychologist thought the behaviorist a rude barbarian for his rejection of concepts reflecting the inner man.

That conflict does not appear explicitly in the research we have reviewed. True, many of the repression studies come from the dynamic tradition, and the conflict research had important behavioristic leanings in its background. These were not, however, research programs with a doctrine to instill, and they appear in this book on their own merits as important conceptual and methodological representatives of experimental personality research. Indeed, I sought to review research that seemed to me to have found a way to avoid the unfortunate excesses of each extreme. We have learned, I believe, that personality is not reducible to a simple situation–behavior analysis. Though the appeal of simplicity is strong, the development of personality psychology will be through conceptual and methodological recognition of situation–person interactions. Turning the point around, persistence in an exclusive concern with person variables—traits—would consign the psychology of personality to limited prediction, weak and disappointing findings, and so to grave narrowness of understanding. Thus, polarization is going to diminish. Neither radical behaviorism nor hidebound trait psychology will flourish in personality psychology, since neither has much to offer.

2. There will be an increasing emphasis on studies of situation–person interactions. I have made much of situation–person interaction throughout this book; my choice of research to review is itself an emphasis and a way of expressing a belief that this is a prominent direction in which experimental research in personality will move. This trend will impose sterner demands in the design of experiments: an experimental group and a control group will no longer suffice. Instead, there will have to be the systematic testing of several points along a dimension, requiring careful theoretical analysis of experimental situations. Personality dispositions will have to be more explicitly conceptualized if they are to be articulated with a refined analysis of situations.

3. The cognitive emphasis that we discussed earlier in this chapter will continue to mark personality research. We now seem to be free to listen to people—to study their thinking, anticipation, and feeling without embarrassment. There was a time when behaviorism rather terrorized psychology into believing that because thinking was a covert process it was not proper scientific grist. Only the overt, only behavior, was a proper subject. Dynamic psychology, for its part, implanted suspicion about cognition in an excess of post-Freudian insistence on the indirectness, circuitousness, and derivativeness of thought. One had to be so fiercely alert to the possibility of hidden

motives as to cast doubt on nearly all cognitive activity. Happily, that era is over, and we can study cognitive processes and their antecedents and consequences without such crippling inhibitions. Though there will continue to be "behavioral" and "dynamic" approaches, cognitive processes are firmly established as necessary to the study of personality.

4. An important stress on behavior of social relevance will be seen. That is presaged in the research of this book by some of the work on internal versus external control, most particularly the social action studies. The very notion of external control, with its intimations of alienation from mass society, is expressive of this emphasis. On this ground, we should expect research on internal–external control to continue, as well as research on such problems of contemporary importance as aggression and the social-sexual roles of men and women. Thus, emerging social concerns and problems will exercise a significant influence on the choice of research problems. There are dangers in that. At the extreme, a too motile responsiveness to social concerns of immediate relevance means the dictation of scientific growth by popular culture. I do not believe it is truly an elitist argument to suggest that a science of human behavior is not well served by subservience of this sort. An important measure of independence is essential to the creative growth of any science.

# References

Aas, A. *Mutilation fantasies and autonomic response*. Oslo, Norway: Oslo University Press, 1958.

Adorno, T. W., Frenkel-Brunswik, E., Levinson, D. J., & Sanford, R. N. *The authoritarian personality*. New York: Harper, 1950.

Alker, H. A. Is personality situationally specific or intrapsychically consistent? *Journal of Personality*, 1972, *40*, 1–16.

Allaman, J. D., Joyce, C. S., & Crandall, V. C. The antecedents of social desirability response tendencies of children and young adults. *Child Development*, 1972, *43*, 1135–1160.

Alper, T. G. Memory for completed and incompleted tasks as a function of personality: An analysis of group data. *Journal of Abnormal and Social Psychology*, 1946, *41*, 403–420.

Alper, T. G. Memory for completed and incompleted tasks as a function of personality: Correlation between experimental and personality data. *Journal of Personality*, 1948, *17*, 104–137.

Alper, T. G. The interrupted task method in studies of selective recall: A reevaluation of some recent experiments. *Psychological Review*, 1952, *59*, 71–88.

American Psychological Association. Ethical principles in the conduct of research with human participants. *American Psychologist*, 1973a, *28*, 79–80.

American Psychological Association, Committee on Ethical Standards in Psychological Research. *Ethical principles in the conduct of research with human participants*. Washington, D. C.:American Psychological Association, 1973b.

Asch, S. Effects of group pressure upon the modification and distortion of judgments. In H. Guetzkow (Ed.), *Groups, leadership, and men; Research in human relations*. Pittsburgh: Carnegie Press, 1951.

Ax, A. F. The physiological differentiation between fear and anger in humans. *Psychomatic Medicine*, 1953, *15*, 433–442.

Barron, F. Some personality correlates of independence of judgment. *Journal of Personality*, 1953, *21*, 287–297.

Barthel, C. E. *The effects of the approval motive, generalized expectancy, and situational cues upon goal setting and social defensiveness*. Unpublished Ph. D. dissertation, Ohio State University, 1963.

Basowitz, H., Persky, H., Korchin, S. J., & Grinker, R. R., Sr. *Anxiety and stress*. New York: McGraw-Hill, 1955.

231

Battle, E. S., & Rotter, J. B.   Children's feelings of personal control as related to social class and ethnic group. *Journal of Personality*, 1963, *31*, 482–490.

Bellow, S.  *Herzog.* New York: Viking Press, 1964.

Bergmann, G.  Semantics. In V. Ferm (Ed.), *A history of philosophical systems*. New York: Philosophical Library, 1950.

Bergmann, G., & Spence, K. W.  The logic of psychophysical measurement. *Psychological Review*, 1944, *51*, 1–24.

Bettelheim, B.  Individual and mass behavior in extreme situations. *Journal of Abnormal and Social Psychology*, 1943, *38*, 417–452.

Bieri, J., Atkins, A. L., Briar, S., Leaman, R. L., Miller, H., & Tripodi, T.  *Clinical and social judgment: The discrimination of behavioral information.* New York: Wiley, 1966.

Bindra, D., Paterson, A. L., & Strzelecki, J.  On the relation between anxiety and conditioning. *Canadian Journal of Psychology*, 1955, *9*, 1–6.

Block, J.  *The challenge of response sets.* New York: Appleton–Century–Crofts, 1965.

Bowers, K. S.  Situationism in psychology: An analysis and a critique. *Psychological Review*, 1973, *80*, 307–336.

Brackbill, G., & Little, K. B.  MMPI correlates of the Taylor Scale of manifest anxiety. *Journal of Consulting Psychology*, 1954, *18*, 433–436.

Brady, J. V., Porter, R. W., Conrad, D. G., & Mason, J. W.  Avoidance behavior and the development of gastrointestinal ulcers. *Journal of the Experimental Analysis of Behavior*, 1958, *1*, 69–72.

Breuer, J., & Freud, S.  *Studies on hysteria. Standard edition of the complete psychological works of Sigmund Freud.* Vol. II. London: Hogarth, 1955 (1895).

Brown, J. S.  *Generalized approach and avoidance responses in relation to conflict behavior.* Unpublished Ph. D. dissertation, Yale University, 1940.

Brown, P. K.  The social desirability variable and verbal learning performance. *Journal of Educational Psychology*, 1960, *51*, 52–59.

Brown, R.  *Social Psychology.* New York: The Free Press, 1965.

Brown, R., & Hanlon, C.  Derivational complexity and order of acquisition in child speech. In J. R. Hayes (Ed.), *Cognition and the development of language*. New York: Wiley, 1970.

Bryan, J. H., & Lichtenstein, E.  Effects of subject attitudes in verbal conditioning. *Journal of Personality and Social Psychology*, 1966, *3*, 188–189.

Buckhout, R.  Need for social approval and attitude change. *Journal of Psychology*, 1965, *60*, 123–128.

Campbell, D. T., & Fiske, D. W.  Convergent and discriminant validation by the multitrait-multimethod matrix. *Psychological Bulletin*, 1959, *56*, 81–105.

Carlson, R.  Where is the person in personality research? *Psychological Bulletin*, 1971, *75*, 203–219.

Caron, A. J., & Wallach, M. A.  Recall of interrupted tasks under stress: A phenomenon of memory or of learning? *Journal of Abnormal and Social Psychology*, 1957, *55*, 372–381.

Cattell, R. B.  Anxiety and motivation: Theory and crucial experiments. In C. D. Spielberger (Ed.), *Anxiety and behavior*. New York: Academic Press, 1966.

Cattell, R. B., & Scheier, I. H.  *The meaning and measurement of neuroticism and anxiety.* New York: Ronald Press, 1961.

Chance, J. E.  Academic correlates and maternal antecedents of children's belief in external or internal control of reinforcement. In J. B. Rotter, J. E. Chance, & E. J. Phares (Eds.), *Applications of a social learning theory of personality*. New York: Holt, Rinehart, and Winston, 1972.

Child, I. L.  Personality. *Annual Review of Psychology*, 1954, *5*, 149–170.

Cohen, A. R.  Some implications of self-esteem for social influence. In C. I. Hovland & I. L. Janis (Eds.), *Personality and persuasibility*. New Haven: Yale University. Press, 1959.

Collins, B. E. Four components of the Rotter Internal–External Control scale: Belief in a difficult world, a just world, a predictable world, and a politically responsive world. *Journal of Personality and Social Psychology*, 1974, *29*, 381–391.

Conger, J. J. The effects of alcohol on conflict behavior in the albino rat. *Quarterly Journal of Studies in Alcoholism*, 1951, *12*, 1–29.

Conn, L. K., & Crowne, D. P. Instigation to aggression, emotional arousal, and defensive emulation. *Journal of Personality*, 1964, *32*, 163–179.

Crandall, V. C. Personality characteristics and social and achievement behaviors associated with children's social desirability response tendencies. *Journal of Personality and Social Psychology*, 1966, *4*, 477–486.

Crandall, V. C. *Differences in parental antecedents of internal–external control in children and in young adulthood.* Paper presented at meetings of the American Psychological Association, Montreal, Canada, August, 1973.

Crandall, V. C., Crandall, V. J., & Katkovsky, W. A children's social desirability questionnaire. *Journal of Consulting Psychology*, 1965, *29*, 27–36.

Crandall, V. C., Katkovsky, W., & Crandall, V. J. Children's beliefs in their own control of reinforcements in intellectual–academic achievement situations. *Child Development*, 1965, *36*, 91–109.

Crandall, V. J., Katkovsky, W., & Preston, A. Motivational and ability determinants of children's intellectual achievement behaviors. *Child Development*, 1962, *33*, 643–661.

Cronbach, L. J. The two disciplines of scientific psychology. *American Psychologist*, 1957, *12*, 671–684.

Cronbach, L. J., & Meehl, P. E. Construct validity in psychological tests. *Psychological Bulletin*, 1955, *52*, 281–302.

Crowne, D.P., Holland, C. H., & Conn, L. K. Personality factors in discrimination learning in children. *Journal of Personality and Social Psychology*, 1968, *10*, 420–430.

Crowne, D. P., & Liverant, S. Conformity under varying conditions of personal commitment. *Journal of Abnormal and Social Psychology*, 1963, *66*, 547–555.

Crowne, D.P., & Marlowe, D. A new scale of social desirability independent of psychopathology. *Journal of Consulting Psychology*, 1960, *24*, 349–354.

Crowne, D. P., & Marlowe, D. *The approval motive: Studies in evaluative dependence.* New York: Wiley, 1964.

Crowne, D. P., & Strickland, B. R. The conditioning of verbal behavior as a function of the need for social approval. *Journal of Abnormal and Social Psychology*, 1961, *63*, 395–401.

Davis, W. L., & Phares, E. J. Parental antecedents of internal–external control of reinforcement. *Psychological Reports*, 1969, *24*, 427–436.

Dixon, T. Experimenter approval, social desirability, and statements of self-reference. *Journal of Consulting and Clinical Psychology*, 1970, *35*, 400–405.

Doctor, R. M. Locus of control of reinforcement and responsiveness to social influence. *Journal of Personality*, 1971, *39*, 542–551.

Dollard, J., & Miller, N. E. *Personality and Psychotherapy.* New York: McGraw-Hill, 1950.

Dulaney, D. E. Awareness, rules, and propositional control: A confrontation with S–R behavior therapy. In T. R. Dixon & D. L. Horton (Eds.), *Verbal behavior and general behavior theory.* Englewood Cliffs, N. J.: Prentice-Hall, 1968.

Edwards, A. L. The relationship between the judged desirability of a trait and the probability that the trait will be endorsed. *Journal of Applied Psychology*, 1953, *37*, 90–93.

Edwards, A. L. *The social desirability variable in personality assessment and research.* New York: Dryden, 1957.

Efran, J. S., & Boylin, E. R. Social desirability and willingness to participate in a group discussion. *Psychological Reports*, 1967, *20*, 402.

Eibl-Eibesfeldt, I. *Ethology—the biology of behavior.* New York: Holt, Rinehart, and Winston, 1970.

Einstein, A. Considerations concerning the fundaments of theoretical physics. *Science*, 1940, *91*, 487–492.

Endler, N. S., & Hunt, J. McV. Sources of behavioral variance as measured by the S–R inventory of anxiousness. *Psychological Bulletin*, 1966, *65*, 336–346.

Endler, N. S., & Hunt, J. McV. Generalizability of contributions from sources of variance in the S–R inventories of anxiousness. *Journal of Personality*, 1969, *37*, 1–24.

Endler, N. S., Hunt, J. McV., & Rosenstein, A. J. An S–R inventory of anxiousness. *Psychological Monographs*, 1962, *76*, No. 17 (Whole No. 536).

Epstein, S. The measurement of drive and conflict in humans: Theory and experiment. In M. R. Jones (Ed.), *Nebraska symposium on motivation*, 1962. Lincoln, Nebr.: University of Nebraska Press, 1962.

Epstein, S., & Fenz, W. D. Theory and experiment on the measurement of approach–avoidance conflict. *Journal of Abnormal and Social Psychology*, 1962, *64*, 97–112.

Erdelyi, M. H. A new look at the new look: Perceptual defense and vigilance. *Psychological Review*, 1974, *81*, 1–25.

Eriksen, C. W., & Davids, A. The meaning and clinical validity of the Taylor anxiety scale and the hysteria-psychasthenia scales from the MMPI. *Journal of Abnormal and Social Psychology*, 1955, *50*, 135–137.

Fenz, W. D., & Epstein, S. Stress: In the air. *Psychology Today*, 1969, *3*, 27–28; 58–59.

Festinger, L. A theory of social comparison processes. *Human Relations*, 1954, 7, 117–140.

Festinger, L. *A theory of cognitive dissonance*. Evanston, Ill.: Row, Peterson, 1957.

Fischer, W. F. *Theories of anxiety*. New York: Harper & Row, 1970.

Fishman, C. G. Need for approval and the expression of aggression under varying conditions of frustration. *Journal of Personality and Social Psychology*, 1965, *2*, 809–816.

Fiske, D. W. *Measuring the concepts of personality*. Chicago: Aldine-Atherton, 1971.

Fiske, D. W. Can a personality construct be validated empirically? *Psychological Bulletin*, 1973, *80*, 89–92.

Folkins, C. H. Temporal factors and the cognitive mediators of stress reaction. *Journal of Personality and Social Psychology*, 1970, *14*, 173–184.

Fowler, H., & Miller, N. E. Facilitation and inhibition of runway performance by hind- and forepaw shock of various intensities. *Journal of Comparative and Physiological Psychology*, 1963, *56*, 801–805.

Franklin, J. C., Schiele, B. C., Brozek, J., & Keys, A. Observations on human behavior in experimental semistarvation and rehabilitation. *Journal of Clinical Psychology*, 1948, *4*, 28–45.

Franks, C.M. Conditioning and personality: A study of normal and neurotic subjects. *Journal of Abnormal and Social Psychology*, 1956, *52*, 143–150.

Freud, S. The neuro-psychoses of defence. *Standard edition of the complete psychological works of Sigmund Freud*. Vol. III. London: Hogarth, 1962 (1894).

Freud, S. Further remarks on the neuro-psychoses of defence. *Standard edition of the complete psychological works of Sigmund Freud*. Vol. III. London: Hogarth, 1962 (1896).

Freud, S. On the history of the psycho-analytic movement. *Standard edition of the complete psychological works of Sigmund Freud*. Vol. XIV. London: Hogarth, 1957 (1914).

Freud, S. Repression. *Standard edition of the complete psychological works of Sigmund Freud*. Vol. XIV. London: Hogarth, 1957, (1915).

Freud, S. Introductory lectures on psycho-analysis. *Standard edition of the complete psychological works of Sigmund Freud*. Vol. XV. London: Hogarth, 1963 (1916).

Freud, S. Analysis terminable and interminable. *Standard edition of the complete psychological works of Sigmund Freud*. Vol. XXIII. London: Hogarth, 1964 (1937).

Freud, S. Some elementary lessons in psycho-analysis. *Standard edition of the complete psychological works of Sigmund Frued*. Vol. XXIII. London: Hogarth, 1964 (1940).

Geer, J. H. The development of a scale to measure fear. *Behavior Research and Therapy*, 1965, *3*, 45–53.

Getter, H. A. A personality determinant of verbal conditioning. *Journal of Personality*, 1966, *34*, 397–405.

Glixman, A. F. An analysis of the use of the interruption–technique in experimental studies of "repression." *Psychological Bulletin*, 1948, *45*, 491–506.

Glixman, A. F. Recall of completed and incompleted activities under varying degrees of stress. *Journal of Experimental Psychology*, 1949, *39*, 281–295.

Glucksberg, S., & King, L. J. Motivated forgetting mediated by implicit verbal chaining: A laboratory analog of repression. *Science*, 1967, *158*, 517–519.

Goldstein, M. J., & Palmer, J. O. *The experience of anxiety.* New York: Oxford University Press, 1963.

Gore, P. M. *Individual differences in the prediction of subject compliance to experimenter bias.* Unpublished Ph. D. dissertation, Ohio State University, 1962.

Gore, P. M., & Rotter, J. B. A personality correlate of social action. *Journal of Personality*, 1963, *31*, 58–64.

Graham, F. K., & Clifton, R. K. Heart-rate change as a component of the orienting response. *Psychological Bulletin*, 1966, *65*, 305–320.

Gray, J. A. *The psychology of fear and stress.* New York: McGraw-Hill, 1971.

Greenspoon, J. The reinforcing effect of two spoken sounds on the frequency of two responses. *American Journal of Psychology*, 1955, *68*, 409–416.

Grinker, R. R., Sr. The psychosomatic aspects of anxiety. In C. D. Spielberger (Ed.), *Anxiety and behavior.* New York: Academic Press, 1966.

Grinker, R. R., & Spiegel, J. *Men under stress.* Philadelphia: Blakiston, 1945.

Guyton, A. C. *Textbook of medical physiology.* 3rd Ed. Philadelphia: Saunders, 1966.

Hamburg, D. A., Hamburg, B., & DeGoza, S. Adaptive problems and mechanisms in severely burned patients. *Psychiatry*, 1953, *16*, 1–20.

Hamsher, J. H., Geller, J. D., & Rotter, J. B. Interpersonal trust, internal–external control, and the Warren Commission Report. *Journal of Personality and Social Psychology*, 1968, *9*, 210–215.

Harter, S. Mastery motivation and need for approval in older children and their relationship to social desirability response tendencies. *Developmental Psychology*, 1975, *11*, 186–196.

Heatherington, E. M., & Wray, M. P. Aggression, need for social approval, and humor preferences. *Journal of Abnormal and Social Psychology*, 1964, *68*, 685–689.

Heider, F. Social perception and phenomenal causality. *Psychological Review*, 1944, *51*, 358–374.

Heider, F. *The psychology of interpersonal relations.* New York: Wiley, 1958.

Hilgard, E. R. Discussion of probabilistic functionalism. *Psychological Review*, 1955, *62*, 226–228.

Hodges, W. F. Effects of ego threat and threat of pain on state anxiety. *Journal of Personality and Social Psychology*, 1968, *8*, 364–372.

Hodges, W. F., & Spielberger, C. D. The effects of threat of shock on heart rate for subjects who differ in manifest anxiety and fear of shock. *Psychophysiology*, 1966, *2*, 287–294.

Hodges, W. F., & Spielberger, C. D. Digit span: An indicant of trait or state anxiety? *Journal of Consulting and Clinical Psychology*, 1969, *33*, 430–434.

Holden, K. B., & Rotter, J. B. A nonverbal measure of extinction in skill and chance situations. *Journal of Experimental Psychology*, 1962, *63*, 519–520.

Horton, D. L., Marlowe, D., & Crowne, D. P. The effect of instructional set and need for social approval on commonality of word association responses. *Journal of Abnormal and Social Psychology*, 1963, *66*, 67–72.

Hull, C. L. The goal gradient hypothesis and maze learning. *Psychological Review*, 1932, *39*, 25–43.

Hull, C. L. *Principles of behavior.* New York: Appleton–Century–Crofts, 1943.

Jackson, D. N., & Bloomberg, R. Anxiety: Unitas or multiplex? *Journal of Consulting Psychology*, 1958, *22*, 225–227.

Jaensch, E. R. *Der gegentypus*. Leipzig: Barth, 1938.

James, W. H. *Internal versus external control of reinforcement as a basic variable in learning theory*. Unpublished Ph. D. dissertation, Ohio State University, 1957.

James, W. H., Woodruff, A. B., & Werner, W. Effect of internal and external control upon changes in smoking behavior. *Journal of Consulting Psychology*, 1965, *29*, 184–186.

Janis, I. L. *Psychological Stress*. New York: Wiley, 1958.

Jessor, R., Graves, T. D., Hanson, R. C., & Jessor, S. L. *Society, personality, and deviant behavior: A study of a tri-ethnic community*. New York: Holt, Rinehart, and Winston, 1968.

Jessor, R., & Hammond, K. R. Construct validity and the Taylor Anxiety Scale. *Psychological Bulletin*, 1957, *54*, 161–170.

*Journal of Abnormal and Social Psychology*, Symposium: Psychoanalysis as seen by analyzed psychologists, 1940, *35*.

Kanfer, F. H., & Marston, A. R. Characteristics of interactional behavior in a psychotherapy analogue. *Journal of Consulting Psychology*, 1964, *28*, 456–467.

Katchmar, L. T., Ross, S., & Andrews, T. G. Effects of stress and anxiety on performance of a complex verbal-coding task. *Journal of Experimental Psychology*, 1958, *55*, 559–564.

Katkin, E. S. Relationship between manifest anxiety and two indices of autonomic response to stress. *Journal of Personality and Social Psychology*, 1965, *2*, 324–333.

Katkovsky, W., Crandall, V. C., & Good, S. Parental antecedents of children's beliefs in internal–external control of reinforcements in intellectual achievement situations. *Child Development*, 1967, *38*, 765–776.

Kelly, G. A. *The psychology of personal constructs*. Vol. I. *A theory of personality*. New York: Norton, 1955.

Kimble, G. A., & Posnick, G. M. Anxiety? *Journal of Personality and Social Psychology*, 1967, *7*, 108–110.

Kuhn, T. S. *The structure of scientific revolutions* (2nd Ed.). Chicago: University of Chicago Press, 1970.

Lacey, J. I. The evaluation of autonomic responses: Toward a general solution. *Annals of the New York Academy of Sciences*, 1956, *67*, 123–164.

Lacey, J. I. Psychophysiological approaches to the evaluation of psychotherapeutic process and outcome. In E. A. Rubenstein & M. B. Parloff (Eds.), *Research in psychotherapy*. Washington, D. C.: American Psychological Association, 1959.

Landis, C., & Hunt, W. A. Adrenalin and emotion. *Psychological Review*, 1932, *39*, 467–485.

Lazarus, R. S. *Psychological stress and the coping process*. New York: McGraw-Hill, 1966.

Lazarus, R. S., & Averill, J. R. Emotion and cognition: With special reference to anxiety. In C. D. Spielberger (Ed.), *Anxiety: Current trends in theory and research*. New York: Academic Press, 1972.

Lazarus, R. S., Opton, E. M., Jr., Nomikos, M. S., & Rankin, N. O. The principle of short-circuiting of threat: Further evidence. *Journal of Personality*, 1965, *33*, 622–635.

Lazarus, R. S., Speisman, J. C., Mordkoff, A. M., & Davison, L. A. A laboratory study of psychological stress produced by a motion picture film. *Psychological Monographs*, 1962, *76*, No. 34 (Whole No. 553).

Lefcourt, H. M. Need for approval and threatened negative evaluation as determinants of expressiveness in a projective test. *Journal of Consulting and Clinical Psychology*, 1969, *33*, 96–102.

Lefcourt, H. M., & Ladwig, G. W. The American Negro: A problem in expectancies. *Journal of Personality and Social Psychology*, 1965, *1*, 377–380.

Lester, L. F., & Crowne, D. P. A strict behavioral test of obedience and some childrearing correlates. *Personality: An International Journal*, 1970, *1*, 85–93.

Lewin, K. Environmental forces in child behavior and development. In C. Murchison (Ed.), *A handbook of child psychology*. Worcester, Mass.: Clark University Press, 1931.

Lewin, K. *A dynamic theory of personality*. New York: McGraw-Hill, 1935.

Lewis, D. J. Partial reinforcement: A selective review of the literature since 1950. *Psychological Bulletin*, 1960, *57*, 1–28.

Loehlin, J. C., Lindzey, G., & Spuhler, J. N. *Race differences in intelligence*. San Francisco: Freeman, 1975.

Losco, J., & Epstein, S. Relative steepness of approach and avoidance gradients as a function of magnitude and valence of incentive. *Journal of Abnormal Psychology*, 1977, *86*, 360–368.

Løvaas, O. I. Supplementary report: The relationship of induced muscular tension to manifest anxiety in learning. *Journal of Experimental Psychology*, 1960, *59*, 205–206.

Madison, P. *Freud's concept of repression and defense, its theoretical and observational language*. Minneapolis: University of Minnesota Press, 1961.

Maher, B. A. *Principles of psychopathology. An experimental approach*. New York: McGraw-Hill, 1966.

Maher, B. A., & Noblin, C. D. *Conflict equilibrium and distance from the goal: A demonstration of irrelevance*. Paper presented at meetings of the Southeastern Psychological Association, Miami Beach, Florida, 1963.

Maher, B. A., & Nuttall, R. *The effect of repeated measures and prior aproach training upon a spatial gradient of avoidance*. Paper presented at meetings of the American Psychological Association, St. Louis, Missouri, 1962.

Malmo, R. B. Studies of anxiety: Some clinical origins of the activation concept. In C. D. Spielberger (Ed.), *Anxiety and behavior*. New York: Academic Press, 1966.

Mandler, G. Helplessness: Theory and research in anxiety. In C. D. Spielberger (Ed.), *Anxiety: Current trends in theory and research*. New York: Academic Press, 1972.

Mandler, G. Consciousness: Respectable, useful, and probably necessary. In R. Solso (Ed.), *Information processing and cognition: The Loyola Symposium*. Hillsdale, N. J.: Lawrence Erlbaum Associates, 1975.

Mandler, G., & Kessen, W. *The language of psychology*. Huntington, N. Y.: Krieger, 1975.

Mandler, G., Mandler, J. M., Kremen, I., & Sholiton, R. D. The response to threat: Relations among verbal and physiological indices. *Psychological Monographs*, 1961, *75*, No. 9 (Whole No. 513).

Mandler, G., & Watson, D. L. Anxiety and the interruption of behavior. In C. D. Spielberger (Ed.), *Anxiety and behavior*. New York: Academic Press, 1966.

Marañon, G. Contribution à l'étude de l'action émotive de l'adrénaline. *Revue Française d'Endocrinologie*, 1924, *2*, 301–325.

Marlowe, D. Need for social approval and the operant conditioning of meaningful verbal behavior. *Journal of Consulting Psychology*, 1962, *26*, 79–83.

Marlowe, D., Beecher, R. S., Cook, J. B., & Doob, A. N. The approval motive, vicarious reinforcement, and verbal conditioning. *Perceptual and Motor Skills*, 1964, *19*, 523–530.

Marlowe, D., & Crowne, D. P. Social desirability and response to perceived situational demands. *Journal of Consulting Psychology*, 1961, *25*, 109–115.

Masserman, J. H., & Yum, K. S. An analysis of the influence of alcohol on experimental neurosis in cats. *Psychosomatic Medicine*, 1946, *8*, 36–52.

McArthur, C. Personalities of public and private school boys. *Harvard Educational Review*, 1954, *24*, 256–262.

McArthur, C. Personality differences between middle and upper classes. *Journal of Abnormal and Social Psychology*, 1955, *50*, 247–254.

McClelland, D. C., Clark, R. A., Roby, T. B., & Atkinson, J. W. The effect of the need for achievement on thematic apperception. In J. W. Atkinson (Ed.), *Motives in fantasy, action, and society*. Princeton, N. J.: Van Nostrand, 1958.

Mednick, S. A. Generalization as a function of manifest anxiety and adaptation to psychological experiments. *Journal of Consulting Psychology*, 1957, *21*, 491–494.

Miller, N., Doob, A. N., Butler, D. C., & Marlowe, D. The tendency to agree: Situational determinants and social desirability. *Journal of Experimental Research in Personality*, 1965, *1*, 78–83.

Miller, N. E. Experimental studies of conflict. In J. McV. Hunt (Ed.), *Personality and the behavior disorders.* Vol. 1. New York: Ronald, 1944.

Miller, N. E. Theory and experiment relating psychoanalytic displacement to stimulus-response generalization. *Journal of Abnormal and Social Psychology,* 1948, *43,* 155-178.

Miller, N. E. Liberalization of basic S-R concepts: Extensions to conflict behavior, motivation, and social learning. In S. Koch (Ed.), *Psychology: A study of a science.* Vol. 2. *General systematic formulations, learning, and special processes.* New York: McGraw-Hill, 1959.

Miller, N. E. Some recent studies of conflict behavior and drugs. *American Psychologist,* 1961, *16,* 12-24.

Mischel, W. *Personality and assessment.* New York: Wiley, 1968.

Mischel, W. Toward a cognitive social learning reconceptualization of personality. *Psychological Review,* 1973, *80,* 252-283.

Mischel, W., Zeiss, R., & Zeiss, A. Internal-external control and persistence: Validation and implications of the Stanford Preschool Internal-External Scale. *Journal of Personality and Social Psychology,* 1974, *29,* 265-278.

Monat, A., Averill, J. R., & Lazarus, R. S. Anticipatory stress and coping reactions under various conditions of uncertainty. *Journal of Personality and Social Psychology,* 1972, *24,* 237-253.

Mosher, D. L. Approval motive and acceptance of "fake" personality test interpretations which differ in favorability. *Psychological Reports,* 1965, *17,* 395-402.

Murray, E. J. A case study in a behavioral analysis of psychotherapy. *Journal of Abnormal and Social Psychology,* 1954, *49,* 305-310.

Murray, E. J., & Berkun, M. M. Displacement as a function of conflict. *Journal of Abnormal and Social Psychology,* 1955, *51,* 47-56.

Neisser, U. *Cognitive psychology.* New York: Appleton-Century-Crofts, 1967.

Nisbett, R. E., & Wilson, T. D. Telling more than we can know: Verbal reports on mental processes. *Psychological Review,* 1977, *84,* 231-259.

Nomikos, M. S., Opton, E. M., Jr., Averill, J. R., & Lazarus, R. S. Surprise versus suspense in the production of stress reaction. *Journal of Personality and Social Psychology,* 1968, *8,* 204-208.

Nowicki, S. *Predicting academic achievement from a locus of control orientation: Some problems and some solutions.* Paper presented at meetings of the American Psychological Association, Montreal, Canada, August, 1973.

Odell, M. *Personality correlates of independence and conformity.* Unpublished master's thesis, Ohio State University, 1959.

Orne, M. T. On the social psychology of the psychological experiment: With particular reference to demand characteristics. *American Psychologist,* 1962, 17, 776-783.

Osgood, C. E. *Method and Theory in Experimental Psychology.* New York: Oxford University Press, 1953.

Palmer, J., & Altrocci, J. Attribution of hostile intent as unconscious. *Journal of Personality,* 1967, *35,* 164-177.

Pervin, L. A., & Lilly, R. S. Social desirability and self-ideal self ratings on the semantic differential. *Educational and Psychological Measurement,* 1967, *27,* 845-853.

Phares, E. J. Expectancy changes in skill and chance situations. *Journal of Abnormal and Social Psychology,* 1957, *54,* 339-342.

Phares, E. J. Perceptual threshold decrements as a function of skill and chance expectancies. *Journal of Psychology,* 1962, *53,* 399-407.

Phares, E. J. Internal-external control as a determinant of amount of social influence exerted. *Journal of Personality and Social Psychology,* 1965, *2,* 642-647.

Phares, E. J. *Locus of control in personality.* Morristown, N. J.: General Learning Press, 1976.

Popper, K. *Conjectures and refutations: The growth of scientific knowledge.* New York: Basic Books, 1962. *Also see:* 2nd Ed. London: Routledge and Kegan Paul, 1965; *and* Torchbooks, 1968.

Postman, L. The probability approach and nomothetic theory. *Psychological Review*, 1955, *62*, 218–225.

Pribram, K. H. *Languages of the brain. Experimental paradoxes and principles in neuropsychology.* Englewood Cliffs, N. J.: Prentice-Hall, 1971.

Rappaport, H., & Katkin, E. S. Relationships among manifest anxiety, response to stress, and the perception of autonomic activity. *Journal of Consulting and Clinical Psychology*, 1972, *38*, 219–224.

Reid, E. C. Autopsychology of the manic-depressive. *Journal of Nervous and Mental disease*, 1910, *37*, 606–620.

Rigby, W. K. Approach and avoidance gradients and conflict behavior in a predominantly temporal situation. *Journal of Comparative and Physiological Psychology*, 1954, *47*, 83–89.

Ritchie, E. & Phares, E. J. Attitude change as a function of internal–external control and communicator status. *Journal of Personality*, 1969, *37*, 429–443.

Rosenzweig, S. An experimental study of "repression" with special reference to need-persistive and ego-defensive reactions to frustration. *Journal of Experimental Psychology*, 1943, *32*, 64–74.

Rosenzweig, S. The investigation of repression as an instance of experimental idiodynamics. *Psychological Review*, 1952, *59*, 339–345.

Rosenzweig, S., & Mason, G. An experimental study of memory in relation to the theory of repression. *British Journal of Psychology*, 1934, *24*, 247–265.

Rotter, J. B. Generalized expectancies for internal versus external control of reinforcement. *Psychological Monographs*, 1966, *80*, No. 1 (Whole No. 609).

Rotter, J. B. A new scale for the measurement of interpersonal trust. *Journal of Personality*, 1967, *35*, 651–665.

Rotter, J. B. Some problems and misconceptions related to the construct of internal versus external control of reinforcement. *Journal of Consulting and Clinical Psychology*, 1975, *43*, 56–67.

Rotter, J. B., Liverant, S., & Crowne, D. P. The growth and extinction of expectancies in chance controlled and skilled tasks. *Journal of Psychology*, 1961, *52*, 161–177.

Rotter, J. B., & Mulry, R. C. Internal versus external control of reinforcement and decision time. *Journal of Personality and Social Psychology*, 1965, *2*, 598–604.

Runquist, W. N., & Ross, L. E. The relation between physiological measures of emotionality and performance in eyelid conditioning. *Journal of Experimental Psychology*, 1959, *57*, 329–332.

Runquist, W. N., & Spence, K. W. Performance in eyelid conditioning related to changes in muscular tension and physiological measures of emotionality. *Journal of Experimental Psychology*, 1959, *58*, 417–422.

Russell, W. A., & Storms, L. H. Implicit verbal chaining in paired-associate learning. *Journal of Experimental Psychology*, 1955, *49*, 287–293.

Salman, A. R. *The need for approval, improvisation, and attitude change.* Unpublished master's thesis, Ohio State University, 1962.

Saltz, E., & Hoehn, A. J. A test of the Taylor–Spence theory of anxiety. *Journal of Abnormal and Social Psychology*, 1957, *54*, 114–117.

Sarason, I. G. The effect of anxiety and two kinds of failure on serial learning. *Journal of Personality*, 1957, *25*, 383–392.

Sarason, S. B., Davidson, K. S., Lighthall, F. F., Waite, R. R., & Ruebush, B. K. *Anxiety in elementary school children.* New York: Wiley, 1960.

Sarbin, T. R., Taft, R., & Bailey, D. E. *Clinical inference and cognitive theory.* New York: Holt, Rinehart, and Winston, 1960.

Schachter, J. Pain, fear, and anger in hypertensives and normotensives. A psychophysiological study. *Psychosomatic Medicine*, 1957, *19*, 17–29.

Schachter, S. The interaction of cognitive and physiological determinants of emotional state. In C. D. Spielberger (Ed.), *Anxiety and Behavior.* New York: Academic Press, 1966.

Schachter, S., & Singer, J. E. Cognitive, social, and physiological determinants of emotional state. *Psychological Review*, 1962, *69*, 379–399.

Schachter, S. & Wheeler, L. Epinephrine, chlorpromazine, and amusement. *Journal of Abnormal and Social Psychology*, 1962, *65*, 121–128.

Schwartz, B. J. An empirical test of two Freudian hypotheses concerning castration anxiety. *Journal of Personality*, 1956, *24*, 318–327.

Sears, R. R. Functional abnormalilties of memory with special reference to amnesia. *Psychological Bulletin*, 1936, *33*, 229–274.

Sears, R. R. Initiation of the repression sequence by experienced failure. *Journal of Experimental Psychology*, 1937, *20*, 570–580.

Sears, R. R. Personality, In C. P. Stone (Ed.), *Annual review of psychology*. Vol. 1. Stanford, Calif.: Annual Reviews, 1950.

Seeman, M. Alienation and social learning in a reformatory. *American Journal of Sociology*, 1963, *69*, 270–284.

Seeman, M. Social learning theory and the theory of mass society. In J. B. Rotter, J. E. Chance, & E. J. Phares (Eds.), *Applications of a social learning theory of personality*. New York: Holt, Rinehart, and Winston, 1972.

Seeman, M., & Evans, J. W. Alienation and learning in a hospital setting. *American Sociological Review*, 1962, *27*, 772–783.

Seligman, M. E. P. *Helplessness. On depression, development, and death*. San Francisco: Freeman, 1975.

Selye, H. *The physiology and pathology of exposure to stress*. Montreal: Acta, 1950.

Selye, H. *The stress of life*. New York: McGraw-Hill, 1956.

Shedletsky, R., & Endler, N. S. Anxiety: The state–trait model and the interaction model. *Journal of Personality*, 1974, *42*, 511–527.

Skinner, B. F. Are theories of learning necessary? *Psychological Review*, 1950, *57*, 193–216.

Skinner, B. F. *Science and human behavior*. New York: The Free Press, 1953.

Skolnick, P., & Heslin, R. Approval dependence and reactions to bad arguments and low credibility sources. *Journal of Experimental Research in Personality*, 1971, *5*, 199–207.

Spence, J. T., & Spence, K. W. The motivational components of manifest anxiety: Drive and drive stimuli. In C. D. Spielberger (Ed.), *Anxiety and behavior*. New York: Academic Press, 1966.

Spence, K. W. The nature of theory construction in contemporary psychology. *Psychological Review*, 1944, *51*, 47–68.

Spence, K. W. *Behavior theory and conditioning*. New Haven, Conn.: Yale University Press, 1956.

Spence, K. W. A theory of emotionally based drive (D) and its relation to performance in simple learning situations. *American Psychologist*, 1958, *13*, 131–141.

Spence, K. W. Anxiety (drive) level and performance in eyelid conditioning. *Psychological Bulletin*, 1964, *61*, 129–139.

Spence, K. W. Cognitive and drive factors in the extinction of the conditioned eye blink in human subjects. *Psychological Review*, 1966, *73*, 445–458.

Spence, K. W., Farber, I. E., & McFann, H. H. The relation of anxiety (drive) level to performance in competitional and noncompetitional paired-associates learning. *Journal of Experimental Psychology*, 1956, *52*, 296–305.

Spence, K. W., Haggard, D. F., & Ross, L. E. UCS intensity and the associative (habit) strength of the eyelid CR. *Journal of Experimental Psychology*, 1958, *55*, 404–411.

Spence, K. W., Taylor, J., & Ketchel, R. Anxiety (drive) level and degree of competition in paired-associates learning. *Journal of Experimental Psychology*, 1956, *52*, 306–310.

Spielberger, C. D. Theory and research on anxiety. In C. D. Spielberger (Ed.), *Anxiety and behavior*. New York: Academic Press, 1966.

Spielberger, C. D. The measurement of state and trait anxiety: Conceptual and methodological issues. In L. Levi (Ed.), *Emotions: Their parameters and measurement*. New York: Raven Press, 1975a.

Spielberger, C. D. Anxiety: State–trait–process. In C. D. Spielberger & I. G. Sarason (Eds.), *Stress and anxiety*. Washington, D. C.: Hemisphere/Wiley, 1975b.

Spielberger, C. D., Berger, A., & Howard, K. Conditioning of verbal behavior as a function of awareness, need for social approval, and motivation to receive reinforcement. *Journal of Abnormal and Social Psychology*, 1963, *67*, 241–246.

Spielberger, C. D., Gorsuch, R. L., & Lushene, R. E. *Manual for the State–Trait Anxiety Inventory*. Palo Alto, Calif.: Consulting Psychologists Press, 1970.

Stephens, M. W., & Delys, P. External control expectancies among disadvantaged children at preschool age. *Child Development*, 1973, *44*, 670–674.

Stevens, S. S. Psychology and the science of science. *Psychological Bulletin*, 1939, *36*, 221–263.

Straits, B., & Sechrest, L. Further support of some findings about the characteristics of smokers and non-smokers. *Journal of Consulting Psychology*, 1963, *27*, 282.

Stricker, L. J. Note on social desirability response style and learning. *Journal of Educational Psychology*, 1963, *54*, 52–56.

Strickland, B. R. The prediction of social action from a dimension of internal–external control. *Journal of Social Psychology*, 1965a, *66*, 353–358.

Strickland, B. R. Need approval and motor steadiness under positive and negative conditions. *Perceptual and Motor Skills*, 1965b, *20*, 667–668.

Strickland, B. R. Individual differences in verbal conditioning, extinction, and awareness. *Journal of Personality*, 1970, *38*, 364–378.

Strickland, B. R. Delay of gratification as a function of race of the experimenter. *Journal of Personality and Social Psychology*, 1972, *22*, 108–112.

Strickland, B. R., & Crowne, D. P. Conformity under conditions of simulated group pressure as a function of the need for social approval. *Journal of Social Psychology*, 1962, *58*, 171–181.

Strickland, B. R., & Crowne, D. P. Need for approval and the premature termination of psychotherapy. *Journal of Consulting Psychology*, 1963, *27*, 95–101.

Taylor, J. A. The relationship of anxiety to the conditioned eyelid response. *Journal of Experimental Psychology*, 1951, *41*, 81–92.

Taylor, J. A. A personality scale of manifest anxiety. *Journal of Abnormal and Social Psychology*, 1953, *48*, 285–290.

Taylor, J. A. Drive theory and manifest anxiety. *Psychological Bulletin*, 1956, *53*, 303–320.

Taylor, J. A., & Maher, B. A. Escape and displacement experience as variables in the recovery from approach-avoidance conflict. *Journal of Comparative and Physiological Psychology*, 1959, *52*, 586–590.

Taylor, S. Aggressive behavior as a function of approval motivation and physical attack. *Psychonomic Science*, 1970, *18*, 195–196.

Trapold, M. A., Miller, N. E., & Coons, E. E. All-or-none versus progressive approach in an approach-avoidance conflict. *Journal of Comparative and Physiological Psychology*, 1960, *53*, 293–296.

Tutko, T. A. *Need for social approval and its effect on responses to projective tests*. Unpublished Ph. D. dissertation, Northwestern University, 1962.

Wachtel, P. L. Psychodynamics, behavior therapy, and the implacable experimenter: An inquiry into the consistency of personality. *Journal of Abnormal Psychology*, 1973, *82*, 324–334.

Weinstein, J., Averill, J. R., Opton, E. M., Jr., & Lazarus, R. S. Defensive style and discrepancy between self-report and physiological indexes of stress. *Journal of Personality and Social Pschychology*, 1968, *10*, 406–413.

Wiggins, J. A., Renner, K. E., Clore, G. L., & Rose, R. J. *The psychology of personality*. Reading, Mass.: Addison-Wesley, 1971.

Willingham, A., & Strickland, B. R. Need for approval and simple motor performance. *Perceptual and Motor Skills,* 1965, *21,* 879-884.

Wolf, S., & Wolff, H. G. *Human gastric function.* New York: Oxford University Press, 1947.

Wolk, S., & DuCette, J. The moderating effect of locus of control in relation to achievement-motivation variables. *Journal of Personality,* 1973, *41,* 59-70.

Zeigarnik, B. Uber das Behalten von erledigten und unerledigten Handlungen. *Psychologische Forschung,* 1927, *9,* 1-85.

Zeller, A. F. An experimental analogue of repression. II. The effect of individual failure and success on memory measured by relearning. *Journal of Experimental Psychology,* 1950, *40,* 411-422.

Zuckerman, M., & Gerbasi, K. C. Dimensions of the I-E scale and their relationship to other personality measures. *Educational and Pscyhological Measurements,* 1977a, *37,* 159-175.

Zuckerman, M., & Gerbasi, K. C. Belief in I-E or belief in a just world? *Journal of Personality,* 1977b, *45,* 356-378.

Zuckerman, M., Gerbasi, K. C., & Marion, S. P. Correlates of the just world factor of Rotter's I-E Scale. *Educational and Psychological Measurements,* 1977b, *37,* 375-381.

# Author Index

*Numbers in italic indicate the page on which the complete reference appears.*

# Subject Index